An **R** and
S-PLUS
COMPANION
to **APPLIED**
REGRESSION

To the memory of my parents,
Joseph and Diana

An R and S-PLUS COMPANION to APPLIED REGRESSION

John Fox
McMaster University

SAGE Publications
International Educational and Professional Publisher
Thousand Oaks ▪ London ▪ New Delhi

Copyright © 2002 by Sage Publications, Inc.

All rights reserved. No part of this book may be reproduced or utilized in any form or by any means, electronic or mechanical, including photocopying, recording, or by any information storage and retrieval system, without permission in writing from the publisher.

For information:

Sage Publications, Inc.
2455 Teller Road
Thousand Oaks, California 91320
E-mail: order@sagepub.com

Sage Publications Ltd.
6 Bonhill Street
London EC2A 4PU
United Kingdom

Sage Publications India Pvt. Ltd.
M-32 Market
Greater Kailash I
New Delhi 110 048 India

Printed in the United States of America

Library of Congress Cataloging-in-Publication Data

Fox, John, 1947–
  An R and S-Plus companion to applied regression/by John Fox.
    p. cm.
    Includes bibliographical references and index.
  ISBN 978-0-7619-2279-7 (hardcover)
  ISBN 978-0-7619-2280-3 (paperback)
  1. Regression analysis - - Data processing. 2. S-Plus. 3. R (Computer program language)
I. Title.
  QA278.2.F628 2002
  519.5'36'0285 - - dc21

                                                                                        2002066787

This book is printed on acid-free paper.

08   09   10   11   12   11   10   9   8   7   6

Acquiring Editor:	C. Deborah Laughton
Editorial Assistant:	Veronica Novak
Production Editor:	Diana Axelsen
Typesetter:	Technical Typesetting Inc.
Print Buyer:	Michelle Lee

Contents

Preface

R and S-PLUS are statistical-computing environments, incorporating implementations of the S programming language. This book aims to teach the use of R and S-PLUS in the context of applied regression analysis—typically studied by social scientists and others in a second course in applied statistics. As the title of the book implies, I assume that the reader is learning or is otherwise familiar with the statistical methods that I describe; thus, this book is a *companion* to a text or course on modern applied regression, such as (but not necessarily) my own *Applied Regression, Linear Models, and Related Methods* (Fox, 1997).[1] Of course, different texts and courses have somewhat different content, and if you encounter a topic that is unfamiliar, or that is not of interest, feel free to skip it or to pass over it lightly.

The availability of cheap, powerful, and convenient computing has revolutionized the practice of statistical data analysis, as it has revolutionized other aspects of our society. Once upon a time, but well within living memory, data analysis was typically performed by statistical "packages" running on mainframe computers. The primary input medium was the punch card, large data sets were stored on magnetic tapes, and printed output was produced by line printers; data were in rectangular "case-by-variable" format. The job of the software was to combine instructions for data analysis with a data set to produce a printed report. Computing jobs were submitted in "batch mode," rather than interactively, and a substantial amount of time—hours, or even days—elapsed between the submission of a job and its completion.

Eventually, batch-oriented computers were superseded by interactive, time-shared, terminal-based computing systems and then successively by personal computers and workstations, networks of computers, and the Internet. But some statistical software still in use traces its heritage to the days of the card reader and line printer. Statistical packages, such as SAS and SPSS, have acquired a variety of accoutrements (such as graphical interfaces and limited programming capabilities), but they are still

---

1. The topics covered in this book correspond closely to those in Fox (1997), and many of the examples are drawn from that source. My regression text also provides a general statistical reference for the methods discussed here.

principally oriented toward combining instructions with rectangular data sets to produce printed output.[2]

This model of statistical computing often works well in the application of standard methods of data analysis. It is relatively difficult, however, to do something that is nonstandard or to add to the capability of a statistical package by programming a new technique. In contrast, programming languages provide access to a variety of data and programming structures. Developing statistical software in traditional programming languages, such as C or FORTRAN, however, is a time-consuming task.

S is a high-level computer programming language designed to facilitate the implementation of statistical methods. It is embedded in a "programming environment," including an interpreter for the S language, with which the user-programmer can interact in a conversational manner.[3] S is one of several statistical programming environments; others include Gauss, Stata, and Lisp-Stat.[4]

In a good statistical programming environment, one can have one's cake and eat it too: Routine data analysis is convenient, but so are programming and the incorporation of new statistical methods. I believe that S balances these factors especially well:

- S is extremely capable "out of the box," incorporating a wide range of standard statistical applications, augmented by an even wider range of freely available add-on libraries (see below).

- The S programming language is easy to use (the easiest programming language that I have encountered) and is finely tuned to the development of statistical applications.

- The S programming language is also very carefully designed from the point of view of computer science as well as statistics. Indeed, John Chambers, the principal designer of S, won the 1998 Software System Award of the Association for Computing Machinery (ACM) for the S System.

---

2. With SAS, in particular, the situation is not so clear-cut, because there are several facilities for programming: The SAS DATA step is a simple programming language for manipulating data sets, the IML ("interactive matrix language") procedure provides a programming language for matrix computations, and the macro facility allows the user to build applications that incorporate DATA steps and calls to SAS procedures. Nevertheless, programming in SAS is substantially less consistent and convenient than in a true statistical programming environment, and it remains fair to say that SAS principally is oriented toward processing rectangular data sets to produce printed output.

3. A *compiler* translates a program written in a programming language into an independently executable program in machine code. In contrast, an *interpreter* translates and executes a program under the control of the interpreter. Although it is in theory possible to write a compiler for a high-level, interactive language such as S, it is difficult to do so. Compiled programs usually execute more efficiently than interpreted programs. In advanced use, R and S-PLUS both have facilities for incorporating compiled programs written in FORTRAN and C.

4. Parallel brief presentations of different statistical-computing environments may be found in Stine and Fox (1997).

■ The two implementations of S—R and S-PLUS—are very solid, incorporating, for example, sound numerical algorithms for statistical computations.

S is a product of Bell Labs, where it was developed, and continues to be developed, by experts in statistical computing, including John Chambers, Richard Becker, and Allan Wilks. Like most good software, S has evolved substantially since its origins in the mid-1970s. The most recent major versions still in use are S3 and S4, which have some significant differences. Although Bell Labs originally distributed S directly, it is now available only as the commercial product S-PLUS, sold by Insightful Corporation. There are implementations of S-PLUS for Windows PCs and for a variety of Unix/Linux systems. The most recent Windows versions as I write this are S-PLUS 2000, which corresponds to the S3 language, and S-PLUS 6.0, which corresponds to the S4 language.

R is an independent, open-source, and free implementation of the S language, developed by an international team of statisticians, now including John Chambers. The current version is R 1.3.1, which runs on Windows PCs, Macintoshes, and various flavors of Unix and Linux. Version 1.3.1 of R is relatively close to S3; version 1.4, still in development, will move R toward S4.[5] There will remain some important differences between the two implementations of the S language, but most are at a relatively deep level and largely will not concern us; when necessary, I discuss differences between R and S-PLUS and between S3 and S4.

Differences Among Versions of S

I point out many small differences between S-PLUS and R and between S3 and S4 in boxes such as this one. The title of the box will tell you whether the information in it is relevant to your version of S.

It is easy to get tangled up in the nomenclature of implementations and versions, so I will adopt the following simple rule for this book: I will use "S" generically to refer both to R and S-PLUS and to the S3 and S4 language versions of S proper. As I mentioned, distinctions will be made as necessary.

One of the great strengths of S is the ability to add new capabilities to the software. Not only is it possible to write functions (programs), but it is convenient to combine related sets of functions and data in

---

5. Version 1.4 of R is due for release in December 2001; currently, three "minor" versions of R (corresponding to the tenths place in the version number) are released yearly, so you will almost surely be working with a newer version than the one described in this book. Significant developments will appear on the Web site for the book.

S-PLUS "library sections" and R "packages" (both of which I will call "libraries"). Currently, for example, there are more than 100 contributed packages available on the R Web site (see below), many of them prepared by experts in various areas of applied statistics, such as resampling methods, mixed models, and survival analysis. In the statistical literature, new methods are often accompanied by implementations in S; indeed, S has become a kind of *lingua franca* of statistical computing—at least among statisticians.[6]

The computer output and graphs in this book were produced with R. Note as well that the title of the book places R first. It may seem peculiar to favor R in this manner—after all, S-PLUS came first—but there are several good reasons to do so:

1. R is *free* software, which makes its use in college and university courses (and other settings where cost is important) especially attractive. It is true that S-PLUS offers generous site-license plans to educational institutions, but this is only helpful if your institution participates.

2. As mentioned, there are implementations of R for Macintoshes, which are still used in many educational institutions.

3. While S-PLUS maintains some advantages—a graphical user interface (GUI), for example—I believe that the current development of R is more dynamic. R has excited a great deal of interest in the statistical-computing community.

It is my expectation that most readers of the book will use a Windows implementation of R or S-PLUS, and the presentation in the text reflects that assumption, but virtually everything should apply equally to other implementations. The Web site for the book, http://www.socsci.mcmaster.ca/jfox/Books/companion/, includes brief instructions for downloading, installing, and using the Windows version of R, and for downloading and installing add-on packages.[7] The home page for R, http://www.r-project.org/, provides access to a panoply of resources and information, including a link to the Comprehensive R Archive Network (CRAN), from which R software can be downloaded. Information about S-PLUS is available from Insightful Corporation at http://www.insightful.com/.

---

6. In econometrics, for example, Stata appears to be more widely used. I hope that this book will help to popularize S among social scientists.

7. If you have difficulty accessing this Web site, please check the Sage Publications Web site at www.sagepub.com for up-to-date information. Search for "John Fox" and follow the links to the Web site for the book.

In addition to instructions for obtaining and installing R, the Web site for the book contains the following materials:

- Downloadable versions of the car (companion to applied regression) library for R and S-PLUS. This library includes software and data sets described in the book.

- An appendix (referred to as the "Web appendix" in the text) containing brief information on using S for various extensions of regression analysis not considered in the main body of the text: nonlinear regression, robust and resistant regression, nonparametric regression, Cox regression for survival data, mixed-effects models, structural-equation models, and bootstrapping. I have relegated this material to a downloadable appendix in an effort to keep the text to a reasonable length. I plan to update the appendix from time to time as new developments warrant.

- Downloadable scripts for all of the examples in the text.

- Some information for instructors using R in their classes.

- Errata and updated information about R and S-PLUS.

This book is not intended as documentation for R and S-PLUS[8]: It is meant to be read, though not necessarily from cover to cover. Various facilities of S are introduced as they are needed in the context of detailed, worked-through examples. If you want to locate information about a particular feature, however, consult the index of functions and operators, or the subject index, at the end of the book; there is also an index of data sets used in the text. Occasionally, more demanding material (e.g., requiring a knowledge of matrix algebra) is marked with an asterisk; this material may be skipped without loss of continuity, as may the footnotes.[9]

Most readers will want to try out the examples in the text. You should therefore install R or S-PLUS (and the car library) before you start to work through the book. As you duplicate the examples in the text, feel free to innovate, experimenting with S commands that do not appear

---

8. S-PLUS comes with extensive documentation. Likewise, thorough documentation for R is available through the R Web site. Both R and S-PLUS have substantial (and overlapping) user communities who contribute to active and helpful e-mail lists. See the previously mentioned Web sites for details. [And remember to observe proper "netiquette": Look for answers in the documentation and frequently-asked-questions (FAQ) lists before posting a question to an e-mail discussion list; the people who answer your question are volunteering their time.]

9. The footnotes to the text include several kinds of material: (1) references to other parts of the text and, occasionally, to other sources; (2) minor elaboration of points in the text; and (3) indications of portions of the text that represent (I hope) innocent distortion for the purpose of simplification. The object is to present more complete and correct information without interrupting the flow of the text and without making the main text overly difficult.

in the examples. You should also be aware that the examples in each chapter are cumulative: Later examples often depend on earlier ones, so do not expect to be able to work the examples starting in the middle of a chapter. The examples in *different* chapters are independent of each other, however.

Here is a brief chapter synopsis:

Chapter 1 explains how to interact with the R or S-PLUS interpreter, introduces basic concepts, and provides a variety of examples, including an extended illustration of the use of S in data analysis. The chapter ends with a brief presentation of S functions for basic statistical methods.

Chapter 2 shows you how to read data into S from several sources and how to work with data sets. There is also a discussion of basic data structures such as vectors, matrices, arrays, and lists.

Chapter 3 discusses the exploratory examination and transformation of data, with an emphasis on graphical displays.

Chapter 4 describes the use of S functions for fitting and testing linear models, including simple and multiple regression, dummy regression, and analysis of variance.

Chapter 5 focuses on generalized linear models in S. Particular attention is paid to generalized linear models for categorical data and to Poisson linear models for counts.

Chapter 6 describes methods—often called "regression diagnostics"— for determining whether linear and generalized linear models adequately describe the data to which they are fit. Many of these methods are implemented in the car library associated with this book.

Chapter 7 contains material on plotting in S, describing a step-by-step approach to constructing complex S graphs.

Chapter 8 is an introduction to programming in S, including a discussions of function definition, operators and functions for handling matrices, control structures, and object-oriented programming.

With the possible exception of the asterisked material, Chapters 1 and 2 contain general information that should be of interest to all readers. Some readers (those who prefer to learn about general principles before seeing concrete applications) may want to read Chapters 7 and 8 before Chapters 3 through 6. Although some topics are obviously logically dependent on others (e.g., regression diagnostics for generalized linear models in Chapter 6 depends on material on generalized linear models in Chapter 5), sections of Chapters 3 through 6 may be read as needed.

I employ a few simple typographical conventions:

■ Computer input and output, as well as S libraries, functions, and variables, are printed in a monospaced `typewriter font`.

■ Occasionally, generic specifications (to be replaced by particular information, such as a variable name) are given in *typewriter italics*.

■ S input and output are printed as they appear on the computer screen, although I sometimes edit output for brevity or clarity; elided material in computer output is indicated by three widely spaced periods (. . .).

■ S input is preceded by the > or + (continuation) prompts, as explained in Chapter 1.

Graphical output is printed in many figures scattered throughout the text; in normal use, graphs typically appear on the computer screen in graphics windows, although both R and S-PLUS provide excellent facilities for saving and printing graphs.

This book deals with the *command-line interface* to R and S-PLUS. S-PLUS additionally employs a *graphical user interface* (*GUI*), which permits the user to access many functions through menus and dialog boxes. It is also possible to program graphical interfaces to user-built applications. Similar facilities for building graphical interfaces exist in R, but they are not as extensive.

I have chosen to ignore the GUI in S-PLUS for several reasons: (1) It is essentially self-explanatory to users familiar with standard Windows software; in fact, this is one of the primary advantages of a menu/dialog-box interface. (2) Many of the facilities of S-PLUS are not available through the GUI. (3) Perhaps most important, I believe that graphical interfaces of this kind are best for casual or occasional use of statistical software. Accomplished users generally prefer the command-line interface, especially if an analysis needs to be repeated or modified (and before we begin, how do we know?). So, be prepared to exercise your typing skills.

There is, of course, much to S beyond its application to regression models. The S3 language is documented in two books: *The New S Language: A Programming Environment for Data Analysis and Graphics* (Becker, Chambers, & Wilks, 1988), which describes the details of S[10]; and an edited volume, *Statistical Models in S* (Chambers & Hastie, 1992), which describes the S3 object-oriented programming system and facilities for specifying and fitting statistical models. Similarly, Chambers's 1998 book, *Programming With Data*, describes the S4 language.

---

10. Actually, *The New S Language* describes S2, which is incorporated in S3.

There are several relatively advanced statistics texts that deal with particular applications of S, such as to survival analysis (Therneau & Grambsch, 2000) and mixed models (Pinheiro & Bates, 2000). Likewise, some statistics texts that do not focus on S are nevertheless associated with S libraries that implement the methods discussed in the book: Examples include resampling methods (Efron & Tibshirani, 1994; Davison & Hinkley, 1997), methods for dealing with missing data (Schafer, 1997), and nonparametric regression and smoothing (Hastie & Tibshirani, 1990; Bowman & Azzalini, 1997; Loader, 1999). Additional sources may be found on the R and S-PLUS Web sites.

Two general texts on S are particularly worthy of mention here: The third edition of *Modern Applied Statistics With S-PLUS* (Venables & Ripley, 1999) demonstrates the use of S for a wide range of statistical applications. The book is associated with several S libraries, including the MASS library, to which I make occasional reference. Venables and Ripley's text is generally more advanced and has a broader focus than my book; there are also some differences in emphasis: For example, the *R and S-PLUS Companion* has more material on diagnostic methods. The same authors' *S Programming* (Venables & Ripley, 2000) provides an advanced, in-depth treatment of programming in the various implementations and versions of the S language.

Acknowledgments

I am grateful to a number of individuals who provided valuable assistance in writing this book: Douglas Bates, Georges Monette, and Sanford Weisberg helped me with the car software that accompanies the book. Michael Friendly and three unusually diligent (and, at the time anonymous) reviewers, Jeff Gill, J. Scott Long, and William Jacoby, made many excellent suggestions for revising the text. C. Deborah Laughton, my editor at Sage through several books, has been informative and supportive, as always. Finally, I wish to express my gratitude to the designers and developers of S and R, and to those who have contributed S and R software, for the wonderful resource that they have created.

CHAPTER 1

Introducing R
and S-PLUS

The purpose of this chapter is to introduce you to the S language and to the R and S-PLUS interpreters. After describing some of the basics of S, I proceed to illustrate its use in analyzing a typical, if small, regression problem. The chapter concludes with a brief description of S functions for familiar operations in basic statistics.

I know that many readers are in the habit of beginning a book at Chapter 1, skipping the Preface. Please read the Preface *before* this first chapter: In particular, I assume that you have installed R or S-PLUS on your computer and that you have access to the car library associated with this book. Moreover, the Preface includes information on typographical and other conventions employed in the text.

S BASICS · 1.1

Figure 1.1 shows the R *"Gui"* (graphical user interface) window immediately after R is started. Under the opening message in the R *Console* is the > ("greater than") prompt. Although there are several ways to interact with the R interpreter (see Section 1.1.6), I will assume, at least for the present, that statements for the interpreter are typed directly into the *R Console*.

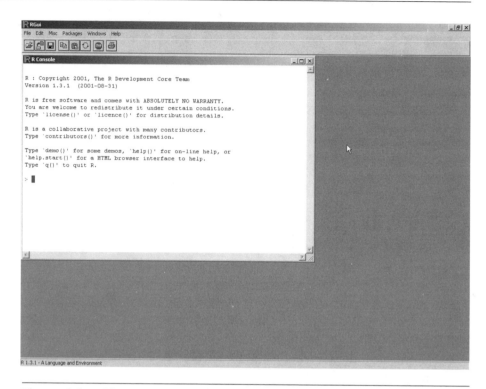

Figure 1.1   The R "Gui" window, showing the *R Console*. (R version 1.3.1.)

The R "Gui"

The *R Gui* (unlike the graphical interface to S-PLUS) does not provide access to statistical functions in R. Because the menus in the *R Gui* have changed significantly from version to version, I defer a discussion of the menus to the Web site for the text. I draw your attention, however, to the Packages menu, which provides a convenient means of installing and updating R libraries.

Figure 1.2 shows the main S-PLUS window at the start of a session. Initially, the *Object Browser* subwindow has the focus, but I have brought the *Commands* subwindow to the front and resized it. The *Commands* window is similar to the *R Console*, and we can shift the focus to this window simply by clicking in it.

1.1.1   Interacting with the Interpreter

Data analysis in S proceeds as an interactive dialog with the interpreter. We type an S statement at the > prompt, press the *Enter* key, and the

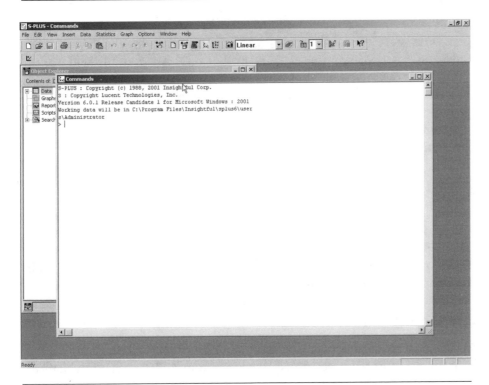

Figure 1.2   The main S-PLUS window, showing *Object Browser* and *Commands* subwindows. The *Commands* window was brought to the front and resized. (S-PLUS version 6.0.1.)

interpreter responds by executing the statement and, as appropriate, returning a result, producing graphical output, or sending output to a file or device.

The S language includes the usual arithmetic operations:

+   addition
−   subtraction
*   multiplication
/   division
^   exponentiation

Here are some simple examples of arithmetic in S:

```
> 2+3
[1] 5
> 2-3
[1] -1
> 2*3
[1] 6
> 2/3
[1] 0.6666667
> 2^3
[1] 8
>
```

Notice that output lines are preceded by [1]: When printed output consists of many values spread over several lines, each line begins with the index (number) of the first element in that line. An example will appear shortly. Notice, as well, that after the interpreter executes a statement and returns a value, it waits for the next statement, as signified by the > prompt.

Several arithmetic operations may be combined to build up more or less complex expressions:

```
> 4^2-3*2
[1] 10
```

In the usual notation, this statement is $4^2 - 3 \times 2$. S employs common conventions for precedence of mathematical operators. So, for example, exponentiation takes place before multiplication, which takes place before subtraction; if two operations have equal precedence (such as addition and subtraction), then they take place from left to right:

```
> 1-6+4
[1] -1
```

You can always explicitly specify the order of evaluation of an expression by using parentheses; thus, the expression 4^2-3*2 is equivalent to

```
> (4^2)-(3*2)
[1] 10
```

Be careful with the unary minus sign, - (negation), which has a higher order of precedence than binary arithmetic operators:

```
> 2^-3
[1] 0.125
> -2--3
[1] 1
> -2 - -3
[1] 1
```

Although spaces are not required to separate the elements of an arithmetic expression, judicious use of spaces can help to clarify the meaning of the expression: Compare the last S statement with the preceding one, for example. Placing spaces around operators usually makes expressions more readable (and, indeed, would improve the readability of some of the preceding examples).

1.1.2   S Functions

In addition to the common arithmetic operators, S includes many (literally hundreds) of functions, for mathematical operations, for statistical data analysis, for making graphs, and for other purposes. Function arguments (values passed to functions) are specified within parentheses after the function name. For example, to calculate the natural log of 100, that is $\log_e 100$ or $\ln 100$, we type:

```
> log(100)
[1] 4.60517
```

To compute the log of 100 to the base 10, we specify:

```
> log(100, base=10)
[1] 2
```

The `log` and `logb` Function in S4

In S4, the `log` function calculates natural logarithms; `logb` (with a base argument) behaves like the `log` function in S3 and R. For example, in S4 the log of 100 to the base 10 is `logb(100, base=10)`.

In general, arguments to S functions may be specified in the order in which they occur in the function definition (to be described shortly) or by name, followed by = (equal sign) and a value. Argument names may be abbreviated, as long as the abbreviation is unique; thus, the previous example may be more compactly rendered as

```
> log(100, b=10)
[1] 2
```

To obtain information about a function, use the `help` function. For example:

```
> help(log)
log                    package:base              R Documentation

Logarithms and Exponentials

Description:

  'log' computes natural logarithms, 'log10' computes common (i.e.,
  base 10) logarithms, and 'log2' computes binary (i.e., base 2)
  logarithms. The general form 'log(x, base)' computes logarithms
  with base 'base' ('log10' and 'log2' are only special cases).
  . . .
Usage:

  log(x)
  log(x, base)
  log10(x)
  log2(x)
  . . .
```

```
Arguments:

  x: a numeric or complex vector.

  base: positive number. The base with respect to which logarithms
        are computed.  Defaults to e='exp(1)'.

Value:

  A vector of the same length as 'x' containing the transformed
  values.  'log(0)' gives '-Inf' (when available).
  . . .
```

An alternative that requires less typing is to use the ? (help) operator, for example, ?log. As explained in the Preface, the three widely separated dots (. . .) mean that I have elided some information. Help information is not printed in the *R Console*, but in a help window. Several help formats are supported by R, including standard Windows help. S-Plus also provides standard Windows help.

Because base is the second argument of the log function, we can also type

```
> log(100,10)
[1] 2
```

An argument to a function may have a *default* value—a value that the argument assumes if it is not explicitly specified in the function call. For example, the base argument to the log function defaults to $e \simeq 2.718$, the base of the natural logarithms.

S is a *functional* programming language: Both the "primitive" programs that comprise the language and the programs that users write are functions. Indeed, the distinction between primitives and user-defined functions is somewhat artificial in S.[1] Even the arithmetic operators in S are really functions and may be used as such:

```
> '+'(2,3)
[1] 5
```

We need to place quotation marks around '+' (either single or double quotes will do) so that the interpreter does not get confused, but our ability to use + and the other arithmetic functions as in-fix operators, as in 2+3, is really just "syntactic sugar," simplifying the construction of S expressions but not fundamentally altering the functional character of the language.

---

1. Section 1.1.4 briefly discusses user-defined functions; the topic is treated in greater depth in Chapter 8. In both S-PLUS and R, experienced programmers can also access programs written in FORTRAN and C.

Vectors and Variables   1.1.3

S would not be very convenient to use if we had to compute one value at a time. The arithmetic operators, and most S functions, can operate on more complex data structures than individual numbers. The simplest of these data structures is a numeric vector, or one-dimensional "list" of numbers.[2] Indeed, in S, an individual number is really a vector with a single element. A simple way to construct a vector is with the c function, which combines its elements:

```
> c(1,2,3,4)
[1] 1 2 3 4
```

Many other functions also return vectors as results. For example, the *sequence operator* (:) generates consecutive numbers, while the seq (sequence) function does much the same thing, but more flexibly:

```
> 1:4
[1] 1 2 3 4

> 4:1
[1] 4 3 2 1

> -1:2
[1] -1  0  1  2

> seq(1,4)
[1] 1 2 3 4

> seq(2, 8, by=2)  # specify interval
[1] 2 4 6 8

> seq(0, 1, by=.1)
 [1] 0.0 0.1 0.2 0.3 0.4 0.5 0.6 0.7 0.8 0.9 1.0

> seq(0, 1, length=11) # specify number of elements
 [1] 0.0 0.1 0.2 0.3 0.4 0.5 0.6 0.7 0.8 0.9 1.0
```

The pound sign (#) signifies a comment: Text to the right of # is ignored by the interpreter.

The standard arithmetic functions and operators apply to vectors on an element-wise basis:

```
> c(1,2,3,4)/2
[1] 0.5 1.0 1.5 2.0
```

---

2. I refer to vectors as "lists" using that term loosely, because lists in S are a distinct data structure (described in Chapter 2).

```
> c(1,2,3,4)/c(4,3,2,1)
[1] 0.2500000 0.6666667 1.5000000 4.0000000

> log(c(0.1, 1, 10, 100), 10)
[1] -1  0  1  2
```

If the operands are of different lengths, then the shorter of the two is extended by repetition [as in c(1,2,3,4)/2 above]; if the length of the longer operand is not a multiple of the length of the shorter, then a warning message is printed, but the interpreter proceeds with the operation:

```
> c(1,2,3,4) + c(4,3)
[1] 5 5 7 7

> c(1,2,3,4) + c(4,3,2)
[1] 5 5 5 8
Warning message:
longer object length
        is not a multiple of shorter object length in:
        c(1, 2, 3, 4) + c(4, 3, 2)
```

Operands of Different Lengths in S4

In S4, performing an arithmetic operation on operands of different lengths produces an error (rather than a warning) when the length of the longer operator is not a multiple of the length of the shorter one.

S would also be of little use if we were unable to save the results returned by functions; we do so by assigning values to variables, as in the following example:

```
> x <- c(1,2,3,4)
> x
[1] 1 2 3 4
```

The left-pointing arrow (<-) is the *assignment operator*; it is composed of the two characters < (less than) and - (dash or minus), with no intervening blanks, and is usually read as *gets*: "The variable x *gets* the value c(1,2,3,4)."

The rule for naming variables in S is simple: Variable names are composed of letters (a–z, A–Z), numerals (0–9), and periods (.), and may be arbitrarily long. The first character must be a letter or a period, but variable names beginning with a period are reserved by convention for special purposes.[3] Names in S are case sensitive; so, for example, x and X are

---

3. Nonstandard names may be used in a variety of contexts, including assignments, by enclosing the names in single or double quotes (e.g., 'first name' <- 'John'). In most circumstances, however, nonstandard names are best avoided.

distinct variables. It is generally a good idea to use descriptive names—for example, `total.income` rather than x2.[4] Typing the name of a variable causes its value to be printed.

Once defined, variables may be used in S expressions in the normal manner:

```
> x/2
[1] 0.5 1.0 1.5 2.0
```

including in the definition of other variables:

```
> y <- sqrt(x)
> y
[1] 1.000000 1.414214 1.732051 2.000000
```

In this example, `sqrt` is the square-root function, so `sqrt(x)` is equivalent to `x^.5`.

Unlike in many programming languages, in S variables are dynamically defined and redefined: We need not tell the interpreter in advance how many values x is to hold; whether it contains integers (whole numbers) or real numbers; or whether it is a numeric variable, a character variable, or something else. Moreover, if we wish, we may *redefine* the variable x:

```
> x <- rnorm(100)  # 100 standard normal random numbers
> x
 [1] -0.04821767 -0.60571637 -0.39322377  0.43416765  0.28387745
 [6]  1.35957233  0.06703925  0.07497876  0.34170083  0.61477147
[11] -0.61420864 -0.46709553  0.41896732 -0.51487725 -0.17473063
[16]  0.20457797 -0.15066077  1.74732395 -0.27819601  1.31427698
[21] -0.61184541 -0.57516762  0.04810963  0.94873165  0.57223627

  . . .

> summary(x)
    Min.  1st Qu.   Median     Mean  3rd Qu.     Max.
 -2.83600 -0.51550  0.03029  0.06216  0.58720  3.99900
```

The `rnorm` function generates standard-normal random numbers—in this case, 100 of them. (Two additional arguments allow us to sample values from a normal distribution with arbitrary mean and standard deviation; the defaults, employed here, are `mean=0` and `sd=1`.) Notice that when a vector prints on more than one line, the number of the leading element of each line is printed in brackets.

The function `summary` is an example of a *generic function*: How it behaves depends on its argument. Applied (as here) to a numeric vector, `summary` prints the minimum and maximum values of the argument, along with the mean, median, and first and third quartiles.

If we wish to print only one of the elements of a vector, we can specify the index of the element within square brackets; for example, `x[21]` is

---

4. Two common naming styles are conventionally employed in S: (1) separating parts of a name by periods, as in `total.income`, or (2) separating by uppercase letters, as in `totalIncome`. I prefer the first style, but this is purely a matter of taste.

the 21st element of the vector x:

```
> x[21]
[1] -0.6118454
```

Indexing in S is quite flexible. We may also specify a vector of indices:

```
> x[11:20]
[1] -0.6142086 -0.4670955  0.4189673 -0.5148772 -0.1747306
[6]  0.2045780 -0.1506608  1.7473240 -0.2781960  1.3142770
```

Negative indices cause the corresponding values of the vector to be *omitted*:

```
> x[-(11:100)]
[1] -0.04821767 -0.60571637 -0.39322377  0.43416765  0.28387745
[6]  1.35957233  0.06703925  0.07497876  0.34170083  0.61477147
```

The parentheses around 11:100 serve to avoid generating numbers from −11 to 100!

A vector may also be indexed by a logical vector of the same length. Logical values are either T (or TRUE) or F (or FALSE), and frequently arise through the use of comparison operators:

==	equals
!=	not equals
<=	less than or equals
<	less than
>	greater than
>=	greater than or equals

Note, in particular, that the double equals (==) is used for testing equality, because = is reserved for specifying function arguments.

Use of = for Assignment in S4

In S4, the equal sign (=) may also be used for assignment in place of the arrow (<−), except inside a function call, where = is exclusively employed to specify arguments by name. Because reserving the equal sign for specification of function arguments leads to clearer S expressions, I encourage you to use the arrow for assignment, even in S4.

Logical values may also be used in conjunction with the logical operators:

&	and
|	or
!	not

Here are some simple examples:

```
> 1 == 2
[1] FALSE
```

```
> 1 != 2
[1] TRUE
> 1 <= 2
[1] TRUE
> 1 < 2
[1] TRUE
> 1 > 2
[1] FALSE
> 1 >= 2
[1] FALSE
> T & T
[1] TRUE
> T & F
[1] FALSE
> F & F
[1] FALSE
> T | T
[1] TRUE
> T | F
[1] TRUE
> F | F
[1] FALSE
> ! c(T, F)
[1] FALSE  TRUE
```

and a somewhat more extended example illustrating the use of the comparison and logical operators:

```
> z <- x[1:10]
> z
 [1] -0.04821767 -0.60571637 -0.39322377  0.43416765  0.28387745
 [6]  1.35957233  0.06703925  0.07497876  0.34170083  0.61477147

> z < -0.5
 [1] FALSE  TRUE FALSE FALSE FALSE FALSE FALSE FALSE FALSE FALSE

> z > 0.5
 [1] FALSE FALSE FALSE FALSE FALSE  TRUE FALSE FALSE FALSE  TRUE

> z < -0.5 | z > 0.5  # note <, > of higher precedence than |
 [1] FALSE  TRUE FALSE FALSE FALSE  TRUE FALSE FALSE FALSE  TRUE

> abs(z) > 0.5  # absolute value
 [1] FALSE  TRUE FALSE FALSE FALSE  TRUE FALSE FALSE FALSE  TRUE

> z[abs(z) > 0.5]
[1] -0.6057164  1.3595723  0.6147715
```

The following points are noteworthy:

■ We need to be careful in typing z < -0.5; although most spaces in
S expressions are optional, the space after < is crucial: z<-0.5 would

assign the value 0.5 to z.[5] (As I mentioned, even when the spaces are not required around operators, they usually help to clarify an S expression.)

■ Logical operators have lower precedence than comparison operators, and so z < -0.5 | z > 0.5 is equivalent to (z < -0.5) | (z > 0.5). When in doubt, parenthesize!

■ The abs function takes the absolute value of its argument.

■ As the last expression illustrates, we can index a vector by a logical vector of the same length, selecting the elements with TRUE indices.

In addition to the vectorized *and* (&) and *or* (|) operators presented here, there are special *and* (&&) and *or* (||) operators that take individual logical values as arguments. These are sometimes useful in writing programs (see Chapter 8).

1.1.4 User-Defined Functions

As you probably guessed, S includes functions for calculating many common statistical summaries, such as the mean of a vector:

```
> mean(x)
[1] 0.06216418
```

Recall that x is a vector of 100 standard-normal random numbers. Were there no mean function, we could have calculated the mean straightforwardly using sum and length:

```
> sum(x)/length(x)
[1] 0.06216418
```

To do this repeatedly every time we need a mean is inconvenient, so—in the absence of the "primitive" function mean—we could define our own mean function:

```
> my.mean <- function(x) sum(x)/length(x)
>
```

---

5. Another occasional (and difficult to diagnose) source of errors is the attempted use of the underscore in variable names, as in
```
> x_1 <- 0
Error in 1 <- 0 : invalid (do_set) left-hand side to assignment
```
  The underscore character (_) is a synonym for the assignment arrow (<-). The offending expression is therefore equivalent to x <- 1 <- 0, which tries to assign the value 0 to the numeral 1 and then to x. Even *correct* use of the underscore leads to difficult-to-read expressions and should therefore be discouraged.

■ We define a function using the function `function`. (I could not resist writing that sentence![6]) The arguments to `function`, here just x, are the *formal arguments* of the function being defined, `my.mean`. As explained below, when the function `my.mean` is called, a *real argument* will appear in the place of the formal argument. The remainder of the function definition is an expression specifying the *body* of the function.

■ The rule for naming functions is the same as that for naming variables. I avoided using the name `mean` because I did not wish to redefine the primitive function `mean`, which is a generic function with greater utility than our simple version. Actually, we cannot damage the definitions of primitive functions, but if we define a function of the same name, our version will be used in place of the standard function, and is said to "shadow" or "mask" the standard function. This behavior is explained in Chapter 2.

■ The bodies of most user-defined functions are more complex than in this example, consisting of a *compound expression* comprising several simple S expressions, enclosed in braces and separated by semicolons or newlines. I introduce additional information about writing functions as required, and take up the topic more systematically in Chapter 8.

Having defined the function `my.mean`, we may use it in the same manner as the primitive functions. Indeed, many of the standard functions in S are not true primitives, but are themselves written in the S language.

```
> my.mean(x)
[1] 0.06216418
> my.mean(y)
[1] 1.536566
> my.mean(1:100)
[1] 50.5
```

As these examples illustrate, there is no necessary correspondence between the name of the formal argument x of the function `my.mean` and the actual argument to the function, which need not be named x. Function arguments are evaluated by the interpreter, and it is the *value* of the argument that is passed to the function, not its name. Function arguments (and any variables that are defined within a function) are *local* to the function: Local variables exist only while the function executes and are distinct from *global* variables of the same name. In the example,

---

6. Actually, `function` is a "special form," not a true function, because its arguments (here, the formal argument x) are not evaluated. The distinction is technical, and it will do no harm to think of `function` as a function that returns a function as its result.

the last call to my.mean passed the value 1:100 to the argument x, but this did not change the contents of the global variable x:

```
> x
 [1] -0.04821767 -0.60571637 -0.39322377  0.43416765  0.28387745
 [6]  1.35957233  0.06703925  0.07497876  0.34170083  0.61477147
[11] -0.61420864 -0.46709553  0.41896732 -0.51487725 -0.17473063
 . . .
```

1.1.5 Cleaning Up

In R, user-defined variables and functions exist in a region of memory called the "workspace." The R workspace can be saved at the end of a session (or even during the session), in which case it is automatically loaded at the start of the next session. Different workspaces can be saved in different directories, as a means of keeping several projects separate. Starting R in a directory loads the corresponding workspace.[7]

The objects function lists the names of variables and functions residing in the R workspace:

```
> objects()
[1] "last.warning" "my.mean" "x" "y" "z"
```

The function objects requires no arguments, but we nevertheless need to type parentheses after the function name. Were we to type only the name of the function, then objects would not be called—instead the *definition* of the objects function would be printed. (Try it!) The variable last.warning was generated automatically by the R interpreter earlier in the current session:

```
> last.warning
$"longer object length
        is not a multiple of shorter object length"
c(1, 2, 3, 4) + c(4, 3, 2)
```

Saving Data in S-PLUS

In S-PLUS, user-defined objects are saved in files in a special data directory (named _data in the Windows version of S3, and .data in S4), and therefore persist from session to session. As in R, projects can be kept separate by using different directories. The objects function lists objects in the S-PLUS data directory.

---

7. See the Web site for the book and the R documentation for additional information on organizing separate projects.

It is natural in the process of using S to define variables—and occasionally functions—that we do not want to retain. It is good general practice in S-PLUS, and in R if you intend to save the workspace, to clean up after yourself from time to time. We may use the `remove` function to delete the variables x, y, and z:

```
> remove(x, y, z)
> objects()
[1] "last.warning" "my.mean"
```

(I am keeping the function my.mean for use in Section 1.1.7.)

Using `remove` in S-PLUS

In S-PLUS, you must specify the *names* of objects as a character vector, rather than the objects themselves, as the argument to `remove`: For example, `remove(c('x', 'y', 'z'))`.

Command Editing and Output Management   1.1.6

In the course of typing an S command, you may find it necessary to correct or modify the command before pressing *Enter*. Both R and S-PLUS support command-line editing:

■ In S-PLUS, you may use the left and right arrow keys or the mouse to move the text-insertion cursor within the current command line; the *Home* key moves the cursor to the beginning of the line, the *End* key to the end of the line.

■ R is somewhat less flexible: You must move the cursor with the left and right arrow, *Home*, and *End* keys.

■ The *Delete* key deletes the character under the cursor in R, and to the right of the cursor in S-PLUS.

■ In both R and S-PLUS, the *Backspace* key deletes the character to the left of the cursor.

■ The standard Windows Edit menu and keyboard shortcuts may be employed, along with the mouse, to block, copy, and paste text.

■ In addition, both R and S-PLUS implement a command-history mechanism that allows you to recall (and edit) previously entered commands without having to retype them. Use the up and down arrow keys to move backward and forward in the command history. Press *Enter* in the normal manner to submit a recalled (and possibly edited) command to the interpreter.

It is advantageous to use an editor to write functions: It is impractical to write any but the simplest function at the command prompt. The *Script* window in S-PLUS incorporates a reasonable, if minimal, programming editor. Moreover, copy-and-paste operations may be used with any plain-text (ASCII) editor, such as Windows Notepad. Simply prepare your program in the editor, block and copy a function definition, and paste this text into the *R Console* or S-PLUS *Commands* window. Alternatively, a program prepared in an editor may be saved to a file and read into R or S-PLUS via the source function.

My personal preference is to use the shareware WinEdt programming editor, which may be set up to work directly with R (see the R Web site for details). Many people prefer the free Emacs editor, which is available for a variety of platforms, including Windows, and which may also be set up to work with R or S-PLUS.

I also use an editor for *data analysis* in S, blocking and submitting commands for execution rather than typing them at the command prompt. (In Notepad, you would block and copy the commands to be submitted, pasting them directly into the *R Console* or S-PLUS *Commands* window.) This mode of operation makes it easy to fix errors, particularly in multiline commands, and to try out alternatives. When I work in the editor, I build a permanent, reusable record of input to my S session as a by-product.

As I work, I save text and graphical output from S in a word-processing (e.g., Word or WordPerfect) document. I simply block and copy text output from R or S-PLUS, pasting it into the word processor, and taking care to use a monospaced (i.e., typewriter) font, such as Courier New. Similarly, I copy and paste graphs. In both R and S-PLUS, right-clicking on a graphics window brings up a menu that allows you to save the graph to a file or copy it to the Windows clipboard; alternatively, you may use the File menu in R or the Edit menu in S-PLUS when a graphics window has the focus. In R, copying the graph to the clipboard as a Windows Metafile (rather than as a bitmap) generally produces a more satisfactory result.

1.1.7 When Things Go Wrong

No one is perfect, and it is impossible to use a computer without making mistakes. Part of the craft of computing is learning to recognize the source of errors. I hope that the following advice and information will help you to fix errors in S commands:

■ Although it never hurts to be careful, do not worry too much about generating errors. An advantage of working in an interactive system is that you can proceed step by step, fixing mistakes as you go.

■ If you are unsure whether a command is properly formulated, or whether it will do what you intend, try it out and carefully examine the result. You can often debug a command, or series of commands, by trying it on a scaled-down problem with an obvious answer. If the answer that you get differs from the one that you expected, focus your attention on the nature of the difference.

■ When you do generate an error, read the error or warning message carefully. It is often possible to figure out the source of the error from the message. Some of the most common errors are simply typing mistakes: For example, when the interpreter tells you that an object is not found, suspect a typing error (or that you have forgotten to attach the library containing the object).

■ Sometimes, however, the source of an error may be subtle, particularly because an S command can generate a sequence of function calls (of one function by another), and the error message may originate deep within this sequence. The `traceback` function (called with no arguments) provides information about the sequence of function calls leading up to an error. Although the format of the output from `traceback` differs among R, S3, and S4, the general nature of the information provided is similar. Here is a simple example employing R:

```
> letters
 [1] "a" "b" "c" "d" "e" "f" "g" "h" "i" "j" "k" "l" "m" "n" "o"
[16] "p" "q" "r" "s" "t" "u" "v" "w" "x" "y" "z"
> my.mean(letters)
Error in sum(..., na.rm = na.rm) : invalid "mode" of
argument
```

The variable `letters` contains the lowercase letters, and, of course, calculating the mean of character data makes no sense. The source of the problem is obvious here, but notice that the error occurs in the `sum` function, not directly in `my.mean`; `traceback` shows the (short) sequence of function calls culminating in the error:

```
> traceback()
2: sum(x)
1: my.mean(letters)
```

■ Remember that not all errors generate error messages. Indeed, the ones that do not are more pernicious, because you may fail to notice them.

Always check your output for reasonableness, and follow up suspicious results.

■ If you need to interrupt the execution of a command, you may do so in R or S-PLUS by pressing the *Esc* (escape) key, or in R by using the mouse to press the *Stop* button in the toolbar.

1.2   AN EXTENDED ILLUSTRATION: DUNCAN'S OCCUPATIONAL-PRESTIGE REGRESSION

In this section, I illustrate how to read data from a file into an S *data frame* (data set), how to draw some simple graphs to examine the data, how to perform a linear least squares regression analysis, and how to check the adequacy of the preliminary regression model using a variety of "diagnostic" methods. It is my intention both to introduce some additional capabilities of S and to convey the flavor of using S for statistical data analysis. All of these topics are treated at length later in the book, so you should not be concerned if you don't understand all of the details.

The data in the file `Duncan.txt` were originally analyzed by Duncan (1961). The first few lines of the data file are as follows:

	type	income	education	prestige
accountant	prof	62	86	82
pilot	prof	72	76	83
architect	prof	75	92	90
author	prof	55	90	76
chemist	prof	64	86	90
minister	prof	21	84	87
professor	prof	64	93	93
dentist	prof	80	100	90
reporter	wc	67	87	52
engineer	prof	72	86	88
	. . .			

The first row of the file consists of variable (column) names: type, income, education, and prestige. Each subsequent row of the file contains data for one observation, with values separated by spaces. In this data set, the observations are occupations, and the first entry in each row is the name of the occupation; note that there is no variable name for the observation-name column. There are 45 occupations in all, only 10 of which are shown.

The variables are defined as follows:

■ type: Type of occupation—bc (blue collar), wc (white collar), or prof (professional or managerial).

- income: Percentage of occupational incumbents in the 1950 U.S. Census who earned more than $3500 per year.

- education: Percentage of occupational incumbents in 1950 who were high-school graduates.

- prestige: Percentage of respondents in a social survey who rated the occupation as good or better in prestige.

Duncan performed a linear least squares regression of prestige on income and education. He proceeded to use the regression equation to predict the prestige levels of occupations for which the income and educational levels were known but for which there were no direct prestige ratings. Duncan did not employ occupational type in his analysis, and I largely ignore the variable here.

Reading the Data   1.2.1

The first step is to read the data into an S data frame, using the read.table function:

```
> Duncan <- read.table('D:/data/Duncan.txt', header=T)
> Duncan
             type income education prestige
accountant   prof     62        86       82
pilot        prof     72        76       83
architect    prof     75        92       90
author       prof     55        90       76
chemist      prof     64        86       90
minister     prof     21        84       87
professor    prof     64        93       93
dentist      prof     80       100       90
reporter       wc     67        87       52
engineer     prof     72        86       88
  . . .
> summary(Duncan)
    type         income          education          prestige
 bc  :21   Min.   : 7.00   Min.   :  7.00   Min.   : 3.00
 prof:18   1st Qu.:21.00   1st Qu.: 26.00   1st Qu.:16.00
 wc  : 6   Median :42.00   Median : 45.00   Median :41.00
           Mean   :41.87   Mean   : 52.56   Mean   :47.69
           3rd Qu.:64.00   3rd Qu.: 84.00   3rd Qu.:81.00
           Max.   :81.00   Max.   :100.00   Max.   :97.00
```

- The initial argument to read.table is the location of the file containing the data to be read. Note that the file name is given in quotes and that forward slashes (/) are used rather than the standard Windows back slashes (\) to separate directories in the path to the file.

- The argument `header=T` tells `read.table` that the first row of the file contains variable names.

- Here, I assign the data frame to the variable `Duncan`. I prefer to begin the names of data frames with uppercase letters, to use lowercase names for variables within data frames, and to name data frames for the files from which the data were read. S enforces none of these conventions, but I find that they help me to keep things straight.

The file `Duncan.txt` is supplied with the `car` library. As explained in the next chapter, this and other data sets in an attached library are available as data frames without being read explicitly. To duplicate the example here, make a copy of `Duncan.txt`.[8]

Typing `Duncan` implicitly invokes the generic `print` function, which prints the data frame in a suitable format. (This is normally how objects get printed in S.)

The generic `summary` function also has a "method" that is appropriate for data frames. As described in Chapter 8, generic functions know how to adapt their behavior to their arguments. Thus, a function such as `summary` may be used appropriately with diverse kinds of objects. Because the column in the data file corresponding to `type` contains character data, the `read.table` function by default made `type` a *factor*—a kind of variable appropriate for categorical data. The `summary` function simply counts the number of observations in each category of the factor. The other variables—`income`, `education`, and `prestige`—are numeric, and the `summary` function reports the minimum, maximum, median, mean, and the first and third quartiles for each numeric variable.

"Attaching" the `Duncan` data frame allows us to access its columns by name, much as if we had directly defined the variables in the data set:

```
> attach(Duncan)
> prestige
 [1] 82 83 90 76 90 87 93 90 52 88 57 89 97 59 73 38 76 81 45 92
[21] 39 34 41 16 33 53 67 57 26 29 10 15 19 10 13 24 20 7 3 16
[41] 6 11 8 41 10
```

Reading and manipulating data is the subject of Chapter 2, where the topic is developed in greater detail.

8. After installing the car library on a Windows system, locate the subdirectory `library\car\data` under the main R directory. The zip archive `Rdata.zip` in this subdirectory contains all the data sets in car. Using a zip utility, extract the file Duncan.txt from the archive. Alternatively, if you are using S-PLUS, the file `Duncan.txt` may be downloaded from the Web site for the book.

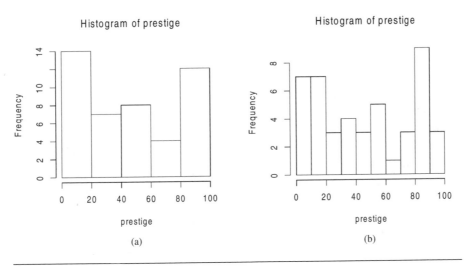

Figure 1.3   Distribution of `prestige`.

Examining the Data   1.2.2

Before fitting a regression model to Duncan's occupational-prestige data, it is advisable to become more intimately acquainted with the data. Figure 1.3(a) shows a histogram for the response variable `prestige`, produced by a call to the `hist` function:

```
> hist(prestige)
>
```

The function `hist` is different from the S functions that we previously encountered in that it does not return a visible result,[9] but rather has the "side effect" of drawing a graph; the graph appears in a separate graphics window, and it may be copied to the Windows clipboard, saved to a file, or printed.

The histogram in Figure 1.3(a) has perhaps too few bins (class intervals) for a data set with $n = 45$ observations. A rough rule is that the number of bins for a variable with fewer than 100 observations should be no more than about $2\sqrt{n}$. (Other, more flexible, rules are described in Chapter 3.) Using S to calculate the recommended maximum number of bins:

```
> 2*sqrt(length(prestige))
[1] 13.41641
```

---

9. The `hist` function does, however, return an *invisible* result—a "list" that contains the information necessary to draw the histogram. To render this list visible, assign it to a variable, e.g., `result <- hist(prestige)`, and then print `result`. Lists are discussed in Chapter 2.

I therefore request 12 bins:

```
> hist(prestige, nclass=12)
>
```

S responds by drawing a histogram with 10 bins (balancing my request against its desire to use "nice" numbers for the endpoints of the bins); the result is shown in Figure 1.3(b). The distribution of prestige appears to be bimodal, with observations stacking up near the lower and upper boundaries. Because prestige is a percentage, this behavior is not altogether unexpected, and we may find later on that we need to use a logit (log-odds) or similar transformation of this variable. As it turns out, however, it will prove unnecessary to transform prestige.

We should also examine the distributions of the predictor variables, along with the relationship between prestige and each predictor, and the relationship between the two predictors. The pairs function in S draws "scatterplot matrices"; the function is quite flexible, and I take advantage of this flexibility by placing histograms for the variables along the diagonal of the graph. To better discern the pairwise relationships among the variables, I augment each scatterplot with a least squares line and with a nonparametric-regression smooth.[10]

```
> pairs(cbind(prestige,income,education),
+     panel=function(x,y){
+         points(x,y)
+         abline(lm(y~x), lty=2)
+         lines(lowess(x,y))
+         },
+     diag.panel=function(x){
+         par(new=T)
+         hist(x, main="", axes=F, nclass=12)
+         }
+     )
>
```

This expression is substantially more complex than the other S function calls that we have encountered, and therefore requires some explanation:

- The cbind (column-bind) function constructs a three-column matrix from prestige, income, and education, as required by the pairs function.

- The panel argument to pairs specifies a function that draws each off-diagonal panel of the scatterplot matrix. The function must have

---

10. Nonparametric regression is discussed in the Web appendix to the book. Here, the method is used simply to pass a smooth curve through the data.

two arguments (which I call x and y), representing the horizontal and vertical variables in each plot. The panel function can be a predefined function or—as here—can be a so-called "anonymous" function, defined "on the fly."[11] My panel function consists of three statements:

1. `points(x,y)` plots the points.

2. `abline(lm(y~x), lty=2)` draws a broken line (specified by the line type,[12] `lty=2`) with intercept and slope given by a linear regression of y on x, computed by the `lm` (linear-model) function. Note the sequence of events here: The `lm` function fits a linear regression of y on x , returning a linear-model object; this object is then passed as an argument to `abline`, which uses the intercept and slope of the regression to draw a line on the plot.

3. `lines(lowess(x,y))` draws a solid line (the default line type) showing the nonparametric regression of y on x. Again, note the sequence of operations: The `lowess` function computes and returns coordinates for points on a smooth curve relating y to x; these coordinates are passed as an argument to `lines`, which connects the points with line segments on the graph.

Because there is more than one statement in the function body, these statements are enclosed as a *block* in curly braces, { and }. Notice how the lines are indented to reveal the structure of the expression; this convention is optional but advisable. If no panel function is specified, then `panel` defaults to `points`: Try simply specifying `pairs(cbind(prestige,income,education))`.

■ The `diag.panel` argument similarly tells `pairs` what, in addition to the variable names, to plot on the diagonal of the scatterplot matrix. The function supplied must take one argument (x), corresponding to the current diagonal variable:

1. `par(new=T)` prevents the `hist` function from trying to clear the graph: High-level S plotting functions, such as `plot`, `hist`, and `pairs`, by default clear the current graphics device prior to drawing a new plot. Other, lower-level plotting functions, such as `points`, `abline`, and `lines`, do not clear the current graphics device by default, but rather add elements to the graph.

2. `hist(x, main="", axes=F, nclass=12)` plots a histogram for x, suppressing both the main title and the axes.

---

11. The function is termed "anonymous" because it literally is never given a name: The function object returned by `function` is left unassigned.

12. Chapter 7 discusses the construction of S graphics, including selection of line types.

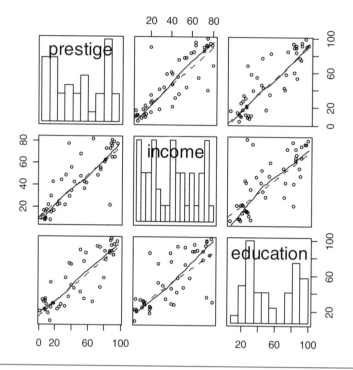

Figure 1.4   Scatterplot matrix for prestige, income, and education.

The scatterplot matrix for prestige, income, and education appears in Figure 1.4. The variable names on the diagonal label the cells: For example, the scatterplot in the upper right-hand corner has education on the horizontal axis and prestige on the vertical axis.

The pairs Function in S-PLUS

The pairs function in S-PLUS does not take a diag.panel argument, so it is not possible to place univariate displays, such as histograms, down the diagonal of the scatterplot matrix.

Like prestige, education appears to have a bimodal distribution. S used rather too many bins in plotting the distribution of income, but some follow-up work (not shown) suggests that the distribution is best characterized as irregular. The pairwise relationships among the variables seem reasonably linear, but two or three observations appear to stand out from the others.

If you frequently want to make scatterplot matrices like this, then it would save work to write a function to do the repetitive parts of the task:[13]

```
> scatmat <- function(..., nclass=NULL) {
+     pairs(cbind(...),
+         panel=function(x,y){
+             points(x,y)
+             abline(lm(y~x), lty=2)
+             lines(lowess(x,y))
+             },
+         diag.panel=function(x){
+             par(new=T)
+             hist(x, main="", axes=F, nclass=nclass)
+             }
+         )
+     }
>
```

Specifying nclass=NULL in the function definition provides a default value for nclass, to be passed as an argument to hist. Note the use of the special formal argument ...; this argument will match any number of real arguments when the function is called. For example:

```
> scatmat(prestige,income,education, nclass=12)
>
```

produces a graph identical to the graph as shown in Figure 1.4. (The scatterplot. matrix function in the car library, described in Chapter 3, is substantially more flexible than the scatmat function just defined.)

It is not convenient in S to identify individual observations in a scatterplot matrix, and so I proceed by drawing a separate scatterplot for the two predictors, education and income:

```
> plot(income, education)

> #   Use the mouse to identify points:
> identify(income, education, row.names(Duncan))
[1]   6 16 27

> row.names(Duncan)[c(6,16,27)]
[1] "minister"     "conductor"     "RR.engineer"
```

The function plot is the workhorse high-level plotting function in S. Called with two vectors as arguments, plot draws a scatterplot. The identify function allows us to label points interactively with a mouse. The first two arguments to identify give the coordinates of the points, and the third argument gives point labels; row.names(Duncan) extracts the observation names from the Duncan data frame to provide point labels. The result is shown in Figure 1.5. Notice that identify returns

---

13. As mentioned, the pairs function in S-PLUS does not take a diag.panel argument, and so scatmat will not work without modification. Try it!

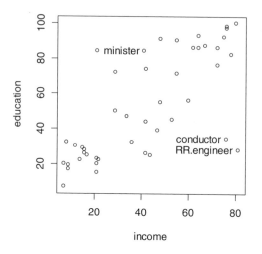

Figure 1.5   Scatterplot of education by income. Three points were labeled interactively with the mouse.

the indices of the identified points [as I verify by indexing into the vector row.names(Duncan)]. To duplicate this figure, you have to move the mouse cursor near each point to be identified, clicking the left mouse button; after identifying the points, click the right mouse button to exit from identify.

Ministers are unusual in combining relatively low income with a relatively high level of education; railroad conductors and engineers are unusual in combining relatively high levels of income with relatively low education. Additional work (not shown) confirms that ministers and conductors are the observations that also stand out in the other scatterplots. None of these observations, however, is an outlier in the *univariate* distributions of the three variables.

1.2.3   Regression Analysis

Duncan's interest in the data was in how prestige is related to income and education in combination. I have thus far addressed the distributions of the three variables and the pairwise (that is, marginal) relationships between them. Following Duncan, I fit a linear least squares regression to the data:

```
> duncan.model <- lm(prestige ~ income + education)
> duncan.model

Call:
lm(formula = prestige ~ income + education)
```

```
Coefficients:
(Intercept)        income     education
    -6.0647        0.5987       0.5458
```

Recall that I attached the Duncan data frame, and consequently I can access the variables in it by name. The argument to lm is a *linear-model formula*, with the response variable on the left of the tilde (~). The right-hand side of the model formula specifies the predictor variables in the regression. We read the formula as "prestige is modeled as income plus education."

The lm function returned a linear-model object, which I assigned to the variable duncan.model. Printing this object (by typing its name) produced a brief report of the results of the regression. The summary function produces a more complete report:

```
> summary(duncan.model)

Call:
lm(formula = prestige ~ income + education)

Residuals:
      Min       1Q    Median       3Q       Max
 -29.5380  -6.4174    0.6546   6.6051   34.6412

Coefficients:
             Estimate Std. Error t value Pr(>|t|)
(Intercept) -6.06466     4.27194  -1.420    0.163
income       0.59873     0.11967   5.003 1.05e-05 ***
education    0.54583     0.09825   5.555 1.73e-06 ***
---
Signif. codes:  0 '***' 0.001 '**' 0.01 '*' 0.05
    '.' 0.1 ' ' 1

Residual standard error: 13.37 on 42 degrees of freedom
Multiple R-Squared: 0.8282,     Adjusted R-squared:  0.82
F-statistic: 101.2 on 2 and 42 degrees of freedom,
      p-value: 1.11e-016
```

Both income and education have highly statistically significant, and rather large, regression coefficients: For example, holding education constant, a 1 percent increase in high-income earners is associated on average with an increase of about 0.6 percent in high prestige ratings.

Notice that S writes very small (and very large) numbers in scientific notation. For example, 1.05e-05 is to be read as 1.05×10^{-5} or 0.0000105, and 1.11e-016 = 1.11×10^{-16} is effectively 0.

If you find the "statistical significance" asterisks that R prints annoying, as I do, you can suppress them by entering

```
> options(show.signif.stars=F)
>
```

Placing this statement in the Rprofile file in R's etc subdirectory will permanently banish the offending asterisks. You can use the same approach to set other options in R.

Linear models are described in greater detail in Chapter 4.

Linear-Model Summaries in S-PLUS

The summary method for linear models in S-PLUS prints the correlation matrix for the coefficient estimates by default. To suppress the coefficient correlations, include the argument correlation = F. As well, S-PLUS does not print significance asterisks.

1.2.4   Regression Diagnostics

Assuming that the regression in the previous section adequately summarizes the data does not make it so. It is therefore wise after fitting a regression model to check the model carefully. S includes some facilities for "regression diagnostics," and the car library associated with this book substantially augments these capabilities. We may attach the car library in the following manner:

```
> library(car)

Attaching package 'car':


        The following object(s) are masked from package:base :

            dfbetas rstudent
```

The warning message indicates that the dfbetas and rstudent functions in car will take precedence over functions with the same names in R's base library. Chapter 2 explains how objects in one library can mask those in another. It is generally bad practice to mask objects in the base library, but the versions of dfbetas and rstudent in car are more general than the standard ones; see Chapter 6 on regression diagnostics for details.

The lm object duncan.model contains a variety of information about the regression. The rstudent function uses some of this information to calculate "studentized" residuals for the model. A histogram of the studentized residuals, in Figure 1.6(a), is unremarkable:

```
> hist(rstudent(duncan.model), nclass=12)
>
```

Histogram of rstudent(duncan.model)

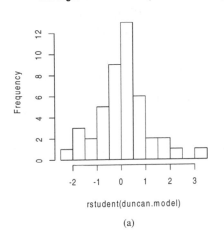

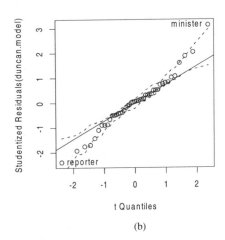

(a) (b)

Figure 1.6 Histogram and t quantile-comparison plot of the studentized residuals from the regression of prestige on income and education.

Observe the sequence of operations here: rstudent takes a linear-model object (previously returned by lm) as an argument, returning studentized residuals, which are passed to hist.

If the errors in the regression are really normally distributed with zero means and constant variance, then the studentized residuals are each t-distributed with $n - p - 1$ degrees of freedom, where p is the number of coefficients in the model (including the regression constant).

The generic qq.plot function (from the car library) has a method for linear models:

```
> qq.plot(duncan.model, labels=row.names(Duncan), simulate=T)
[1] 9 6
```

The resulting plot is shown in Figure 1.6(b). The function extracts the studentized residuals and plots them against the quantiles of the appropriate t distribution; if the studentized residuals are t-distributed, then the plot should be approximately linear. The comparison line on the plot is drawn through the quartiles of the two distributions. In this case, the residuals pull away from the comparison line at both ends, suggesting that the residual distribution is relatively heavy tailed, and raising the possibility that we might do better here with a method of robust or resistant regression than with least squares.[14]

Setting simulate=T in the call to qq.plot produces a bootstrapped pointwise 95 percent confidence envelope for the studentized residuals.

---

14. Robust and resistant regression in S are described in the Web appendix to the book.

The residuals stray near the boundaries of the envelope at both ends of the distribution. Specifying the labels argument to qq.plot allows us to identify points interactively; I identified the most extreme residual at each end of the distribution—the occupations reporter and minister. The qq.plot function returns the indices of the two identified points.

To duplicate this graph, point the mouse successively at the two extreme observations, clicking the left mouse button when the cursor is near each point. After identifying the points, exit from qq.plot by clicking the right mouse button.

I proceed to check for high-leverage and influential observations by calculating hat values and Cook's distances, plotting these statistics against the observation indices:

```
> plot(hatvalues(duncan.model))
> abline(h = c(2,3)*3/45)
> identify(1:45, hatvalues(duncan.model), row.names(Duncan))
[1]   6 16 27

> plot(cookd(duncan.model))
> abline(h = 4/(45-3))
> identify(1:45, cookd(duncan.model), row.names(Duncan))
[1]   6  9 16 27
```

The plots are shown in Figure 1.7. The horizontal lines in the plot of hat values, drawn by abline, are at twice and three times the average hat value, p/n—rough cutoffs for noteworthy values. The horizontal line in the index plot of Cook's distances is at $4/(n - p)$, a rough cutoff for this influence measure. As before, I used the identify function to label interesting observations with the mouse; in each case, identify returns the indices of the identified points. Our attention is drawn in particular to the occupations minister and conductor.

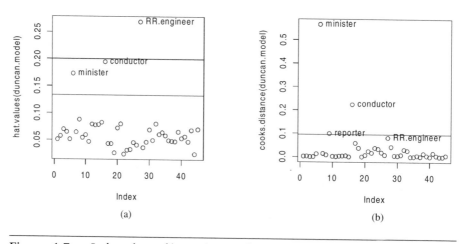

Figure 1.7   Index plots of hat values and Cook's distances from the regression of prestige on income and education.

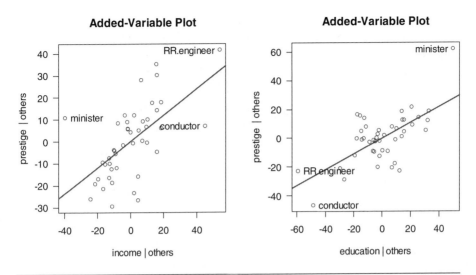

Figure 1.8   Added-variable plots for income and education in Duncan's occupational-prestige regression.

Because observations in a regression can be jointly as well as individually influential, I also examine added-variable (partial-regression) plots for the predictors:

```
> av.plots(duncan.model, labels=row.names(Duncan))

1:(Intercept)
2:income
3:education
Selection: 2

1:(Intercept)
2:income
3:education
Selection: 3

1:(Intercept)
2:income
3:education
Selection: 0
>
```

The av.plots function in car presents the user with a numbered menu to select plots; I chose added-variable plots for the income and education coefficients, and ignored the regression constant (intercept).[15] In each plot, av.plots gave me an opportunity to identify points interactively with the mouse. The added-variable plots, which appear in Figure 1.8,

---

15. Including the argument ask=F to av.plots draws all the plots on a single page.

confirm and strengthen our previous observations: We should be concerned about the occupations minister and conductor, which work together to decrease the income coefficient and increase the education coefficient. The occupation RR.engineer has relatively high leverage on these coefficients, but is more in line with the rest of the data.

I next use the cr.plots function to generate component-plus-residual (partial-residual) plots for income and education:

```
> cr.plots(duncan.model)

1:income
2:education
Selection: 1

1:income
2:education
Selection: 2

1:income
2:education
Selection: 0
>
```

The cr.plots function also interacts with the user through a text menu. The component-plus-residual plots appear in Figure 1.9. Each plot includes a least squares line (representing the regression plane viewed edge on in the direction of the corresponding predictor) and a

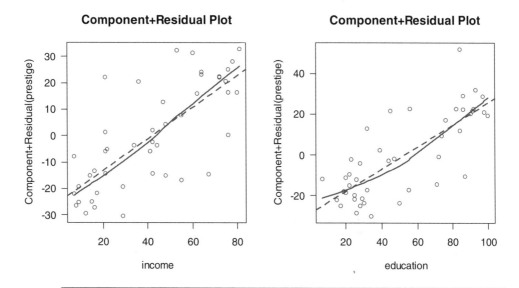

Figure 1.9   Component-plus-residual plots for income and education in Duncan's occupational-prestige regression. The span of the nonparametric-regression smoother was set to 0.7.

Spread-Level Plot for duncan.model

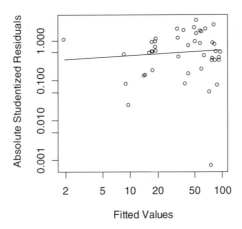

Figure 1.10   Spread-level plot of studentized residuals from Duncan's regression of prestige on income and education.

nonparametric-regression smooth (with the span of the smoother set to 0.7—see Section 3.2). The purpose of these plots is to detect nonlinearity, evidence of which is slight here.

I check whether the size of the residuals changes with the fitted values, using the spread.level.plot function, which has a method for linear models:

```
> spread.level.plot(duncan.model)

Suggested power transformation:  0.8653151
```

The graph produced by spread.level.plot, in Figure 1.10, shows little association of residual spread with level, and the suggested power transformation of the response variable, prestige$^{0.87}$, is essentially no transformation at all. Using the ncv.test function in car, I follow up with score tests for nonconstant variance, checking for an association of residual spread with fitted values and with *any* linear combination of the predictors:

```
> ncv.test(duncan.model)
Non-constant Variance Score Test
Variance formula: ~fitted.values
Chisquare = 0.3810967    Df = 1     p = 0.5370169

> ncv.test(duncan.model, var.formula= ~ income + education)
Non-constant Variance Score Test
Variance formula: ~ income + education
Chisquare = 0.6976023    Df = 2     p = 0.7055334
```

Both tests are far from statistically significant.

Finally, on the basis of the influential-data diagnostics, I try removing the observations `minister` and `conductor` from the regression:

```
> remove <- which.names(c('minister', 'conductor'), Duncan)
> remove
[1]   6 16
> duncan.model.2 <- update(duncan.model, subset=-remove)
> summary(duncan.model.2)

Call:
lm(formula = prestige ~ income + education, subset = -remove)

Residuals:
    Min      1Q  Median      3Q     Max
-28.612  -5.898   1.937   5.616  21.551

Coefficients:
            Estimate Std. Error t value Pr(>|t|)
(Intercept) -6.40899    3.65263  -1.755   0.0870
income       0.86740    0.12198   7.111 1.31e-08
education    0.33224    0.09875   3.364   0.0017

Residual standard error: 11.42 on 40 degrees of freedom
Multiple R-Squared: 0.876,      Adjusted R-squared: 0.8698
F-statistic: 141.3 on 2 and 40 degrees of freedom,
        p-value:    0
```

Note the use of the `which.names` function in `car` to determine the indices of `minister` and `conductor`; actually, I knew from my previous work that these are observations 6 and 16. Rather than respecifying the regression model from scratch, I refit it using the `update` function, removing the two observations via the `subset` argument to `update`. The coefficients of `income` and `education` have changed substantially with the deletion of these two observations. Further work (not shown) suggests that removing the occupations `RR.engineer` and `reporter` does not make much of a difference.

Chapter 6 has more extensive information on regression diagnostics in S, including use of functions in the `car` library.

1.3   S FUNCTIONS FOR BASIC STATISTICS

The focus of this book is on using S for regression analysis, broadly construed. In the course of developing this subject, we will encounter, and indeed have encountered, a variety of S functions for basic statistical methods (`mean`, `hist`, etc.), but the topic is not addressed systematically.

Table 1.1   S Functions for basic statistical methods. All functions are present in both R and S-PLUS, unless marked [R] for R only or [S] for S-PLUS only. All functions are in the R base library, unless the library is shown explicitly. Chapter references are to the current text.

Method	S Function(s)	R Library	Reference
Histogram	hist		Chapter 3
Stem-and-leaf display	stem		Chapter 3
Boxplot	boxplot		Chapter 3
Scatterplot	plot		Chapter 3
Time-series plot	ts.plot	ts	
Mean	mean		
Median	median		
Quantiles	quantile		
Extremes	range, min, max		
Variance	var		
Standard deviation	stdev [S], sd [R]		
Covariance matrix	var		
Correlations	cor		
Basic statistical distributions: normal, t, F, chi-square, binomial, etc.	dnorm, dt, df, dchisq, dbinom, etc. pnorm, pt, pf, pchisq, pbinom, etc. qnorm, qt, qf, qchisq, qbinom, etc. rnorm, rt, rf, rchisq, rbinom, etc.		Chapter 3
Simple regression	lm		Chapter 4
Multiple regression	lm		Chapter 4
Analysis of variance	aov, lm, anova		Chapter 4
Contingency tables	table, xtabs [R], crosstabs [S]		Chapter 5
Generating random samples	sample, rnorm, etc.		
t tests for means	t.test		
Tests for proportions	prop.test, binom.test	ctest	
chi-square test for independence	chisq.test	ctest	
Various nonparametric tests	friedman.test, kruskal.test, wilcox.test, etc.	ctest	

Because I expect that most readers of the book will be new to S, it is worthwhile to draw an orienting road map of S functions for familiar statistical operations. Rather than describing the use of S for basic applied statistics at length, however, I simply provide in tabular form (Table 1.1) the names of some of the S functions that implement these operations, referring the interested reader to the on-line documentation (accessible, recall, through the help command and ? operator). This table is not meant to be complete.

All the functions listed are in libraries attached by default to the S-PLUS search path. As indicated under *R Library*, some of these functions are in R libraries other than the base library; these other libraries are not attached by default, but are part of the basic R distribution. Where there is a substantial discussion of a function later in the present text, this is indicated under *Reference*. Functions present only in one of R or S-PLUS are marked [R] or [S], as appropriate; other functions are common to R and S-PLUS, although the details of their implementation may differ.

CHAPTER 2

Reading and Manipulating Data

A s I mentioned in the Preface, a traditional statistical computer package, such as SAS or SPSS, is designed primarily to transform rectangular data sets into printed reports and graphs. A rectangular data set has rows representing observations and columns representing variables. S, in contrast, is a programming language embedded in a statistical computing environment; it is designed to transform data objects into other data objects, (generally brief) printed reports, and graphs.

S supports rectangular data sets, in the form of *data frames*, but as a programming language, it also supports a variety of other data structures. One by-product of this generality is flexibility: It is typically much easier to accomplish tasks not directly designed into the software in S than in a statistical package. Another by-product of generality, however, is complexity. In this chapter, I attempt to cut through the complexity to explain what you need to know about data in S in order to work efficiently as a statistical data analyst:

■ There are often many ways to accomplish a task in S. For common tasks—reading data into an S data frame from a text file, for example—I generally explain one or two good ways to proceed rather than aiming at an exhaustive treatment.

■ I limit the presentation to those aspects of the S language that are most useful to practicing data analysts. For example, I avoid a fully general exposition of S modes and classes.

■ I suggest that users of S adopt conventions that will facilitate their work and minimize confusion, even when the S language does not enforce these conventions. For example, I begin the names of data frames with uppercase letters and the names of variables in data frames with lowercase letters.

Section 2.1 describes how to read data into S variables and data frames. Section 2.2 explains how to work with data stored in data frames. Section 2.3 introduces matrices, higher-dimensional arrays, and lists. Finally, Section 2.4 deals more abstractly with the organization of data in S, introducing the notions of data modes, attributes, and classes.

2.1   DATA INPUT

Although there are many ways to read data into R and S-PLUS, I will concentrate on just four: typing data directly at the keyboard, reading data from an ASCII (plain-text) file into an S data frame, "importing" data saved by a statistical package, and accessing data from a library. In addition, I will explain how to generate certain kinds of patterned data.

2.1.1   Keyboard Input

It is impractical to enter large data sets directly at the keyboard, and it is wasteful to reenter data that are already available in machine-readable form. It is occasionally convenient, however, to enter small data sets directly, and we frequently find it necessary to enter a few numbers, for example, in the process of augmenting a graph.

We saw in the previous chapter how to use the c (combine) function to enter a vector of numbers:

```
> x <- c(1,2,3,4)
> x
[1] 1 2 3 4
```

The same procedure works for vectors of other types, such as character data or logical data:

```
> names <- c('John', 'Georges', 'Mary')
> names
[1] "John"    "Georges" "Mary"

> v <- c(T,F)
> v
[1]  TRUE FALSE
```

Character strings may be input between single or double quotation marks: for example, 'John' and "John" are equivalent.

Entering data in this manner works well for very short vectors. Although entries may be continued over several lines simply by omitting the terminal right parenthesis until the data are complete,[1] it is more convenient to use the scan function, which prompts with the index of the next entry.

To illustrate, consider the data in the following table, which originates in an experiment conducted by Fox and Guyer (1978):

Condition	Sex	
	Male	Female
Public Choice	49	54
	64	61
	37	79
	52	64
	68	29
Anonymous	27	40
	58	39
	52	44
	41	34
	30	44

In this experiment, 20 four-person groups of subjects played 30 trials of a game in which each subject could make either cooperative or competitive choices. Half the groups were composed of women and half of men. Half the groups of each sex were randomly assigned to a public-choice condition in which the choices of all individuals were made known to the group after each trial; the other groups were assigned to an anonymous-choice condition in which only the aggregated choices were revealed. The data in the table give the number of cooperative choices made in each group, out of $30 \times 4 = 120$ choices in all.

To enter the number of cooperative choices as a vector:

```
> cooperation <- scan()
1: 49 64 37 52 68 54
7: 61 79 64 29
11: 27 58 52 41 30 40 39
18: 44 34 44
21:
Read 20 items
```

---

1. You may have noticed in some of the previous examples that when an S statement is continued on additional lines, the > prompt is replaced by the interpreter with the + (plus) prompt on the continuation lines. S recognizes that a line is to be continued when it is syntactically incomplete—for example, when a left parenthesis needs to be balanced by a right parenethesis or when the right argument to a binary operator, such as *, has not yet been entered.

```
> cooperation
 [1] 49 64 37 52 68 54 61 79 64 29 27 58 52 41 30 40 39 44
[19] 34 44
```

The number before the colon on each input line is the index of the next observation to be entered; entering a blank line terminates scan. I entered the data for the Male, Public-Choice treatment first, followed by the data for the Female, Public-Choice treatment, and so on.

I could enter the condition and sex of each group in a similar manner, but because the data are patterned, it is more economical to use the rep (replicate) function. The first argument to rep specifies the data to be repeated; the second argument specifies the number of repetitions:

```
> rep(5,3)
[1] 5 5 5


> rep(c(1,2,3), 2)
[1] 1 2 3 1 2 3
```

When the first argument to rep is a vector, the second argument can be a vector of the same length, specifying the number of times to repeat each entry of the first argument:

```
> rep(1:3, 3:1)
[1] 1 1 1 2 2 3
```

In the current context, we may proceed as follows:

```
> condition <- rep(c('public', 'anonymous'), c(10,10))
> condition
 [1] "public"    "public"    "public"    "public"
 [5] "public"    "public"    "public"    "public"
 [9] "public"    "public"    "anonymous" "anonymous"
[13] "anonymous" "anonymous" "anonymous" "anonymous"
[17] "anonymous" "anonymous" "anonymous" "anonymous"

> sex <- rep(rep(c('male', 'female'), c(5,5)), 2)
> sex
 [1] "male"   "male"   "male"   "male"   "male"   "female"
 [7] "female" "female" "female" "female" "male"   "male"
[13] "male"   "male"   "male"   "female" "female" "female"
[19] "female" "female"
```

To construct the vector sex, I used rep twice—first to generate five 'male' character strings followed by five 'female' character strings, and then to repeat this pattern of 10 strings two times.

Finally, it is convenient to put the three variables together in a data frame:

```
> Guyer <- data.frame(cooperation, condition, sex)
> Guyer
  cooperation condition   sex
1          49    public  male
```

```
2              64     public    male
3              37     public    male
. . .
19             34  anonymous  female
20             44  anonymous  female
```

In the process, `condition` and `sex` are converted from character variables into factors. The distinction is discussed in Section 2.2.3.

Both R and S-PLUS have spreadsheet-like data editors that may be used to enter, examine, and modify data frames. I find these editors useful primarily for viewing the contents of data frames and for modifying individual values, for example, to fix an error in the data. In R, to enter data into a new data frame, we may type:

```
> Guyer <- edit(as.data.frame(NULL))
>
```

This opens the data editor, into which we may type variable names and data values. Figure 2.1 shows the editor after the data values have been entered. (Out of laziness, I entered `condition` as P or A, and `sex` as M or F.) An existing data frame can be viewed or edited by using the `fix` function, as in `fix(Guyer)`.

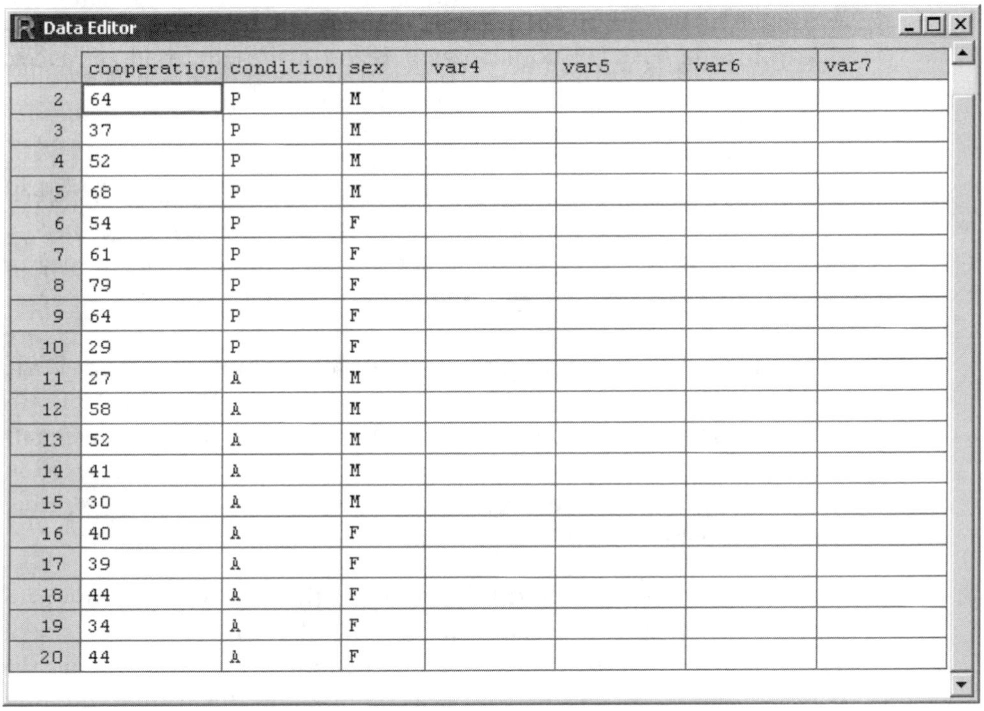

	cooperation	condition	sex	var4	var5	var6	var7
2	64	P	M				
3	37	P	M				
4	52	P	M				
5	68	P	M				
6	54	P	F				
7	61	P	F				
8	79	P	F				
9	64	P	F				
10	29	P	F				
11	27	A	M				
12	58	A	M				
13	52	A	M				
14	41	A	M				
15	30	A	M				
16	40	A	F				
17	39	A	F				
18	44	A	F				
19	34	A	F				
20	44	A	F				

Figure 2.1 The R data editor.

The Data Editor in S-PLUS

In S-PLUS, we may enter a new data frame in the data editor by selecting **New** $\longrightarrow$ **Data Set** from the **File** menu. To view or edit an existing data frame, double-click on its name in the *Object Explorer* window.

2.1.2 File Input to a Data Frame

Delimited Data

The previous example shows how to construct a data frame from preexisting variables. More frequently, as illustrated in Chapter 1, we read data from an ASCII (plain-text) file into an S data frame using the `read.table` function. I assume that the input file is organized in the following manner:

■ The first line of the file gives the names of the variables separated by "white space" (one or more blanks or tabs); these names are valid S variable names and, in particular, contain no embedded blanks. If the first variable in the data file is to provide row names for the data frame, then there is one fewer variable name than columns of data; otherwise, there is one variable name for each column. I prefer to use variable names that begin with lowercase letters.

■ Each subsequent line contains data for one observation, with the data values separated by white space. The data values in each line need not appear in the same place as long as the *number* of values in each line is the same; ensuring that the data values line up neatly in columns makes it easier to examine the input file, however. Character data either contain no embedded blanks (my preference) or are enclosed in single or double quotes. Thus, for example, `white.collar`, `'white collar'`, and `"white collar"` are valid character-data values, but `white collar` is not. Character and logical data are automatically converted to factors on input. You may avoid this conversion by specifying the argument `as.is=T` to `read.table`, but representing categorical data as factors is generally desirable.

■ One variation on this simple scheme is worth mentioning: Many programs, such as spreadsheets, create ASCII files with data values separated by commas—so-called "comma-delimited files." Supplying the argument `sep=','` to `read.table` accommodates this form of data. In comma-delimited data, blanks *may* be included in unquoted character strings, but commas may not.

■ Missing data appear explicitly, preferably encoded by the characters NA (not available); in particular, missing data are *not* left blank. There is, therefore, the same number of data values in each line of the input file even when some of the values represent missing data. If different characters are used to encode missing data, and it is inconvenient to replace them in an editor, then you may specify the missing-data code in the na.strings argument to read.table. For example, both SAS and SPSS recognize the period (.) as an input missing-data indicator; to read a file with period encoding missing data, use na.strings='.'. For more details, see the on-line documentation for read.table.

This specification is more rigid than it needs to be, but it is clear and usually is easy to satisfy. Most spreadsheet, database, and statistical programs are capable of producing ASCII files of this format, or produce files that can be put in this form with minimal editing. Use an ASCII editor (such as Windows Notepad or a programming editor) to edit data files. If you use a word-processing program (such as Word or WordPerfect), be careful to save the file as an ASCII file; read.table cannot read data saved in the default formats employed by word-processing programs.

I use the data in the file Prestige.txt to illustrate.[2] This data set is similar to the Duncan occupational-prestige data employed as an example in the previous chapter, with occupations as observations. Here are a few lines of the data file (recall that the ellipses represent omitted lines—there are 102 occupations in all):

	education	income	women	prestige	census	type
GOV.ADMINISTRATORS	13.11	12351	11.16	68.8	1113	prof
GENERAL.MANAGERS	12.26	25879	4.02	69.1	1130	prof
ACCOUNTANTS	12.77	9271	15.70	63.4	1171	prof
. . .						
COMMERCIAL.ARTISTS	11.09	6197	21.03	57.2	3314	prof
RADIO.TV.ANNOUNCERS	12.71	7562	11.15	57.6	3337	wc
ATHLETES	11.44	8206	8.13	54.1	3373	NA
SECRETARIES	11.59	4036	97.51	46.0	4111	wc
. . .						
ELEVATOR.OPERATORS	7.58	3582	30.08	20.1	6193	bc
FARMERS	6.84	3643	3.60	44.1	7112	NA
FARM.WORKERS	8.60	1656	27.75	21.5	7182	bc
ROTARY.WELL.DRILLERS	8.88	6860	0.00	35.3	7711	bc
. . .						

The variables in the data set are defined as follows:

■ education: the average number of years of education for occupational incumbents in the 1971 Census of Canada.

---

2. As in Chapter 1, you can extract this file from the car library or download it from the Web site for the book.

- income: the average income of occupational incumbents, in dollars, in the 1971 Census.

- women: the percentage of occupational incumbents in the 1971 Census who were women.

- prestige: the average prestige rating for the occupation obtained in a sample survey conducted in Canada in 1966.

- census: the code of the occupation in the standard 1971 Census occupational classification.

- type: professional and managerial (prof), white-collar (wc), blue-collar (bc), or missing (NA).

To read the data into S, I enter[3]:

```
> Prestige <- read.table('D:/data/Prestige.txt', header=T)
> Prestige
                     education income women prestige census type
GOV.ADMINISTRATORS       13.11  12351 11.16     68.8   1113 prof
GENERAL.MANAGERS         12.26  25879  4.02     69.1   1130 prof
ACCOUNTANTS              12.77   9271 15.70     63.4   1171 prof
   . . .
COMMERCIAL.ARTISTS       11.09   6197 21.03     57.2   3314 prof
RADIO.TV.ANNOUNCERS      12.71   7562 11.15     57.6   3337   wc
ATHLETES                 11.44   8206  8.13     54.1   3373   NA
SECRETARIES              11.59   4036 97.51     46.0   4111   wc
   . . .
ELEVATOR.OPERATORS        7.58   3582 30.08     20.1   6193   bc
FARMERS                   6.84   3643  3.60     44.1   7112   NA
FARM.WORKERS              8.60   1656 27.75     21.5   7182   bc
ROTARY.WELL.DRILLERS      8.88   6860  0.00     35.3   7711   bc
   . . .
```

Even though I am running R on a Windows system, directories in the file system are separated by a / (forward slash) rather than by the standard Windows \ (back slash); this is because the back slash has special meaning in an S character string.[4] To keep things tidy, I prefer to name a data frame for the file from which the data were read, and to begin the name of the data frame with an uppercase letter.

---

3. Including the argument header=T is unnecessary in R when, as here, the first row of the data file, containing variable names, has one fewer entry than the data lines that follow. In this setup, the first entry on each data line represents the row label for the corresponding observation. Nevertheless, it does not hurt to specify header=T, and getting into the habit of doing so will save you grief when you read a file with variable names but without row names.

4. The back slash serves as a so-called "escape" character, indicating that the next character has special meaning: For example, \n represents a new-line character (i.e., go to the beginning of the next line), while \t is the tab character. Such special characters can be useful in creating printed output. A back slash may be entered in a character string as \\.

Occasionally, when we try to read a data set from a text file, some of the input lines contain the wrong number of elements, producing an error in `read.table`. To simulate this condition, I prepared a version of the `Prestige.txt` data file in which missing values (i.e., NAs) were erroneously replaced by blanks. Trying to read this file yields the following result:

```
> Prestige <- read.table('D:/data/Prestige-bugged.txt', header=T)
Error in scan(file = file, what = what, sep = sep, quote = quote,
    skip = 0, : line 34 did not have 7 elements
```

Having determined that the data file `Prestige-bugged.txt` contains at least one error, it is convenient to use the `count.fields` function to discover whether there are other errors as well, and, if there are, to determine their location:

```
> counts <- count.fields('D:/data/Prestige-bugged.txt')
> counts
 [1] 7 7 7 7 7 7 7 7 7 7 7 7 7 7 7 7 7 7 7 7 7 7 7 7 7 7 7 7 7 7
[31] 7 7 7 6 7 7 7 7 7 7 7 7 7 7 7 7 7 7 7 7 7 7 7 6 7 7 7 7 7 7
[61] 7 7 7 6 7 7 7 6 7 7 7 7 7 7 7 7 7 7 7 7 7 7 7 7 7 7 7 7 7 7
[91] 7 7 7 7 7 7 7 7 7 7 7 7

> which(counts != 7)
[1] 35 54 64 68
```

Once we know the location of the errors, it is simple the fix the input file in a text editor that keeps track of line numbers. (Notice that `read.table` reports that the 34th data line is in error, and that this corresponds to the 35th line in the file, since the first line is the header.)

Fixed-Format Data

You may find it necessary to read data from a *fixed-format* input file in which the data values are not separated by delimiters such as white space or commas. To illustrate the process of reading these kinds of data, I have created a fixed-format version of the Canadian occupational-prestige data set, which I placed in the file `Prestige-fixed.txt`. The file looks like this:

```
GOV.ADMINISTRATORS       13.111235111.1668.81113prof
GENERAL.MANAGERS         12.2625879 4.0269.11130prof
ACCOUNTANTS              12.77 927115.7063.41171prof
    . . .
TYPESETTERS              10.00 646213.5842.29511bc
BOOKBINDERS               8.55 361770.8735.29517bc
```

The first 25 characters in each line are reserved for the `occupation` name, the next five spaces for the `education` value, the next five for `income`, and so on. Notice how many of the data values run together, making the file difficult to decipher: If you have a choice, fixed-format input is best avoided. We may use the `read.fwf` (read fixed-width-format files) function to input the data into an R data frame:

```
> Prestige <- read.fwf('d:/data/Prestige-fixed.txt',
+     row.names='occupations',
+     col.names=c('occupation', 'education', 'income', 'women',
          'prestige', 'census', 'type'),
+     widths=c(25, 5, 5, 5, 4, 4, 4))
>
```

The `col.names` argument to `read.fwf` supplies names for the variables; `row.names` indicates that one of the variables (here, `occupation`) should be used to define row names; and the `widths` argument gives the *field width* of each variable in the input file.

Reading Fixed-Format Data in S-PLUS

S-PLUS does not have `read.fwf`, but much the same task may be accomplished with the `scan` function. Creating a data frame is a two-step process, using `scan` to read the data into a list of data vectors and then converting this list into a data frame. For example:

```
> Prestige <- data.frame(scan('d:/data/Prestige-fixed.txt',
+     list(occupation="", education=0, income=0, women=0,
+         prestige=0, census=0, type=""),
+     widths=c(25, 5, 5, 5, 4, 4, 4)))
>
```

The second argument to `scan` is a list defining variable names and types, with `""` (an empty character string—or any character string) indicating character data and `0` (or any number) indicating numeric data. The `widths` argument works as for `read.fwf` in R. It should be possible to specify a `row.names` argument to `data.frame`, but I have not been able to get this to work properly in S-PLUS.

2.1.3   Importing Data

You will doubtless encounter data sets that have been prepared in another statistical system, such as SAS or SPSS. If you have access to the other program, then it is generally straightforward to "export" the data as an ASCII file, subsequently reading the data into S with `read.table`, as described in the preceding section. Alternatively, R provides facilities for "importing data" from other programs through functions in the `foreign`

library (which may be downloaded from the R Web site). Currently, functions are available for importing data files from S3, SAS, SPSS, Minitab,
and Stata. There is also an R interface to the Excel spreadsheet program.[5]

Importing Data in S-PLUS

In S-PLUS, it is most straightforward to import data via the graphical interface: Select **Import Data**⟶ **From File** from the **File** menu. S-PLUS will
read data from several statistical programs, including SAS, SPSS, Minitab
(S4 only), Stata, and Systat, the mathematical programs Gauss and Matlab,
and a variety of spreadsheet and database programs.

Accessing Data in S Libraries   2.1.4

Many S libraries, including the car library, contain data sets. In R, which
stores working data in memory, it is necessary to use the data function to
read a data frame from an attached library into memory. Then the data
frame may be attached in the normal manner. For example, to access the
Duncan data frame from the car library in R:

```
> library(car)
. . .
> data(Duncan)
> Duncan
              type income education prestige
accountant    prof    62        86       82
pilot         prof    72        76       83
architect     prof    75        92       90
author        prof    55        90       76
chemist       prof    64        86       90
minister      prof    21        84       87
professor     prof    64        93       93
. . .
janitor         bc     7        20        8
policeman       bc    34        47       41
waiter          bc     8        32       10

> attach(Duncan)
>
```

---

5. In addition, both R and S-PLUS have sophisticated facilities for accessing data stored in binary
formats, in database-management systems, on the Internet, and in other locations. These facilities
are described in the manuals for R and S-PLUS.

Accessing Data in S-PLUS Libraries

In S-PLUS, it is sufficient to attach a library, via the `library` function, to make the data sets in the library accessible. If the data set is a data frame, then the data frame may simply be attached in the normal manner. That is, the `data` function is not needed and is not used in S-PLUS.

I have defined several variables in the course of this section, some of which are no longer needed, so it is time to clean up:

```
> objects()
[1] "Duncan"      "Guyer"       "Prestige"    "condition"
[5] "cooperation" "names"       "sex"         "v"
[9] "x"
> remove(names, v, x)
>
```

I retain the data frames `Duncan`, `Guyer`, and `Prestige` and the vectors `condition`, `cooperation`, and `sex` for subsequent illustrations in this chapter.

Reminder: Removing Objects in S-PLUS

Remember that in S-PLUS the *names* of objects to be removed must be given as a character vector: for example, `remove(c('names', 'x', 'y'))`.

2.1.5   Getting Data *Out* of S

I hope and expect that you will rarely have to get your data out of S to use with another program, but doing so is nevertheless straightforward. As in the case of reading data, there are many ways to proceed, but a particularly simple approach is to use the `write.table` function to output a data frame to an ASCII file. The syntax for `write.table` is essentially the reverse of that for `read.table`. For example, the following command writes the `Duncan` data frame to a file:

```
> write.table(Duncan, 'c:/temp/Duncan.txt')
>
```

By default, row labels and variable names are included in the file. In R, data values are separated by blanks, and all character strings are quoted, whether or not they contain blanks. This default behavior can be changed—see the documentation for `write.table`.

Exporting Data from S-PLUS

In S-PLUS, data values exported by `write.table` are separated by commas, and strings are not quoted. S-PLUS can also export data in a variety of other formats: Select **Export Data**⟶**To File** from the **File** menu.

WORKING WITH DATA FRAMES   2.2

It is perfectly possible in S to analyze data stored in vectors, but I generally prefer to begin with a data frame, typically read from a file via the `read.table` function, or accessed from an S library. Almost all the examples in this book use data frames from the `car` library.

In many statistical packages, such as SPSS, a single data set is active at any given time; in other packages, such as SAS, individual statistical procedures draw their data from a single source. This is not the case in S, where data may be used simultaneously from several sources, providing substantial flexibility, but also the possibility of interference and confusion.

The Search Path   2.2.1

When you type the name of a variable or a function, the R interpreter looks for an object of that name in the locations specified by the *search path*. To view the current search path, use the `search` function:

```
> search()
[1] ".GlobalEnv"    "Duncan"         "package:car"
[4] "Autoloads"     "package:base"
```

If, therefore, I type the name of the variable `prestige`, R will look first in the "global environment" (the region of memory in which R stores working data), then in the data frame `Duncan` (which I attached to the search path in the preceding section), then in the `car` library (which I previously attached via the `library` function), then in a special list of objects whose loading from libraries can take place automatically (and which I will subsequently ignore), and, finally, in the R base library. Because there is no variable named `prestige` in the working data, but there is such a variable in the Duncan data frame, when I type prestige, I get the prestige variable from Duncan, as we may readily verify:

```
> prestige
 [1] 82 83 90 76 90 87 93 90 52 88 57 89 97 59 73 38 76 81
[19] 45 92 39 34 41 16 33 53 67 57 26 29 10 15 19 10 13 24
[37] 20  7  3 16  6 11  8 41 10

> Duncan[,'prestige']
 [1] 82 83 90 76 90 87 93 90 52 88 57 89 97 59 73 38 76 81
[19] 45 92 39 34 41 16 33 53 67 57 26 29 10 15 19 10 13 24
[37] 20  7  3 16  6 11  8 41 10
```

Typing Duncan[,'prestige'] directly extracts the column named prestige from the Duncan data frame.[6]

Suppose, now, that I attach the Prestige data frame to the search path. The default behavior of the attach function is to attach a data frame in the *second* position of the search path, after the global environment:

```
> attach(Prestige)
> search()
[1] ".GlobalEnv" "Prestige" "Duncan"
[4] "package:car" "Autoloads" "package:base"
```

Consequently, the data frame Prestige is attached *before* the data frame Duncan; and if I now simply type prestige, then the prestige variable in Prestige will be located before the prestige variable in Duncan is encountered:

```
> prestige
  [1] 68.8 69.1 63.4 56.8 73.5 77.6 72.6 78.1 73.1 68.8
 [11] 62.0 60.0 53.8 62.2 74.9 55.1 82.3 58.1 58.3 72.8
 [21] 84.6 59.6 66.1 87.2 66.7 68.4 64.7 34.9 72.1 69.3
      . . .
 [91] 38.9 36.2 29.9 42.9 26.5 66.1 48.9 35.9 25.1 26.1
[101] 42.2 35.2
```

The prestige variable in Duncan is still there—it is just being "shadowed" or "masked" (that is, hidden) by prestige in Prestige:

```
> Duncan[,'prestige']
 [1] 82 83 90 76 90 87 93 90 52 88 57 89 97 59 73 38 76 81
[19] 45 92 39 34 41 16 33 53 67 57 26 29 10 15 19 10 13 24
[37] 20  7  3 16  6 11  8 41 10
```

---

6. Information on indexing data frames is presented in Section 2.3.4.

Because variables in one data frame can shadow variables in another, it is generally good practice to attach only one data frame at a time—unless there is a valid reason for accessing data simultaneously from two data frames. You can remove a data frame from the search path with the detach function:

```
> detach(Prestige)
> search()
[1] ".GlobalEnv" "Duncan" "package:car"
[4] "Autoloads" "package:base"
```

Calling detach with no arguments detaches the second entry in the search path.

Using detach in S-PLUS

In S-PLUS, you need to specify the *name* of the data frame to be detached as a character string, rather than the object itself: e.g., detach('Prestige'). This usage also works in R.

Now that Prestige has been detached, prestige again refers to the variable by that name in the Duncan data frame:

```
> prestige
[1] 82 83 90 76 90 87 93 90 52 88 57 89 97 59 73 38 76 81
[19] 45 92 39 34 41 16 33 53 67 57 26 29 10 15 19 10 13 24
[37] 20 7 3 16 6 11 8 41 10
```

Because the working data are the first item in the search path, globally defined variables shadow variables of the same names anywhere else along the path. This is why I use an uppercase letter at the beginning of the name of a data frame. Had I, for example, named the data frame prestige rather than Prestige, then the variable prestige within the data frame would have been shadowed by the data frame itself. To access the variable would then require a relatively awkward construction, such as prestige[,'prestige'].

Our focus here is on manipulating data, but it is worth mentioning that S locates functions in the same way that it locates data. Consequently, functions earlier on the path can shadow functions of the same name later on the path.

In the previous chapter, I defined a function called my.mean, avoiding the name mean so that the mean function in the base library would not be shadowed. To understand the consequences of failing to take this precaution, note that the mean function in the base library can calculate "trimmed" means as well as the ordinary arithmetic mean. For example:

```
> mean(prestige)
[1] 47.68889

> mean(prestige, trim=0.1)
[1] 47.2973
```

Specifying mean(prestige, trim=0.1) removes the largest and smallest 10 percent of the data, calculating the mean of the middle 80 percent of observations. Trimmed means provide more efficient estimates of the center of a heavy-tailed distribution—for example, when outliers are present; in this example, trimming makes little difference.

Suppose that I define my own mean function, making no provision for trimming:

```
> mean <- function(x){
+      warning('The mean function in the base package is shadowed')
+      sum(x)/length(x)
+      }
>
```

The first line in my mean function prints a warning message. The purpose of the warning is simply to verify that this function executes in place of the mean function in the base library. Had I *carelessly* shadowed the base mean function, I would not have politely provided a warning:

```
> mean(prestige)
[1] 47.68889
Warning message:
The mean function in the base package is shadowed in: mean(prestige)
```

The essential point here is that because my mean function resides in the global environment, it is encountered on the search path before the mean function in the base package. Shadowing the base mean function is inconsequential as long as my function is equivalent; but if, for example, I try to calculate a trimmed mean, my function does not work:

```
> mean(prestige, trim=0.1)
Error in mean(prestige, trim = 0.1) : unused argument(s) (trim ...)
```

Shadowing standard S functions is a practice generally to be avoided. Suppose, for example, that a robust-regression function tries to calculate a trimmed mean, but fails because the base mean function is shadowed by my redefined mean function. If we are not on the lookout for this problem, the resulting error message may prove cryptic.

Illustrating Function Shadowing in S4

The standard mean function is a generic function, and S4 does not permit a nongeneric version of a function to shadow the generic. (Try it.) To illustrate one function shadowing another in S4, let us instead use stdev:

```
> stdev <- function (x) {
+     warning("The standard stdev function is shadowed")
+     sqrt(var(x))
+     }
Warning: Conflicting definitions of "stdev" on databases
 "C:\Program Files\Insightful\splus6\users\Administrator"
 and "splus"

> stdev (prestige)
Warning in stdev(prestige): The standard stdev function
is shadowed

[1] 17.204

> remove('stdev')
>
```

Note that S4 warns us of the conflict when our stdev is defined. Remember to remove stdev when you are finished.

We can, however, use the same name for a variable and a function, as long as the two do not reside in the working data. Consider the following example:

```
> mean <- mean(prestige)  # uses then overwrites our mean function
Warning message:
The mean function in the base package is shadowed in: mean(prestige)

> mean
[1] 47.68889
```

Recall that everything to the right of the # (pound sign) is a comment, ignored by the S interpreter. Specifying mean <- mean(prestige) causes our mean function to calculate the mean prestige and then stores the result in a variable called mean, which has the effect of destroying our mean function (and good riddance to it). The *variable* mean in the working data does not, however, shadow the *function* mean in the base library:

```
> mean(prestige, trim=.1)
[1] 47.2973
```

Before proceeding, let us tidy up a bit:

```
> remove(mean)
> detach(Duncan)
>
```

The Search Path in S-PLUS

A word on the difference in the search path between R and S-PLUS: Data and functions in S-PLUS are stored in files, which reside in data and function directories. Here is an example of a search path in S-PLUS:

```
> search()
[1]  "C:\\Program Files\\Insightful\\splus6\\users\\Administrator"
[2]  "Duncan"
[3]  "car"
[4]  "splus"
[5]  "stat"
[6]  "data"
[7]  "trellis"
[8]  "nlme3"
[9]  "menu"
[10] "sgui"
[11] "winspj"
[12] "main"
>
```

This example uses S-PLUS version 6, based on S4; the listing of the search path in S-PLUS 2000, based on S3, looks different. The first directory contains the working data, and is therefore analogous to the global environment in R. (The concept of an environment in R does not correspond precisely to a data base in S-PLUS—an environment is more nearly a list of data bases—but the distinction is subtle, and I will not pursue it here.) The Duncan data frame, added to the search path via the attach function, is in the second position, followed by the car library. Notice that several libraries appear by default at the end of the path.

2.2.2 Missing Data

Missing data are a regrettably common feature of real data sets. Two kinds of issues arise in handling missing data:

■ There are relatively deep statistical issues concerning how best to use available information in the presence of missing data (see, for example, Little & Rubin, 1987; Schafer, 1997). I will ignore these issues here, except to remark that S is well designed to exploit sophisticated approaches to missing data (and, indeed, the methods described in Schafer, 1997, are available in S[7]).

---

7. See the missing library for S-PLUS 6 and the less extensive norm library for R.

■ There are intellectually trivial but often practically vexing mechanical issues concerning computing with missing data in S. These are the subject of the present section. Partly these issues arise because of the diverse data structures and kinds of functions available simultaneously to the S user, but partly similar issues arise in all statistical computing systems, although they may sometimes be disguised.

As we have seen, on data input, missing values are typically encoded by the characters NA (not available). The same characters are used to print missing information. Many functions in S know how to handle missing data, although sometimes they have to be explicitly told what to do.

To illustrate, let us access the data set Freedman in the car library; because the car library is already in the search path, all I need to do in R is to use the data and attach functions; I also print out the first few rows of Freedman:

```
> data(Freedman)
> attach(Freedman)
> Freedman[1:10,]   # first 10 rows
            population nonwhite density crime
AKRON              675      7.3     746  2602
ALBANY             713      2.6     322  1388
ALBUQUERQUE         NA      3.3      NA  5018
ALLENTOWN          534      0.8     491  1182
ANAHEIM           1261      1.4    1612  3341
ATLANTA           1330     22.8     770  2805
BAKERSFIELD        331      7.0      41  3306
BALTIMORE         1981     21.6     877  4256
BEAUMONT           315     20.7     240  2117
BINGHAMTON         305      0.6     147  1063
```

These data, on 110 U.S. metropolitan areas, are originally from the *1970 Statistical Abstract of the United States*, and were employed by Freedman (1975) as part of a wide-ranging study of the social and psychological effects of crowding. (Freedman argues, by the way, that high density tends to intensify social interaction, and thus the effects of crowding are not simply negative.) The variables in the data set are as follows:

■ population: total 1968 population, in thousands.

■ nonwhite: percentage nonwhite population in 1960.

■ density: population per square mile in 1968.

■ crime: number of serious crimes per 100,000 residents in 1969.

Some of Freedman's data are missing (for example, the population and density for Albuquerque). Here are the values for density:

```
> density
   [1]  746   322    NA   491  1612   770    41   877   240
  [10]  147   272  1831  1252   832   630    NA    NA   328
  [19]  308  1832   640  1361    NA   583   194   320   215
   . . .
 [100]   NA    NA   123   132  1170   166   383   419   405
 [109]  220   513
```

Suppose, now, that I try to calculate the median density. (As we will see shortly, the density values are highly positively skewed, so using the mean as a measure of the center of the distribution would be a bad idea.)

```
> median(density)
[1] NA
```

S tells me that the median density is missing. This is the pedantically correct answer: Several of the density values are missing, and consequently we cannot, in the absence of those values, know the median, but this is probably not what I had in mind when I asked for the median density. By setting the na.rm (NA-remove) argument of median to TRUE, I instruct S to calculate the median of the remaining, nonmissing values:

```
> median(density, na.rm=T)
[1] 412
```

Several other S functions that calculate statistical summaries, such as mean and var (variance), also work like this, but not all S functions handle missing data in this manner.

Most plotting functions simply ignore missing data. For example, to construct a scatterplot of crime against density, including only the observations with valid data for both variables, simply enter:

```
> plot(density, crime)
> identify(density, crime, row.names(Freedman))
[1] 50 67 73
```

The resulting plot, including three observations identified with the mouse, appears in Figure 2.2. (Recall that you identify observations by pointing at them with the mouse and clicking the left mouse button; you exit from identify by clicking the right mouse button.) It is apparent that density is highly positively skewed, making the plot very difficult to read. I would like to try plotting crime against the log of density, but wonder whether the missing data will spoil the computation. The log function in S behaves sensibly, however: The result has a missing entry wherever—and only where—there was a missing entry in the argument:

```
> log(c(1,10,NA,100), base=10)
[1]  0  1 NA  2
```

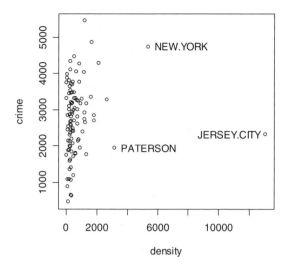

Figure 2.2   Scatterplot of crime by density for Freedman's data on crowding and crime. Three cities with high density were identified interactively with the mouse.

Logs in S4

Remember, in S4, you must use the function logb in place of log to calculate logs to an arbitrary base.

Other functions that compute on vectors in an element-wise fashion—such as the arithmetic operators—behave similarly.

I, therefore, may proceed as follows, producing the graph in Figure 2.3:

```
> plot(log(density, base=10), crime)
>
```

This graph is much easier to read, and it now appears that there is a weak, positive relationship between crime and density. (I will address momentarily how to produce the lines in the plot.)

Statistical modeling functions in S have a special argument, na.action, which specifies how missing data are to be handled; na.action is set to a function that takes a data frame as an argument and returns a similar data frame composed entirely of valid data. The simplest na.action is na.omit, which removes all observations with missing data on *any* variable in the computation. An alternative, for example, would be to supply an na.action that imputes the missing values.

The prototypical statistical modeling function in S is lm (linear model), which is described extensively in Chapter 4. For example, to fit a linear

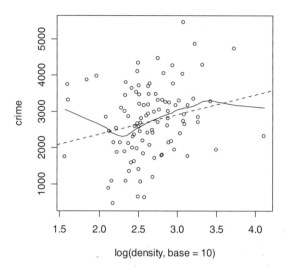

Figure 2.3   Scatterplot of crime by $\log_{10}$density, showing linear least squares and nonparametric-regression (lowess) lines.

regression of crime on the log of density, removing observations with missing data on either crime or density, enter:

```
> lm(crime ~ log(density, base=10))

Call:
lm(formula = crime ~ log(density, base = 10))

Coefficients:
        (Intercept)   log(density, base = 10)
             1297.3                     542.6
```

The lm function returns a linear-model object; because the returned object was not saved in a variable, the interpreter simply printed a brief report of the regression. To plot the least squares line on the scatterplot in Figure 2.3:

```
> abline(lm(crime ~ log(density, base=10)), lty=2)
>
```

The linear-model object returned by lm is passed to abline, which draws the regression line; specifying lty=2 (line type 2) produces a broken line.

In R, the default na.action is given by the na.action option, which is initially set to na.omit:

```
> options('na.action')
$na.action
[1] "na.omit"
```

There is another na.action function named na.exclude, which is similar to na.omit in that it removes observations with missing data from a statistical model. When quantities such as residuals are calculated, however, na.exclude causes entries corresponding to observations with missing data to be NA, rather than simply absent from the result. Filling out results with NAs can be advantageous because it preserves the number of observations in the data set—for example, in plotting residuals against a predictor, we need do nothing special to ensure that both variables have the same number of entries. I suggest that you adopt na.exclude as the default na.action. If you run across a modeling function that does not yet support na.exclude, then you can use na.omit.

---

na.action in S-PLUS

In S-PLUS, in contrast to R, there is no preset global na.action, although one can be set with the option command. The default na.action for statistical modeling functions such as lm is na.fail, which reports an error when missing data are encountered. To change this behavior, supply an appropriate na.action argument, such as na.omit or na.exclude. The na.exclude function is available in S4 but not in S3.

Some functions in S, particularly older ones, make no provision for missing data, and simply fail if an argument has a missing entry. In these cases, we need somewhat tediously to handle the missing data ourselves. A relatively straightforward way to do so is to use the is.na function to test for missing data, and then to exclude the missing data from the calculation.

For example, to locate all observations with valid data for both crime and density, I enter:

```
> good<-!(is.na(density) | is.na(crime))
> good
 [1]  TRUE TRUE FALSE  TRUE  TRUE  TRUE  TRUE  TRUE  TRUE
[10]  TRUE TRUE TRUE   TRUE  TRUE  TRUE FALSE FALSE  TRUE
  . . .
```

I then use good to select the valid observations by indexing (a topic described in Section 2.3.4). For example, it is convenient to use the lowess function to add a nonparametric-regression smooth to a scatterplot (see Figure 2.3), but lowess makes no provision for missing data:

```
> lines(lowess(log(density[good], base=10), crime[good]))
>
```

By indexing density and crime with the logical vector good, I extract only the observations that have valid data for *both* variables.

Suppose, as is frequently the case, that we analyze a data set with a complex pattern of missing data, fitting several statistical models to the data. If the models do not all employ exactly the same variables, then it is likely that they will be fit to different subsets of nonmissing observations. Then if we compare models, for example, with an incremental *F* test or a likelihood-ratio test, the comparison will be invalid.

To avoid this problem, we can first use na.omit to filter the data frame for missing data, including all variables that we intend to use in our data analysis. For example, for Freedman's data, we may proceed as follows, assuming that we want to use all four variables in the data frame:

```
> detach(Freedman)
> Freedman.good <- na.omit(Freedman)
> attach(Freedman.good)
> Freedman.good[1:10,]  # first 10 observations
            population nonwhite density crime
AKRON              675      7.3     746  2602
ALBANY             713      2.6     322  1388
ALLENTOWN          534      0.8     491  1182
ANAHEIM           1261      1.4    1612  3341
ATLANTA           1330     22.8     770  2805
BAKERSFIELD        331      7.0      41  3306
BALTIMORE         1981     21.6     877  4256
BEAUMONT           315     20.7     240  2117
BINGHAMTON         305      0.6     147  1063
BIRMINGHAM         739     32.1     272  2285

> dim(Freedman.good)
[1] 100    4
```

Notice that I detach Freedman because there is no need to access variables in both data frames simultaneously (and the variables in Freedman.good, now in position 2 on the search list, will shadow those in Freedman in any event): As mentioned, it is generally advisable to have only one data frame attached at a time, unless there is a specific reason to access data from several sources at once. The dim (dimension) function tells us that there are 100 observations and 4 variables in the Freedman.good data frame; all missing data have been removed.

2.2.3 Numeric Variables and Factors

If you construct S data frames as I have suggested, by reading data from files using read.table, or from numeric and character vectors using data.frame, your data frames will consist of two kinds of data: numeric variables and factors. Both read.table and data.frame by default translate character data into factors.

Before proceeding, let us clean up a bit:

```
> detach(Freedman.good)
```

```
> objects()
 [1] "Duncan"        "Freedman"       "Freedman.good" "Guyer"
 [5] "Prestige"      "condition"      "cooperation"   "good"
 [9] "last.warning"  "sex"

> remove(good, Freedman.good)
>
```

Near the beginning of this chapter, I entered data from Fox and Guyer's experiment on anonymity and cooperation into the "global" variables cooperation, condition, and sex. (Variables created by assignment at the command prompt are global variables defined in the working data.) The latter two variables are character vectors, as we may verify for condition:

```
> condition
 [1] "public"    "public"    "public"    "public"    "public"
 [6] "public"    "public"    "public"    "public"    "public"
[11] "anonymous" "anonymous" "anonymous" "anonymous" "anonymous"
[16] "anonymous" "anonymous" "anonymous" "anonymous" "anonymous"

> is.character(condition)
[1] TRUE
```

Note the use of the "predicate" function is.character. Types of data are discussed more systematically in Section 2.4.

After entering the data, I defined the data frame Guyer, which also contains variables named cooperation, condition, and sex. I now attach the data frame, but before doing so, I remove the global variables so that they do not shadow the variables of the same names in the data frame:

```
> remove(cooperation, condition, sex)
> attach(Guyer)
>
```

There is, by the way, a general lesson here: Because the global environment is the first entry on the search path, global variables in general shadow variables by the same names in data frames on the path. You can take advantage of this fact, or it can be a source of trouble and confusion. For example, when we make a change to a variable in an attached data frame (e.g., cooperation[1] <- NA) the change is actually made to a *copy* of the variable in the working data. Likewise, the assignment cooperation <- cooperation makes a copy of cooperation in the working data.

Let us take a look at the variable condition in the attached data frame:

```
> condition
 [1] public    public    public    public    public    public
 [7] public    public    public    public    anonymous anonymous
[13] anonymous anonymous anonymous anonymous anonymous anonymous
```

```
[19] anonymous anonymous
Levels:  anonymous public

> is.character(condition)
[1] FALSE
> is.factor(condition)
[1] TRUE
```

As promised, the version of `condition` in the data frame is a *factor* rather than a character vector. A factor is a representation of a categorical variable; factors are stored more economically than character vectors, and the manner in which they are stored saves information about the *levels* (category set) of a factor. When a factor is printed, its values are not quoted (as they would be for a character vector), and (in R) the levels are listed.

Most important, many functions in S, including the statistical modeling functions such as `lm`, know how to deal with factors. For example, when the generic `summary` function is called with a data frame as its argument, it prints various statistics for a numeric variable but simply counts the number of observations in each level of a factor:

```
> summary(Guyer)
   cooperation          condition        sex
  Min.    :27.00    anonymous:10    female:10
  1st Qu.:38.50    public   :10    male  :10
  Median :46.50
  Mean    :48.30
  3rd Qu.:58.75
  Max.    :79.00
```

Factors have unordered levels. An extension, called *ordered factors*, is discussed (along with factors) in Chapter 4 on linear models.

2.2.4   Modifying Data

For the most part, data modification in S occurs naturally and unremarkably. When I wanted to plot `crime` against the log of `density` in Freedman's data, for example, I simply specified `log(density, base=10)`; in this case, I did not even have to create a new variable, say `log.density`, as one would have to do in a typical statistical package like SAS or SPSS.[8] Similarly, in regressing `crime` on the log of `density`, I just used `log(density, base=10)` on the right-hand side of the linear model.

---

8. An alternative would have been to plot `crime` against `density`, using a log axis for `density`. See Chapters 3 and 7 for general discussions of plotting data in S.

Creating new variables is similarly straightforward. Unless we take explicit steps to the contrary, assignments in S create global variables in the working data. So, for example, with the Guyer data frame attached (as is currently the case), let us calculate the percentage of cooperative choices in each group. Recall that the variable cooperation counts the number of cooperative choices out of 120 choices in all:

```
> perc.coop <- 100*cooperation/120
>
```

The variable perc.coop resides in the working data, not in the Guyer data frame. It is generally harmless, and even desirable, to create global variables from a currently attached data frame, as long as we are careful to clean up after we are finished.

Suppose, instead, that I *replace* the variable cooperation in the data frame with the percentage of cooperative choices:

```
> Guyer$cooperation <- 100*cooperation/120
> Guyer
    cooperation condition    sex
1      40.83333    public   male
2      53.33333    public   male
3      30.83333    public   male
. . .
20     36.66667 anonymous female
```

Note the use of the $ (dollar sign) for indexing a variable in a data frame: This "list-like" indexing is discussed in Section 2.3.4. Although the variable cooperation in the data frame has been modified, the attached version of the data frame is unaffected, as we may readily verify:

```
> cooperation
 [1] 49 64 37 52 68 54 61 79 64 29 27 58 52 41 30 40 39 44 34 44
```

Detaching and reattaching the data frame makes the definition of cooperation current:

```
> detach(Guyer)                    .
> attach(Guyer)
> cooperation
 [1] 40.83333 53.33333 30.83333 43.33333 56.66667 45.00000
 [7] 50.83333 65.83333 53.33333 24.16667 22.50000 48.33333
[13] 43.33333 34.16667 25.00000 33.33333 32.50000 36.66667
[19] 28.33333 36.66667
```

A similar procedure may be employed to add a *new* variable to a data frame. The following statement, for example, adds the logit (log-odds) of cooperation to the Guyer data frame:

```
> Guyer$logit.coop <- log(cooperation/(100-cooperation))
> Guyer
   cooperation condition    sex  logit.coop
1     40.83333    public   male -0.37085958
2     53.33333    public   male  0.13353139
3     30.83333    public   male -0.80792270
 . . .

20    36.66667 anonymous female -0.54654371
```

The assignment takes place in the global version of Guyer, however, rather than in the previously attached version, and consequently the new variable logit.coop is not immediately available:

```
> logit.coop
Error: Object "logit.coop" not found
> detach(Guyer)
> attach(Guyer)
> logit.coop
 [1] -0.37085958  0.13353139 -0.80792270 -0.26826399  0.26826399
 [6] -0.20067070  0.03333642  0.65587579  0.13353139 -1.14356368
[11] -1.23676263 -0.06669137 -0.26826399 -0.65587579 -1.09861229
[16] -0.69314718 -0.73088751 -0.54654371 -0.92798677 -0.54654371
```

Because of the awkwardness of detaching and reattaching the data frame, and the attendant possibility of error, I generally prefer to create new and modified variables in the working data rather than directly in an attached data frame. If I want to save the new or modified variables in the data frame, then I can assign them to the data frame when I clean up.

Transforming numerical data is usually a straightforward operation, simply employing mathematical operators and functions. Categorizing numerical data and recoding categorical variables are often more complicated matters. A number of functions in S are employed to create and to deal with categorical data, but I limit discussion to two that I find particularly useful: the standard S function cut and the function recode in the car library.

The cut function dissects the range of a numerical variable into class intervals. The first argument to the function is the variable to be categorized; the second argument gives either the number of equal-width intervals or a vector of cut points at which the division is to take place. For example, to divide the range of cooperation into four equal-width intervals, I specify:

```
> coop.4 <- cut(cooperation, 4)
> summary(coop.4)
(22.5,33.3] (33.3,44.2]   (44.2,55]   (55,65.9]
         6           7           5           2
```

R responds by creating a factor, the levels of which are named for the intervals. Because cooperation is not uniformly distributed across its range, the several levels of coop.4 contain different numbers of observations.

Suppose, alternatively, that we want to dissect cooperation into three levels containing roughly equal numbers of observations[9] and to name these levels 'low', 'med', and 'high'; we may proceed as follows:

```
> coop.groups <- cut(cooperation,
+     quantile(cooperation, c(0, 1/3, 2/3, 1)),
+     include.lowest=T,
+     labels=c('low', 'med', 'high'))

> summary(coop.groups)
 low  med high
   7    6    7
```

Note the use of the quantile function to locate the cut points. Had we wished to divide cooperation into four groups, for example, we would simply have specified different quantiles: c(0, .25, .5, .75, 1).

The cut Function in S-PLUS

In S-PLUS, the cut function creates a *category* variable rather than a factor. A category is an older S representation for categorical data. It is a simple matter to "coerce" a category to a factor: For example, coop.4 <- as.factor(cut(cooperation, 4)).

The recode function may also be used to dissect a quantitative variable into class intervals. For example:

```
> coop.2 <- recode(cooperation, 'lo:50=1; 50:hi=2')
> coop.2
 [1] 1 2 1 1 2 1 2 2 2 1 1 1 1 1 1 1 1 1 1 1
```

The recode function works as follows:

- The first argument is the variable to be recoded, here cooperation.

- The second argument is a character string (i.e., enclosed in single or double quotes) containing the recode specifications.

- Recode specifications are of the form *old.values=new.value*; there may be several recode specifications separated by semicolons.

- The "old values" may be a single value, including NA; a range, of the form *minimum:maximum*, as in the example (where the special values lo and hi may be used to stand in for the smallest and largest values of the variable); a vector of values, typically specified with the

---

9. *Roughly* equal numbers of observations in the three intervals are the best we can do, because $n = 20$ is not evenly divisible by 3.

c (combine) function; or the special symbol else, which, if present, should appear last.

- An observation that fits into more than one recode specification is assigned the value of the first one encountered. For example, a group with cooperation exactly equal to 50 would get the "new" value 1.

- Character data may appear as both "old" and "new" values. You must be careful with quotation marks, however: If single quotes are employed to enclose the recode specifications, then double quotes must be used for the values (and vice versa).

- When a factor is recoded, the "old" values should be specified as character strings; the result is a factor, even if the "new" values are numbers, unless the argument as.factor.result is set to FALSE.

- Character data may be recoded to numeric and vice versa. To recode a character or numeric variable to a factor, set as.factor.result=TRUE.

- If an observation satisfies none of the recode specifications, then the "old" value for that observation is carried over into the result.

To provide a richer context for some further illustrations of the use of recode, I detach the Guyer data frame, do some housecleaning, and attach the Womenlf data frame from the car library:

```
> detach(Guyer)
> remove(perc.coop, coop.4, coop.groups, coop.2)
> data(Womenlf)
> attach(Womenlf)

> sample.20 <- sort(sample(nrow(Womenlf), 20))  # 20 random obs.
> sample.20
 [1]  14  28  41  47  51  56  66  72  76  80  99 104 117 118
[15] 129 131 153 177 188 224

> Womenlf[sample.20,]  # 20 randomly selected rows
        partic hincome children   region
14   not.work       9  present  Prairie
28   not.work      19  present  Ontario
41   not.work       9  present       BC
47   not.work       7  present  Ontario
51   parttime      10  present  Prairie
56   not.work      17   absent Atlantic
66   not.work      15  present  Ontario
72   not.work      17  present  Ontario
76   parttime      38  present  Ontario
80   parttime      19  present       BC
99   fulltime      15   absent  Ontario
104  not.work      15   absent       BC
```

```
117 not.work      19   absent        BC
118 not.work      19   absent        BC
129 parttime      13   present   Prairie
131 parttime      19   present   Ontario
153 not.work       5   absent        BC
177 not.work      15   present   Ontario
188 not.work       7   present        BC
224 not.work      19   present    Quebec
```

The `sample` function is used to pick a random sample of 20 rows in the data frame, selecting 20 random numbers without replacement from 1 to the number of rows in `Womenlf`; the numbers are placed in ascending order by the `sort` function.

The data in `Womenlf` originate in a social survey of the Canadian population conducted in 1977. The data pertain to married women between the ages of 21 and 30, with variables defined as follows:

- `partic`: labor-force participation, `parttime`, `fulltime`, or `not.work` (not working outside the home).

- `hincome`: husband's income, in $1000s (actually, family income minus wife's income).

- `children`: presence of children in the household: `present` or `absent`.

- `region`: `Atlantic`, `Quebec`, `Ontario`, `Prairie`, `BC` (British Columbia).

Now consider the following recodes:

```
> working <- recode(partic,
+ " c('parttime', 'fulltime')='yes'; 'not.work'='no' ")
> working[sample.20]  # 20 sampled observations
 [1] no  no  no  no  yes no  no  no  yes yes yes no  no  no
[15] yes yes no  no  no  no
Levels:  no yes

> working.alt <- recode(partic,   # equivalent to previous recode
+ " c('parttime', 'fulltime')='yes'; else='no' ")
> all(working == working.alt)     # check
[1] TRUE

> fulltime <- recode(partic,
+ " 'fulltime'='yes'; 'parttime'='no'; 'not.work'=NA ")
> fulltime[sample.20]  # 20 sampled observations
 [1] NA  NA  NA  NA  no  NA  NA  NA  no  no  yes NA  NA  NA
[15] no  no  NA  NA  NA  NA
Levels:  no yes

> region.4 <- recode(region, " c('Prairie','BC')='West' ")
> region.4[sample.20]  # 20 sampled observations
 [1] West     Ontario  West     Ontario  West     Atlantic
```

```
[7] Ontario  Ontario  Ontario  West     Ontario  West
[13] West     West     West     Ontario  West     Ontario
[19] West     Quebec
Levels:  Atlantic Ontario Quebec West
```

In all these examples, factors (either `partic` or `region`) are recoded, and consequently `recode` returns factors as results.

- The first two examples yield identical results, with the second example illustrating the use of `else`. To verify that all of the values in `working` and `working.alt` are the same, I use the `all` function along with the element-wise comparison operator `==` (equals).

- In the third example, a factor `fulltime` is created, indicating whether a woman who works outside of the home works full time or part time; `fulltime` is `NA` (missing) for women who do not work outside the home.

- The fourth and final example illustrates how values that are not recoded (here `Atlantic`, `Quebec`, and `Ontario` in the factor `region`) are simply carried over to the result.

I once more clean up before proceeding:

```
> detach(Womenlf)
> remove(working, working.alt, fulltime, region.4, sample.20)
>
```

2.3 MATRICES, ARRAYS, AND LISTS

We have thus far encountered and used several data structures in S:

- *Vectors*: One-dimensional arrays of numbers, character strings, or logical values (i.e., TRUE or FALSE). Single numbers, character strings, or logical values in S are treated as vectors of length 1.

- *Factors*: One-dimensional arrays of levels.

- *Data frames:* Two-dimensional data tables, with the rows defining observations and the columns defining variables. Data frames are heterogeneous in the sense that some columns may be numeric and others may be factors (or may even contain character data or logical data).

In this section, I describe three other common data structures: *matrices, arrays,* and *lists.*

Matrices   2.3.1

You may be aware that much of applied statistics is naturally expressed mathematically using vectors and matrices. Matrices in S are two-dimensional arrays of elements all of which are of the same *mode*—for example, numbers, character strings, or logical values.

Matrices may be constructed using the matrix function, which reshapes its first argument into a matrix with the specified number of rows (the second argument) and columns (the third argument). For example:

```
> A <- matrix(1:12, 3, 4)  # 3 rows, 4 columns
> A
     [,1] [,2] [,3] [,4]
[1,]   1    4    7   10
[2,]   2    5    8   11
[3,]   3    6    9   12

> B <- matrix(c('a','b','c'), 4, 3, byrow=T)
> B
     [,1] [,2] [,3]
[1,] "a"  "b"  "c"
[2,] "a"  "b"  "c"
[3,] "a"  "b"  "c"
[4,] "a"  "b"  "c"
```

A matrix is filled by columns, unless the optional argument byrow is set to TRUE. The second example illustrates that if there are fewer elements in the first argument than in the matrix being defined, then the elements are simply recycled.

A defining characteristic of a matrix is that it has a dim (dimension) *attribute* with two elements: the number of rows and the number of columns. A vector, in contrast, does not have a dim attribute[10]:

```
> dim(A)
[1] 3 4
> dim(B)
[1] 4 3

> v <- sample(10,10)  # permutation of 1 to 10
> v
 [1] 10  4  7  9  5  3  2  6  8  1
> dim(v)
NULL
```

---

10. More correctly, a matrix is a vector with a two-element dim attribute.

Note that sample(10,10) produces a random permutation of the numbers from 1 to 10.

For more on attributes in S, see Section 2.4. S includes extensive facilities for matrix computation, some of which are described in Chapter 8.

2.3.2 Arrays

Higher-dimensional arrays of homogeneous elements may be created with the array function; here is an example employing a three-dimensional array:

```
> array.3 <- array(1:24, c(4,3,2))   # 4 rows, 3 columns, 2 layers
> array.3
, , 1

     [,1] [,2] [,3]
[1,]    1    5    9
[2,]    2    6   10
[3,]    3    7   11
[4,]    4    8   12


, , 2

     [,1] [,2] [,3]
[1,]   13   17   21
[2,]   14   18   22
[3,]   15   19   23
[4,]   16   20   24


> dim(array.3)
[1] 4 3 2
```

The order of the dimensions is row, column, and "layer," and the array is filled with the index of the first dimension "moving" most quickly. We will seldom require higher-dimensional arrays in this book.

2.3.3 Lists

Lists are one-dimensional data structures composed of potentially heterogeneous elements. Indeed, the elements of a list may themselves be—and usually are—complex data structures, including other lists. Here is an example of a list, constructed with the list function:

```
> list.1 <- list(mat.1=A, mat.2=B, vec=v)   # 3-item list
```

```
> list.1
$mat.1
     [,1] [,2] [,3] [,4]
[1,]    1    4    7   10
[2,]    2    5    8   11
[3,]    3    6    9   12

$mat.2
     [,1] [,2] [,3]
[1,] "a"  "b"  "c"
[2,] "a"  "b"  "c"
[3,] "a"  "b"  "c"
[4,] "a"  "b"  "c"

$vec
 [1] 10  4  7  9  5  3  2  6  8  1
```

This list contains a numeric matrix, a character matrix, and a numeric vector. Notice that I named the elements in the call to the list function; these are arbitrary names that I chose, not standard arguments to list. Because they permit us to collect related information regardless of its form, lists provide the foundation for the class-based object system in S. Classes are described in Section 2.4 and in Chapter 8. Data frames, for example, are lists with some special properties that permit them to behave somewhat like matrices.

Indexing   2.3.4

A common operation in S is to extract some of the elements of a vector, matrix, array, or list by specifying the indices of the elements to be extracted. Indices are specified between square brackets—[and]. I have already used this construction on several occasions, and it is now time to consider indexing more systematically.

As we saw in the first chapter, a vector may be indexed by a single number or by a vector of numbers; indeed, indices may be specified out of order, and an index may be repeated to extract the corresponding element more than once:

```
> v
 [1] 10  4  7  9  5  3  2  6  8  1
> v[2]
[1] 4
> v[c(4,2,6)]
[1] 9 4 3
> v[c(4,2,4)]
[1] 9 4 9
```

Specifying negative indices suppresses the corresponding elements of the vector:

```
> v[-c(2,4,6,8,10)]
[1] 10  7  5  2  8
```

If a vector has a names attribute, then we can also index the elements by name[11]:

```
> names(v) <- letters[1:10]
> names(v)
 [1] "a" "b" "c" "d" "e" "f" "g" "h" "i" "j"

> v[c('f','i','g')]
f i g
3 8 2
```

Finally, a vector may be indexed by a logical vector of the same length:

```
> v < 6
    a     b     c     d     e     f     g     h     i     j
FALSE  TRUE FALSE FALSE  TRUE  TRUE  TRUE FALSE FALSE  TRUE

> v[v < 6]   # all entries less than 6
b e f g j
4 5 3 2 1
```

Any of these forms of indexing may be used on the left-hand side of the assignment operator to replace elements of a vector. For example:

```
> vv <- v   # make copy of v
> vv
 a  b  c  d  e  f  g  h  i  j
10  4  7  9  5  3  2  6  8  1

> vv[c(1,3,5)] <- c(1,2,3)
> vv
a b c d e f g h i j
1 4 2 9 3 3 2 6 8 1

> vv[c('b','d','f','h','j')] <- 0
> vv
a b c d e f g h i j
1 0 2 0 3 0 2 0 8 0

> remove(vv)
>
```

---

11. The vector letters contains the 26 lowercase letters from 'a' to 'z'; LETTERS similarly contains the uppercase letters.

Indexing extends straightforwardly to matrices and to higher-dimensional arrays. Indices corresponding to different dimensions of the array are separated by commas; if the index for a dimension is left unspecified, then all of the elements along that dimension are selected.

I demonstrate with the matrix A:

```
> A
     [,1] [,2] [,3] [,4]
[1,]   1    4    7   10
[2,]   2    5    8   11
[3,]   3    6    9   12

> A[2,3]   # element in row 2, column 3
[1] 8

> A[c(1,2), 2]   # rows 1 and 2, column 2
[1] 4 5

> A[c(1,2), c(2,3)] # rows 1 and 2, columns 2 and 3
     [,1] [,2]
[1,]   4    7
[2,]   5    8

> A[c(1,2),]   # rows 1 and 2, all columns
     [,1] [,2] [,3] [,4]
[1,]   1    4    7   10
[2,]   2    5    8   11
```

Notice that the second example, A[2,3], returns a single-element vector rather than a 1×1 matrix; likewise, the third example, A[c(1,2), 2], returns a vector with two elements rather than a 2×1 matrix. More generally in indexing a matrix or array, dimensions of extent 1 are automatically dropped. Specifying drop=F circumvents this behavior:

```
> A[c(1,2), 2, drop=F]   # returns 1-column matrix
     [,1]
[1,]   4
[2,]   5
```

Negative indices, row or column names (if they are defined), and logical vectors of the appropriate length may also be used to index a matrix or a higher-dimensional array:

```
> A[,-c(1,3)]   # omit columns 1 and 3
     [,1] [,2]
[1,]   4   10
[2,]   5   11
[3,]   6   12
```

```
> A[-1,-2]     # omit row 1 and column 2
     [,1] [,2] [,3]
[1,]    2    8   11
[2,]    3    9   12

> rownames(A) <- c('one', 'two', 'three')  # set row names
> colnames(A) <- c('w','x','y', 'z')       # set column names
> A
      w x y  z
one   1 4 7 10
two   2 5 8 11
three 3 6 9 12

> A[c('one','two'), c('x','y')]
    x y
one 4 7
two 5 8

> A[c(T,F,T),]
      w x y  z
one   1 4 7 10
three 3 6 9 12
```

Used on the left of the assignment arrow, we may replace indexed elements in a matrix or array:

```
> AA <- A  # make a copy of A
> AA
      w x y  z
one   1 4 7 10
two   2 5 8 11
three 3 6 9 12

> AA[1,] <- 0  # set first row to zeros
> AA
      w x y  z
one   0 0 0  0
two   2 5 8 11
three 3 6 9 12

> remove(AA)
>
```

Lists may be indexed much as vectors, but some special considerations apply. Recall the list that I constructed earlier:

```
> list.1
$mat.1
     [,1] [,2] [,3] [,4]
[1,]    1    4    7   10
[2,]    2    5    8   11
[3,]    3    6    9   12
```

```
$mat.2
      [,1] [,2] [,3]
[1,] "a"  "b"  "c"
[2,] "a"  "b"  "c"
[3,] "a"  "b"  "c"
[4,] "a"  "b"  "c"

$vec
 [1] 10  4  7  9  5  3  2  6  8  1

> list.1[c(2,3)]  # elements 2 and 3
$mat.2
      [,1] [,2] [,3]
[1,] "a"  "b"  "c"
[2,] "a"  "b"  "c"
[3,] "a"  "b"  "c"
[4,] "a"  "b"  "c"

$vec
 [1] 10  4  7  9  5  3  2  6  8  1

> list.1[2]  # returns a one-element list
$mat.2
      [,1] [,2] [,3]
[1,] "a"  "b"  "c"
[2,] "a"  "b"  "c"
[3,] "a"  "b"  "c"
[4,] "a"  "b"  "c"
```

Even when we specify a single element of the list, as in the last example, we get a single-element list rather than (in this case) a matrix. To extract the matrix in position 2 of the list, we may use double-bracket notation:

```
> list.1[[2]]  # returns a matrix
      [,1] [,2] [,3]
[1,] "a"  "b"  "c"
[2,] "a"  "b"  "c"
[3,] "a"  "b"  "c"
[4,] "a"  "b"  "c"
```

The distinction between a one-element list and the element itself is subtle, but it can occasionally trip us up if we are not careful.

If the list elements are named, then we can use the names in indexing the list:

```
> list.1['mat.1']  # produces a one-element list
$mat.1
      [,1] [,2] [,3] [,4]
[1,]    1    4    7   10
[2,]    2    5    8   11
[3,]    3    6    9   12
```

```
> list.1[['mat.1']]   # extracts a single element
     [,1] [,2] [,3] [,4]
[1,]   1    4    7   10
[2,]   2    5    8   11
[3,]   3    6    9   12
```

An element name may also be used (either quoted, or if it is a legal S name, unquoted) after the $ (dollar sign) to extract a list element:

```
> list.1$mat.1
     [,1] [,2] [,3] [,4]
[1,]   1    4    7   10
[2,]   2    5    8   11
[3,]   3    6    9   12
```

Used on the left-hand side of the assignment arrow, dollar-sign indexing allows us to replace list elements, to define new elements, or to delete an element:

```
> list.1$mat.1 <- matrix(1, 2, 2)      # replace element
> list.1$title <- 'an arbitrary list'  # new element
> list.1$mat.2 <- NULL                  # delete element
> list.1
$mat.1
     [,1] [,2]
[1,]   1    1
[2,]   1    1

$vec
 [1] 10  4  7  9  5  3  2  6  8  1

$title
[1] "an arbitrary list"
```

Data frames may be indexed either as lists or as matrices. Recall the Guyer data frame:

```
> Guyer
   cooperation condition      sex  logit.coop
1      40.83333    public     male -0.37085958
2      53.33333    public     male  0.13353139
3      30.83333    public     male -0.80792270
 . . .
19     28.33333 anonymous   female -0.92798677
20     36.66667 anonymous   female -0.54654371

> attach(Guyer)
>
```

Because no row names were specified when I entered the data, the row names are simply the character representation of the row numbers.

Indexing Guyer as a matrix:

```
> Guyer[,1]   # first column
 [1] 40.83333 53.33333 30.83333 43.33333 56.66667 45.00000
 [7] 50.83333 65.83333 53.33333 24.16667 22.50000 48.33333
[13] 43.33333 34.16667 25.00000 33.33333 32.50000 36.66667
[19] 28.33333 36.66667

> Guyer[,'cooperation']   # equivalent
 [1] 40.83333 53.33333 30.83333 43.33333 56.66667 45.00000
 [7] 50.83333 65.83333 53.33333 24.16667 22.50000 48.33333
[13] 43.33333 34.16667 25.00000 33.33333 32.50000 36.66667
[19] 28.33333 36.66667

> Guyer[c(1,2),]   # rows 1 and 2
  cooperation condition  sex logit.coop
1    40.83333    public male -0.3708596
2    53.33333    public male  0.1335314

> Guyer[c('1','2'), 'cooperation']
[1] 40.83333 53.33333

> Guyer[-(6:20),]   # drop rows 6 through 20
  cooperation condition  sex logit.coop
1    40.83333    public male -0.3708596
2    53.33333    public male  0.1335314
3    30.83333    public male -0.8079227
4    43.33333    public male -0.2682640
5    56.66667    public male  0.2682640

> Guyer[sex == 'female' & condition == 'public',]
   cooperation condition    sex  logit.coop
6     45.00000    public female -0.20067070
7     50.83333    public female  0.03333642
8     65.83333    public female  0.65587579
9     53.33333    public female  0.13353139
10    24.16667    public female -1.14356368
```

Alternatively, indexing the data frame Guyer as a list:

```
> Guyer$cooperation
 [1] 40.83333 53.33333 30.83333 43.33333 56.66667 45.00000
 [7] 50.83333 65.83333 53.33333 24.16667 22.50000 48.33333
[13] 43.33333 34.16667 25.00000 33.33333 32.50000 36.66667
[19] 28.33333 36.66667

> Guyer[['cooperation']]
 [1] 40.83333 53.33333 30.83333 43.33333 56.66667 45.00000
 [7] 50.83333 65.83333 53.33333 24.16667 22.50000 48.33333
[13] 43.33333 34.16667 25.00000 33.33333 32.50000 36.66667
[19] 28.33333 36.66667
```

```
> Guyer['cooperation']
   cooperation
1     40.83333
2     53.33333
3     30.83333
 . . .
20    36.66667
```

Notice that specifying `Guyer['cooperation']` returns a one-column data frame rather than a vector.

As has become my habit, I clean up before continuing:

```
> detach(Guyer)
> remove(A, B, v, array.3, list.1)
>
```

2.4 DATA ATTRIBUTES, MODES, AND CLASSES*

This section deals more abstractly with data in S. I aim to introduce the topic rather than to cover it exhaustively. The information here is occasionally useful in routine data analysis, and certainly useful for programming in S, but you may safely skip the section on first reading.

All objects in S have at least two "attributes": *mode* and *length*. For example, numeric data are of mode `numeric` and character data of mode `character`:

```
> x <- 1:10
> mode(x)
[1] "numeric"
> length(x)
[1] 10

> y <- c("one", "two", "three")
> mode(y)
[1] "character"
> length(y)
[1] 3
```

Lists are of mode `list`, as are data frames and the objects produced by statistical modeling functions such as `lm` (linear model):

```
> list.2 <- list(x, y)
> mode(list.2)
[1] "list"
> length(list.2)
[1] 2
```

```
> mode(Guyer)
[1] "list"
> length(Guyer)
[1] 4

> attach(Duncan)
> mod <- lm(prestige ~ income + education)  # regression model
> mod

Call:
lm(formula = prestige ~ income + education)

Coefficients:
(Intercept)        income      education
    -6.0647        0.5987         0.5458

> mode(mod)
[1] "list"
> length(mod)
[1] 12
> names(mod)
 [1] "coefficients"  "residuals"      "effects"
 [4] "rank"          "fitted.values" "assign"
 [7] "qr"            "df.residual"   "xlevels"
[10] "call"          "terms"         "model"
```

There is a distinction between the printed representation of an object (such as the linear-model object mod) and its internal structure. We do not normally interact directly with an object produced by a modeling function, and therefore do not need to see its internal structure; interaction with the object is the province of functions created for that purpose (for example, the generic summary function).

Because *all* objects in S have a mode and a length, so do functions (and even S expressions):

```
> mode(mean)
[1] "function"
> length(mean)
[1] 1
```

Objects may have attributes beyond mode and length, as we may discover with the attributes function. For example, a matrix has a dim (dimension) attribute of length two, and may have a dimnames (dimension names) attribute as well:

```
> A<-matrix(1:15, 3, 5)  # 3 rows, 5 columns
> A
     [,1] [,2] [,3] [,4] [,5]
[1,]    1    4    7   10   13
[2,]    2    5    8   11   14
[3,]    3    6    9   12   15
```

```
> rownames(A)<-c('a','b','c')
> colnames(A)<-c('v','w','x','y','z')
> attributes(A)
$dim
[1] 3 5

$dimnames
$dimnames[[1]]
[1] "a" "b" "c"

$dimnames[[2]]
[1] "v" "w" "x" "y" "z"
```

The class-based, object-oriented programming system in S3 and R is driven by objects that have a `class` attribute. For example, data frames are of class `data.frame` (and also have other attributes appropriate to this kind of object):

```
> attributes(Duncan)
$names
[1] "type"      "income"     "education" "prestige"

$class
[1] "data.frame"

$row.names
  [1] "accountant"      "pilot"
  [3] "architect"       "author"
  [5] "chemist"         "minister"
  . . .
 [43] "janitor"         "policeman"
 [45] "waiter"
```

Likewise, factors, such as the variable `type` in the currently attached Duncan data frame, are of class `factor` (and also have a `levels` attribute):

```
> type
 [1] prof prof prof prof prof prof prof prof wc   prof prof
[12] prof prof prof prof wc   prof prof prof prof wc   wc
[23] wc   wc   bc   bc   bc   bc   bc   bc   bc   bc   bc
[34] bc   bc   bc   bc   bc   bc   bc   bc   bc   bc   bc
[45] bc
Levels:  bc prof wc

> attributes(type)
$levels
[1] "bc"   "prof" "wc"

$class
[1] "factor"
```

To discover whether an object has a class (and, if so, what that class is), you can use the `class` function:

```
> class(Duncan)
[1] "data.frame"

> class(type)
[1] "factor"

> class(A)
NULL
```

The variable A, recall, is a matrix, and matrices in S3 and R have no class. (That may be a bad pun, but if it is, I don't quite understand it.) Object-oriented programming in S is taken up briefly in Chapter 8.

Standard S functions exist to create data of different modes and for many classes (*constructor functions*), to test for modes and classes (*predicate functions*), and to convert data to a particular mode or class (*coercion functions*).

Constructor functions conventionally have the same name as their mode or class. For example:

```
> num <- numeric(5)  # create numeric vector of zeros of length 5
> num
[1] 0 0 0 0 0

> fac <- factor(c('a','b','c','c','b','a'))  # create factor
> fac
[1] a b c c b a
Levels:  a b c
```

By convention, predicates in S prefix the characters "is." to the name of the mode or class:

```
> is.numeric(num)  # predicate for mode numeric
[1] TRUE

> is.numeric(fac)
[1] FALSE

> is.factor(fac)  # predicate for class factor
[1] TRUE
```

The names of coercion functions employ the prefix "as.":

```
> char <- as.character(fac)  # coerce to mode character
> char
[1] "a" "b" "c" "c" "b" "a"

> as.numeric(fac)  # coerce to mode numeric
[1] 1 2 3 3 2 1

> as.numeric(char)
[1] NA NA NA NA NA NA
```

```
Warning message:
NAs introduced by coercion
```

The last two examples illustrate that coercion may cause information to be lost.

Constructor, predicate, and coercion functions are occasionally available for types of objects that, strictly speaking, are neither modes nor classes. For example:

```
> B <- matrix(1:9, 3, 3)  # matrix constructor
> B
  [,1] [,2] [,3]
[1,] 1 4 7
[2,] 2 5 8
[3,] 3 6 9

> is.matrix(B)  # matrix predicate
[1] TRUE

> as.vector(B)  # coerce to vector
[1] 1 2 3 4 5 6 7 8 9
```

I do not bother to clean up at the end of the current chapter, because I will not save the R workspace. More generally, in this book I assume that each chapter represents an independent S session.

Data Storage and Housekeeping in S-PLUS

Because all globally defined objects are stored in files in the working-data directory, they normally persist from session to session. S-PLUS can be set to prompt for saving global objects when the session is terminated, and housekeeping can be performed at that point.

2.4.1   Data in S4

The preceding sections describe the organization of data in R and S3. Data in S4 are organized in a somewhat different manner, though the differences are mostly transparent in everyday use. Most fundamentally, all objects in S4 have a *class*, as well as a *mode* and *length*. For example[12]:

```
> vec <- 1:10
> char.vec <- letters[1:5]
> mat <- matrix(1:12, 3, 4)
```

---

12. By the way, this is true not only of data objects, but of other objects as well—such as functions and expressions. In S3 and R, all objects have a length and a mode, but not necessarily a class. The ability to manipulate objects such as expressions and functions is very powerful in advanced use of S. I invite the reader to apply the class, mode, and length functions to a variety of objects.

```
> vec
 [1]  1  2  3  4  5  6  7  8  9 10

> char.vec
[1] "a" "b" "c" "d" "e"

> mat
     [,1] [,2] [,3] [,4]
[1,]    1    4    7   10
[2,]    2    5    8   11
[3,]    3    6    9   12

> class(vec)
[1] "integer"
> mode(vec)
[1] "numeric"
> length(vec)
[1] 10

> class(char.vec)
[1] "character"
> mode(char.vec)
[1] "character"
> length(char.vec)
[1] 5

> class(mat)
[1] "matrix"
> mode(mat)
[1] "numeric"
> length(mat)
[1] 12
```

The predicate and coercion functions familiar from S3 work in S4 as well, but S4 also provides the general functions is and as for these purposes:

```
> is.matrix(mat)
[1] T

> is.matrix(vec)
[1] F

> is(mat, 'matrix')
[1] T

> as.vector(mat)
 [1]  1  2  3  4  5  6  7  8  9 10 11 12

> as(mat, 'vector')
 [1]  1  2  3  4  5  6  7  8  9 10 11 12
```

Finally, classes in S4 are not implemented via a `class` attribute (although the S3 class system, based on the `class` attribute, is still supported for "backwards compatibility"). The S4 class system is described briefly in Chapter 8.

CHAPTER 3

Exploring and Transforming Data

E xamination—particularly graphical examination—of data is an
important prelude to statistical modeling, and a step that is skipped
at the peril of the data analyst. Although it employs a very simple graphical approach, which imposes some limitations on the kinds of graphs
that can be created, S provides very strong facilities for constructing statistical graphs. Indeed, the original developers of S were also important
innovators in statistical graphics (see, for example, Chambers, Cleveland,
Kleiner, & Tukey, 1983).

This chapter assumes general familiarity with standard procedures for
exploratory data analysis, statistical graphics, and data transformation,
and shows how these procedures are implemented in S. I make occasional reference to freely available S libraries, including the car library
associated with this book. The chapter takes up the following topics:

■ Distributional displays, including histograms, stem-and-leaf displays,
density estimates, boxplots, and quantile-comparison plots.

■ Plots of the relationship between two variables, including various versions of scatterplots, scatterplot smoothers, bivariate density estimates,
and parallel boxplots.

■ Multivariate displays, including scatterplot matrices, coplots, and
(briefly) dynamic three-dimensional scatterplots.

■ Transformations of data to symmetry, constant spread, and linearity.

The general focus is on graphical tools that are broadly useful in statistical data analysis.

3.1   EXAMINING DISTRIBUTIONS

3.1.1   Histograms and Stem-and-Leaf Displays

The most common graph of the distribution of a quantitative variable is the *histogram*, which dissects the range of the variable into class intervals, called *bins* (usually of equal width), and counts the number of observations falling in each bin. The counts (or percentages, proportions, or densities, calculated from them) are plotted in a bar graph. An example, constructed by the following S commands, appears in Figure 3.1:

```
> library(car)
. . .
> data(Prestige)
> attach(Prestige)
> Prestige[1:5,]   # first 5 obs.
                   education income women prestige census type
GOV.ADMINISTRATORS     13.11   12351 11.16     68.8   1113 prof
GENERAL.MANAGERS       12.26   25879  4.02     69.1   1130 prof
ACCOUNTANTS            12.77    9271 15.70     63.4   1171 prof
PURCHASING.OFFICERS    11.42    8865  9.11     56.8   1175 prof
CHEMISTS               14.62    8403 11.68     73.5   2111 prof

> hist(income)
>
```

The Canadian occupational-prestige data set, on which this example is based, was introduced in the previous chapter.

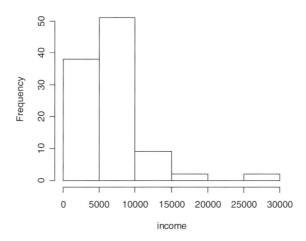

Figure **3.1**   Histogram of income in the Canadian occupational-prestige data.

Histogram of income

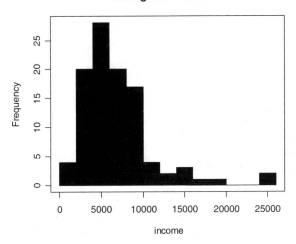

Figure 3.2   Revised histogram of income.

I find that the rule that R uses to determine the number of bins, together with its effort to produce "nice" cut points between the bins, often produces too few bins. The function n.bins in car implements a number of rules for calculating the desired number of bins; the default rule used by n.bins, from Freedman and Diaconis (1981), sets the recommended number of bins to

$$\left\lceil \frac{n^{1/3}(\text{max} - \text{min})}{2(Q_3 - Q_1)} \right\rceil,$$

where n is the number of observations, $\text{max} - \text{min}$ is the range of the data, $Q_3 - Q_1$ is the interquartile range, and the "ceiling" brackets indicate rounding up to the next integer. Applying this rule to income in the Canadian occupational-prestige data produces the histogram in Figure 3.2:

```
> n.bins(income)
[1] 15
> hist(income, nclass=n.bins(income), col=1)
> box()
>
```

The nclass argument to hist suggests the number of bins to employ, and col=1 specifies that the histogram bars are to be drawn in black; finally, box() draws a rectangle around the histogram.[1] Alternatively, you can use the breaks argument to hist to set the endpoints of the bins, as in breaks=seq(0, 30000, 2500). Note that the lowest and highest break

---

1. Chapter 7 includes a discussion of color use in R and S-PLUS.

points should include all of the data. The break points do not have to be evenly spaced (but histograms with unequal-width bins are difficult to interpret). You may also wish to take a look at the truehist function in the MASS library.

The stem function in S creates *stem-and-leaf displays*:

```
> stem(income)
The decimal point is 3 digit(s) to the right of the |
  0 | 6979
  2 | 44689001125556667999
  4 | 0122334567778811111234566889
  6 | 01233556679901145679
  8 | 000012334488999936
 10 | 4004
 12 | 45
 14 | 026
 16 | 5
 18 | 3
 20 |
 22 |
 24 | 39
```

---

hist and stem in S-PLUS

The hist function in S-PLUS does a better job, in my experience, of picking the number of bins for a histogram; moreover, the S-PLUS version of the function incorporates several rules as options for suggesting the number of bins, rendering the n.bins function in car unnecessary. The S-PLUS version of stem is also more capable than the R version, and allows, for example, for trimming outliers.

3.1.2 Density Estimates

Nonparametric density estimation often produces a more satisfactory representation of a distribution by smoothing the histogram. The *kernel-density estimate* at the value x of a variable X is defined as

$$\hat{p}(x) = \frac{1}{nh} \sum_{i=1}^{n} K\left(\frac{x - x_i}{h}\right),$$

where the x_i are the n observations on the variable; K is a *kernel function*—a symmetric, single-peaked density function, such as the normal density; and h is a *bandwidth parameter*, which controls the degree

Histogram of income

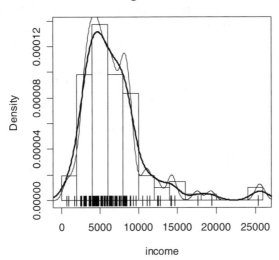

Figure 3.3 Nonparametric kernel-density estimates for the distribution of income, using the default bandwidth (heavier line) and half the default bandwidth (lighter line).

of smoothing: Larger values of the bandwidth produce smoother density estimates. The factor $1/nh$ ensures that the density estimate encloses an area of 1.

The density function in S implements kernel-density estimation, by default using a normal kernel[2]:

```
> hist(income, nclass=n.bins(income), probability=T,
+     ylab='Density')
> lines(density(income), lwd=2)
> points(income, rep(0, length(income)), pch="|")
> box()
> lines(density(income, adjust=.5), lwd=1)
>
```

This example, which produces Figure 3.3, illustrates how an S graph can be built up by successive calls to graphics functions.[3] The hist function constructs the histogram, with probability=T specifying density scaling (i.e., the areas of the histogram bars sum to 1) and ylab='Density' furnishing the label for the vertical axis of the graph. The lines function draws the density estimate on the graph, the coordinates of which are calculated by the call to density; lwd=2 specifies a line of double thickness.

---

2. Several freely available S libraries provide sophisticated facilities for density estimation. See, in particular, the sm library (Bowman & Azzalini, 1997) and the locfit library (Loader, 1999). Nonparametric density estimation is extensively described in Silverman (1986).

3. Chapter 7 describes in more detail how to construct graphs in S.

The `points` function is used to draw a one-dimensional scatterplot (or "rugplot") at the bottom of the graph, using a vertical bar as the plotting symbol, with the horizontal coordinates given by `income` and the vertical coordinates all 0s. The second call to `density`, with `adjust=0.5`, specifies a bandwidth half the default value and therefore produces a rougher density estimate (shown in the figure as a lighter line, `lwd=1`).

Density Estimation in S-PLUS

The function `density` in S-PLUS does not take an `adjust` argument, but several methods are available to select the bandwidth for the density estimate. See `help(density)` for details.

3.1.3   Quantile-Comparison Plots

We often want to compare the distribution of a variable with a theoretical reference distribution, such as the normal distribution. An effective graphical means of doing so is provided by the *quantile-comparison plot*, plotting the ordered data against the corresponding quantiles of the reference distribution. If the data conform to the reference distribution, then the quantile-comparison plot should be linear, within sampling error. S provides the `qqnorm` function for making quantile-comparison plots against the normal distribution, but I prefer the `qq.plot` function in the car library. By default, `qq.plot` compares the data to the normal distribution, and provides a 95 percent pointwise confidence envelope around a line fit to the plot:

```
> qq.plot(income, labels=row.names(Prestige))
[1] 26 17 24  2
```

The resulting graph is shown in Figure 3.4. The argument `labels=row.names(Prestige)` allows us to label points interactively by their occupation names: Placing the mouse cursor near a point and clicking the left button causes the point label to appear on the plot; clicking the right mouse button exits from `qq.plot`. Notice that `qq.plot` returns the indices of the labeled points.

The `qq.plot` function can also be used to plot the data against any reference distribution for which there are quantile and density functions in S, which includes just about any distribution that you may wish to use. Simply specify the "root" word for the distribution. For example, the root for the normal distribution is `norm` (with density function `dnorm` and quantile function `qnorm`); the root for the chi-square distribution is

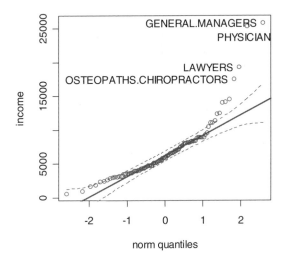

Figure 3.4   Normal quantile-comparison plot for `income`. The broken lines give a pointwise 95 percent confidence envelope around the fitted solid line. Several points were labeled interactively with the mouse.

`chisq` (`dchisq` and `qchisq`). Root words for some other commonly used distributions are `binom`, for the binomial distribution; `f` for the *F* distribution; `t` for the *t* distribution; and `unif` for the uniform distribution.

In addition to density and quantile functions, S also provides cumulative distribution functions (CDFs, prefix p) and pseudo-random-number generators (prefix r): For example, `pnorm` gives cumulative probabilities for the normal distributions, while `rnorm` generates normal random variables. Table 3.1 summarizes the principal arguments to these probability functions.

To illustrate, I use the `rchisq` function to generate a random sample from the chi-square distribution with 3 degrees of freedom, and plot the sample against the distribution from which it was drawn (producing Figure 3.5):

```
> qq.plot(rchisq(100,3), distribution='chisq', df=3)
>
```

Boxplots   3.1.4

Finally, among these univariate displays, Figure 3.6 shows a *boxplot* of `income`, produced by the following S commands:

```
> boxplot(income, ylab='income')
> identify(rep(1,length(income)), income, row.names(Prestige))
[1] 2 17 24 25 26
```

Table 3.1   Arguments for some standard probability functions in S. Most of the arguments are self-explanatory. For the binomial distribution, size represents the number of binomial trials, while prob represents the probability of success on each trial. Not all arguments are shown for all functions; consult the R or S-PLUS on-line documentation for details.

Distribution	Density Function	Quantile Function
Normal	dnorm(x, mean=0, sd=1)	qnorm(p, mean=0, sd=1)
Chi-square	dchisq(x, df)	qchisq(p, df)
F	df(x, df1, df2)	qf(p, df1, df2)
t	dt(x, df)	qt(p, df)
Binomial	dbinom(x, size, prob)	qbinom(p, size, prob)
Uniform	dunif(x, min=0, max=1)	qunif(p, min=0, max=1)

Distribution	Distribution Function	Random Number Function
Normal	pnorm(q, mean=0, sd=1)	rnorm(n, mean=0, sd=1)
Chi-square	pchisq(q, df)	rchisq(n, df)
F	pf(q, df1, df2)	rf(n, df1, df2)
t	pt(q, df)	rt(n, df)
Binomial	pbinom(q, size, prob)	rbinom(n, size, prob)
Uniform	punif(q, min=0, max=1)	runif(n, min=0, max=1)

The call to boxplot is self-explanatory. The identify function is used to label points on the plot interactively; I take advantage of the fact that in R the points in a boxplot are all graphed at the horizontal coordinate 1, while the vertical coordinates are given by the variable plotted, here income.

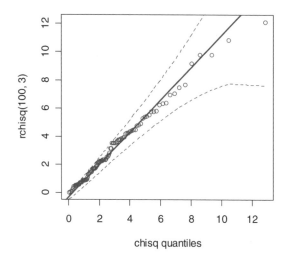

Figure 3.5   Quantile-comparison plot of a sample of size $n = 100$ from $\chi^2(3)$ against the distribution from which the sample was drawn.

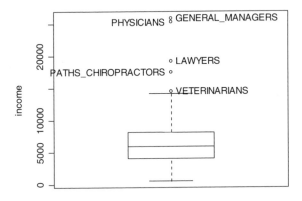

Figure 3.6   Boxplot of income. Several observations were labeled interactively with the mouse.

***

Point Labels for Boxplots in S-PLUS

The same general approach works in S-PLUS, but the points are plotted at horizontal coordinates of 50, rather than 1. That is, we enter `rep(50, length(income))` to specify horizontal coordinates to `identify`.

EXAMINING RELATIONSHIPS   3.2

Scatterplots   3.2.1

The scatterplot, possibly the most useful of all statistical graphs for data analysis, is the standard graph for examining the relationship between two quantitative variables. I will show you how to make several kinds of scatterplots in S.

When it is presented with two numeric-vector argument, which it interprets as giving horizontal and vertical coordinates, respectively, the default behavior of the `plot` function is to make a scatterplot.[4] Continuing, with the Canadian occupational-prestige data, I enter (producing Figure 3.7):

```
> plot(income, prestige)
>
```

***

4. `plot` is a generic function, and so, as explained in more detail in Chapter 8, its behavior depends on the class of its first argument.

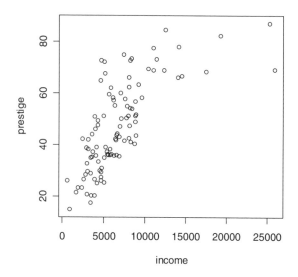

Figure 3.7   Simple scatterplot of prestige by income for the Canadian occupational-prestige data.

Interpretation of a scatterplot is often assisted by enhancing the plot with least squares and nonparametric-regression lines. The scatterplot function in car does this by default, and also adds marginal boxplots for the two variables (as in Figure 3.8):

```
> scatterplot(income, prestige, span=.6, lwd=3,
+    labels=rownames(Prestige))
[1]  2 17 21 24
```

- The nonparametric-regression curve on the plot is drawn by a local-regression smoother. Local regression works by fitting a least squares line in the neighborhood of each observation, placing greater weight on points closer to the focal observation. A fitted value for the focal observation is extracted from each local regression, and the resulting fitted values are connected to produce the nonparametric-regression line. The proportion of observations included in each local fit, called the *span* of the local regression (and specified by the span argument to scatterplot, here span=.6), controls the smoothness of the result: Larger spans produce smoother regression curves.[5]

- The labels argument supplies names for the points, permitting us to identify observations interactively with the mouse: Point the mouse at an observation and click the left button; click the right button to exit from scatterplot, which returns the indices of the identified points.

---

5. Nonparametric regression is described in much more detail in the Web appendix to the book.

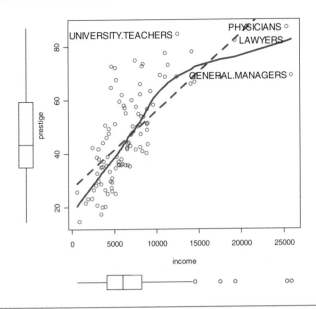

Figure 3.8   Enhanced scatterplot of prestige by income. Several points were identified interactively with the mouse.

■ Finally, specifying the line width as lwd=3 makes the regression lines on the plot thicker than they would be by default (lwd=1).

Coded Scatterplots

A categorical variable can be encoded on a scatterplot by using a different plotting symbol or color for each of its categories. The scatterplot function in car may be used to create coded scatterplots, for example, for prestige by income, coded by type of occupation (Figure 3.9):

```
> scatterplot(prestige ~ income | type, span=.8)
>
```

The variables for the scatterplot are given in a *formula*, as $y \sim x \,|\, groups$. I selected span=.8 because of the relatively small number of observations in the occupational groups: Using a small span in a small data set tends to produce a nonparametric-regression curve that is too rough. The legend on the graph, automatically generated by the scatterplot function, is placed interactively with the mouse: Click the left button to position the upper-left corner of the legend. Although the reproduction of the graph in Figure 3.9 is in monochrome, in the original graph each group is plotted in a different color.

The overall scatterplot of prestige by income (Figure 3.8) suggests a nonlinear relationship between the two variables, but the coded scatterplot indicates that the relationship between prestige and income may well be linear within occupational types. The slope of the relationship

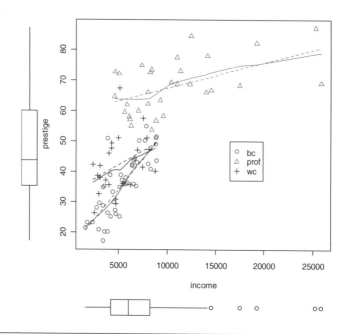

Figure 3.9   Scatterplot of prestige by income, coded by type of occupation.

looks steepest for blue-collar occupations, and least-steep for professional and managerial occupations.

Jittering Scatterplots

Discrete, quantitative variables typically result in uninformative scatterplots. The example in Figure 3.10(a) was produced by the following S statements:

```
> detach(Prestige)
> data(Vocab)
> attach(Vocab)
> plot(education, vocabulary)
>
```

The data for this illustration come from the 1989 U.S. General Social Survey, conducted by the National Opinion Research Center. The two variables in the plot are education in years (education) and the respondent's score on a 10-word vocabulary test (vocabulary). Because education can only take on 21 distinct values, and vocabulary only 11 distinct values, many of the nearly 1000 observations in the data set are overplotted; indeed, in a larger data set, all of the possible $11 \times 21 = 231$ plotting positions might be occupied, producing a meaningless rectangular grid of dots.

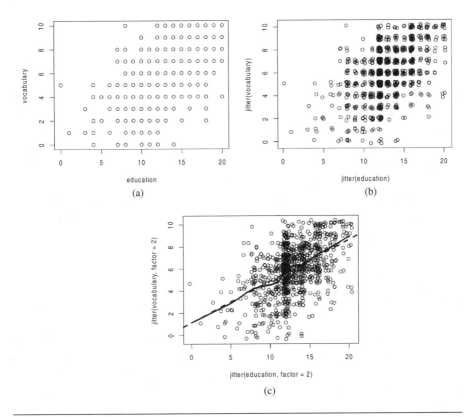

Figure 3.10 Scatterplots of vocabulary by education: (a) unjittered; (b) default jittering; (c) twice default jittering, with least squares and lowess lines.

Jittering the data by adding a small random quantity to each coordinate (Cleveland, 1994) serves to separate the overplotted points. We can use the `jitter` function in S for this purpose:

```
> plot(jitter(education), jitter(vocabulary))
>
```

The result is shown in Figure 3.10(b). We can control the degree of jittering via the argument `factor`; for example, specifying `factor=2` doubles the jitter (yielding, in my opinion, a more satisfactory result for the current example):

```
> plot(jitter(education, factor=2), jitter(vocabulary, factor=2))
>
```

To complete the picture, I add least squares and nonparametric-regression lines (using, note, the original, unjittered data for these computations), producing Figure 3.10(c):

```
> abline(lm(vocabulary ~ education), lwd=3, lty=2)
> lines(lowess(education, vocabulary, f=.2), lwd=3)
>
```

The least squares line on the graph is computed by `lm` and drawn by `abline`; the argument `lwd` to `abline` sets the width of the regression line, while the line type `lty=2` specifies a broken line. The `lowess` function (an acronym for `locally weighted regression`) returns coordinates for the local-regression curve, which is drawn by `lines`; the span of the local regression is set by the argument `f` to `lowess`. Of course, I could have more conveniently used the `scatterplot` function in `car` to make the graph in Figure 3.10(c), but I wanted to demonstrate how to construct a simple plot from its components (a topic described in detail in Chapter 7).

The relationship between `vocabulary` and `education` appears nearly linear, and we can also discern other features of the data that previously were hidden by overplotting, such as the relatively large number of respondents with 12 years of education.

3.2.2   Bivariate Density Estimates

Another context in which scatterplots are frequently uninformative is in large data sets, particularly where the relationship between the two variables in the plot is weak, and therefore much of the plot is filled. An example, using a moderately large data set, appears in Figure 3.11, and is produced with the following S commands:

```
> detach(Vocab)
> data(SLID)
> attach(SLID)
> plot(education, wages)
>
```

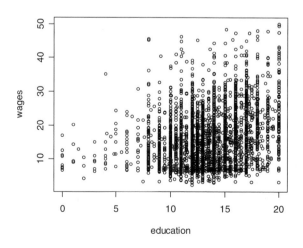

Figure 3.11   Scatterplot of `wages` by `education` in the SLID/Ontario data.

The SLID data are drawn from the 1994 Canadian Survey of Labour and Income Dynamics; the data set includes only respondents from the province of Ontario. The two variables in the scatterplot are years of education (education) and the individuals' composite hourly wage rate, in dollars (wages). Examination of the data reveals that education is measured to the nearest tenth of a year and that there are only 126 different values of this variable among the roughly 4000 individuals who have valid data on both education and wages. In contrast, there are more than 1500 distinct values of wages:

```
> valid <- !(is.na(wages) | is.na(education))
> sum(valid)
[1] 4014
> sort(unique(education[valid]))
  [1]  0.0  1.0  1.5  2.0  3.0  4.0  4.1  4.5  4.8  5.0  5.5  6.0
 [13]  6.4  6.5  7.0  7.3  7.5  7.6  8.0  8.2  8.3  8.5  8.8  9.0
 [25]  9.1  9.2  9.4  9.5  9.6  9.8  9.9 10.0 10.1 10.2 10.3 10.4
 . . .
[109] 18.0 18.1 18.2 18.3 18.4 18.5 18.6 18.7 18.8 19.0 19.1 19.2
[121] 19.3 19.4 19.5 19.7 19.9 20.0

> length(.Last.value)  # number of distinct values
[1] 126
> length(unique(wages[valid]))
[1] 1533
```

A simpler R equivalent to the first command is:

```
> valid <- complete.cases(wages, education)
>
```

Summing a logical variable counts the number TRUE: In evaluating sum(valid), S "coerces" the logical variable valid to a numeric vector of 0s and 1s. The automatic variable .Last.value allows us to access the previous result without recomputing it.

We can improve this scatterplot somewhat by jittering education and by making the plotting symbols smaller, but the graph still conveys a relatively poor impression of the relationship between wages and education. Figure 3.12 employs both of these strategies, but also adds a bivariate kernel-density plot to the graph, using the sm.density function in the sm library (described in detail in Bowman & Azzalini, 1997):

```
> library(sm)
> sm.density(cbind(education[valid], wages[valid]),
+     display='image', xlab='Education',
+     ylab='Wages', col=gray(seq(1, 0, length=100)))

> points(jitter(education, amount=.25), wages, cex=.15)
> box()
```

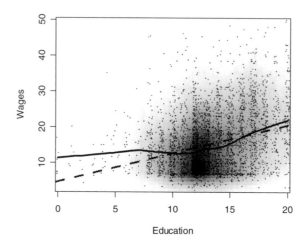

Figure 3.12   Bivariate density estimate for education and wages. A jittered scatterplot, least squares line, and lowess line are added to the plot.

```
> lines(lowess(education[valid], wages[valid], f=1/3), lwd=3)
> abline(lm(wages ~ education), lty=2, lwd=3)
> remove(valid)
>
```

To create a bivariate density plot, the sm.density function expects a matrix as its first argument, which I construct from education and wages with cbind ("bind columns"); display='image' and col=gray(seq(1, 0, length=100)) produce a gray-scale plot, with darker values indicating a higher density of data.[6] I add the jittered observations to the density plot with the points function, specifying cex=.15 to shrink the points to 15 percent of their normal size.[7] The rest of the commands are familiar from previous examples.

3.2.3   Parallel Boxplots

Parallel boxplots help us to visualize the relationship between a quantitative response variable and a categorical predictor. An illustration, based on data from Ornstein (1976) on interlocking directorates among 248 major Canadian corporations, appears in Figure 3.13. The figure was

---

6. Color specification works differently in S-PLUS, as described in Chapter 7.

7. The graphics parameter cex denotes character expansion; graphics parameters are discussed in Chapter 7.

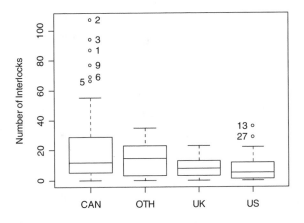

Figure 3.13   Parallel boxplots of `interlocks` by `nation` of control for Ornstein's interlocking-directorate data.

produced by the following S statements:

```
> detach(SLID)
> data(Ornstein)
> attach(Ornstein)
> Ornstein[sort(sample(248,5)),]  # sample 5 obs.
    assets sector nation interlocks
73    3879    WOD    CAN        27
152    809    MAN     UK         0
174    589    MIN    OTH        23
193    495    MAN    CAN         0
217    359    AGR     US         0

> boxplot(interlocks ~ nation, ylab='Number of Interlocks')
> identify(as.numeric(nation), interlocks)
[1]  1  2  3  5  6  9 13 27
```

The variables in the data set include the `assets` of the corporation (in millions of dollars), the corporation's `sector` of operation, the `nation` in which the firm is controlled, and the number of interlocking directorate and executive positions (`interlocks`) maintained between each company and others in the data set. The `identify` function is used to label individual points interactively; because the names of the companies were not given in the original source, there is no third argument to `identify`, and the firms are labeled simply by position within the data set, which is in descending order by `assets`: The identified points, which have low observation numbers, are therefore among the largest firms in the data set. Specifying `as.numeric(nation)` converts the factor `nation` into numbers suitable for plotting as horizontal coordinates.

Parallel Boxplots in S-PLUS

The `boxplot` function in S-PLUS does not support specifying the plot as a formula. Instead, the `split` function may be used to divide the data into groups for plotting, as in `boxplot(split(interlocks, nation))`. Because of the manner in which `boxplot` in S-PLUS scales the horizontal axis, it is relatively inconvenient to identify individual points in the plot.

3.3 EXAMINING MULTIVARIATE DATA

Because the media on which we draw graphs (paper, computer displays) are two dimensional, examining multivariate data is intrinsically more difficult than examining univariate or bivariate data. Three-variable data are a special case, however, and features such as perspective and motion can convey a sense of depth in a three-dimensional scatterplot. The most effective software of this kind allows the user to manipulate—for example, rotate or rock—the display, to mark points, and to plot surfaces, such as regression surfaces, along with points.

Dynamic three-dimensional displays are currently absent from R, although one can construct three-dimensional static graphs (three-dimensional surface plots appear in Chapter 7, for example), and a link is provided to the independent XGobi and GGobi systems for visualizing data in three and more dimensions (Swayne, Cook, & Buja, 1998). Relatively primitive facilities for three-dimensional dynamic graphics are available in S-PLUS; see, in particular, the `spin` and `brush` functions.

Partly because it is difficult to convey the use of dynamic-graphics systems on the printed page, and partly because these facilities are relatively underdeveloped in S, I do not pursue the topic here. I refer the interested reader to the S-PLUS documentation and to other software. In addition to XGobi and GGobi, Cook and Weisberg's (1999) Arc system, built on the Lisp-Stat statistical computing environment (Tierney, 1990), is particularly noteworthy for its three-dimensional dynamic regression graphics, providing much more than is currently available in S.

3.3.1 Scatterplot Matrices

Scatterplot matrices show the pairwise (i.e., marginal) relationships among a set of variables. In S, scatterplot matrices are constructed by the

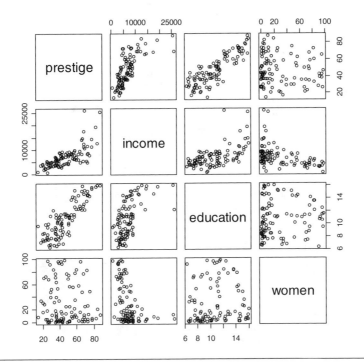

Figure 3.14   Scatterplot matrix for the Canadian occupational-prestige data.

pairs function. An example, using the Canadian occupational-prestige data, appears in Figure 3.14:

```
> detach(Ornstein)
> attach(Prestige)
> pairs(cbind(prestige, income, education, women))
>
```

I usually want to augment the scatterplots in a scatterplot matrix and place distributional displays, such as density estimates, on the diagonal. The `pairs` function supports these features through its `panel` and `diag.panel` arguments (as illustrated in Chapter 1 using Duncan's occupational-prestige data). Because it is tedious to define panel functions each time, however, I prefer to let the `scatterplot.matrix` function in car do most of the work:

```
> scatterplot.matrix(cbind(prestige, income, education, women),
+     diagonal='density', span=.75)
>
```

The result is shown in Figure 3.15. Other values for the `diagonal` argument to `scatterplot.matrix` are `'boxplot'`, `'histogram'`, and `'qqplot'` (all of which may be abbreviated—e.g., `diag='hist'` or even `d='h'`).

Incidentally, the general rule for abbreviating the name of an argument to a function is that you must supply as many characters as are

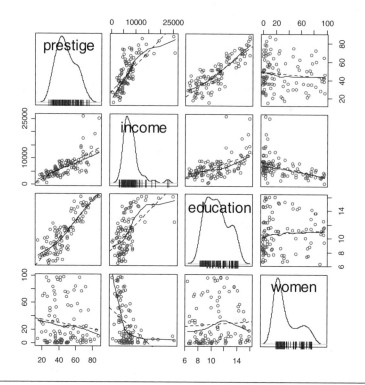

Figure 3.15   Scatterplot matrix for the Canadian occupational-prestige data, with density estimates on the diagonal, created by the `scatterplot.matrix` function.

necessary to identify the argument uniquely. Because no other argument to `scatterplot.matrix` begins with the letter "d," for example, d is a suitable abbreviation for `diagonal`. I adopt a similar convention for character-string arguments to functions in `car` (such as the value `'histogram'` for the argument `diagonal`). My general practice in the text, however, is to spell out arguments and their values fully.

The `scatterplot.matrix` function also supports marking points by groups: Type `help(scatterplot.matrix)` for details.

Trellis Graphics in S-PLUS and Lattice Graphics in R

S-PLUS includes the relatively new "Trellis graphics" system for drawing multipanel graphical displays, such as scatterplot matrices and conditioning plots (described in the next section). The Trellis graphics function for scatterplot matrices is called `splom`. Most of Trellis graphics, including `splom`, has been implemented in the `lattice` library for R, which, as I write this, is still in a preliminary form.

Conditioning Plots   3.3.2

Tracing out the average value of a response variable conditional on one or several predictors is the essence of regression analysis. Often, we focus on the relationship between the response and one predictor, holding other predictors constant at particular values—that is, conditionally fixing the values of other predictors. This idea of "statistical control" is typically realized in a statistical model that makes more-or-less strong assumptions about the nature of the relationship of the response to the predictors, such as an assumption of linearity. Indeed, fitting regression models in S is the principal focus of this text.

Conditioning plots (*coplots*), due to Cleveland (1993), implement statistical control graphically in the absence of a statistical model. To construct a coplot, we focus on a particular predictor, and set each other predictor to a relatively narrow range of values (if the predictor is quantitative) or to a specific value (if it is categorical). The subranges for a quantitative predictor are typically set to overlap (and are termed "shingles") rather than to partition the data into disjoint subsets (or bins). Then, for each combination of values of the conditioning predictors, we construct a scatterplot relating the response to the focal predictor, arranging these scatterplots in an array. Because each panel of a coplot describes a subset of the data, this method works best for large data sets, which can be subdivided without producing sparse subsets. Moreover, if we condition on more than two, or perhaps three, predictors, the array of coplots becomes unwieldy and difficult to comprehend. The coplot function in S permits at most two conditioning predictors, although we can always subset the data ourselves and construct a coplot for each part.[8]

To illustrate coplots, I return to the SLID data set, plotting the log of wages against education, conditioning on the numeric variable age and the factor sex:

```
> detach(Prestige)
> attach(SLID)
> coplot(log(wages) ~ education | age + sex, panel=panel.car,
+     col=gray(.5), lwd=3, cex=0.4)

Missing rows: 3 5 7 8 10 11 13 15 16 17 18 19 21  . . .
```

Using the log transformation of wages serves to reduce the skew in this variable and to make its partial relationship to education more nearly linear: See the next section of the chapter, on transformations.

---

8. Trellis graphics, mentioned in the previous section, powerfully generalize coplots, permitting any number of conditioning variables. We do not require Trellis graphics for the applications described in this book.

As in `pairs`, the `panel` argument to `coplot` specifies a function to draw the panels. The default in R is `points`, which produces a bare scatterplot. The `panel.car` function draws a lowess line and a least squares line on each scatterplot. Note the use of `col=gray(.5)`, `cex=0.4`, and `lwd=3` to tone down the points and emphasize the lines in the plots. The marginal panels at the right and top give, respectively, the levels at which `sex` and `age` are fixed. Thus, the top row of the plot array pertains to males and the bottom row to females; `age` increases from left to right. The age ranges overlap (by default, the overlap includes 50 percent of the observations in adjacent panels), with a roughly equal number of observations in each column of the plot array. The coplot appears in Figure 3.16.

The `coplot` function in S-PLUS

In S-PLUS, the default panel function for `coplot` is `panel.smooth`, which adds a lowess line to each panel (and which is also available in R). Specifying the point color as `col=gray(.5)` does not work in S-PLUS, where colors must be given by number. (Color selection in R and S-PLUS is discussed in Chapter 7.)

3.4   TRANSFORMING DATA

Variable transformations serve a variety of purposes in data analysis, and are used in particular to make distributions more symmetric or normal, to stabilize spread (variation), and to render relationships between variables more nearly linear. These purposes frequently, but not necessarily, harmonize with one another.

The *"family" of powers and roots*, where a variable x is replaced by $x' = x^p$, is often useful in these contexts. For example, $x' = x^2$ when $p = 2$, $x' = \sqrt{x}$ when $p = 1/2$, and $x' = 1/x$ when $p = -1$.

It is sometimes convenient to replace these simple powers and roots with the essentially similar *Box-Cox family* of transformations (Box & Cox, 1964):

$$x' = x^{(p)} = \begin{cases} \dfrac{x^p - 1}{p} & \text{when } p \neq 0, \\ \log_e x & \text{when } p = 0. \end{cases}$$

We may, in any event, treat the log transformation (to any base) as a kind of "zeroth" power.

The family of powers and roots and the Box-Cox family only make sense when all of the data values are positive, a characteristic that we

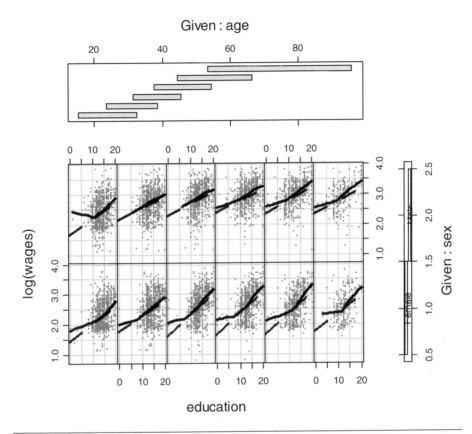

Figure 3.16   Conditioning plot (coplot) of `wages` by `education`, controlling for `age` and `sex`, for the SLID data.

can always impose on the data by adding a sufficiently large constant (called a *start*) to each data value. Because their effect on the shape of the distribution of a variable is the same, we treat ordinary powers and corresponding Box-Cox powers interchangeably.

Powers and roots are easy to calculate directly in S, as is the Box-Cox family. For convenience, `car` provides the `box.cox` function, which automatically computes a suitable start when there are negative or zero values in the data:

```
> box.cox(1:5, 2)
[1]  0.5  2.0  4.5  8.0 12.5

> box.cox(0:5, 2)
[1]  0.0078125  0.6328125  2.2578125  4.8828125  8.5078125
[6] 13.1328125
Warning message:
start = 0.125 added to data prior to transformation in:
  box.cox(0:5, 2)
```

Proportions that get close to the boundaries of 0 and 1 (or percentages that get close to 0 and 100) often do not respond well to power transformations. Among several similar, generally useful, transformations of proportions—the logit transformation, the probit transformation, the inverse-arcsine transformation, and some others—the *logit transformation* is the most commonly employed:

$$\text{logit}(p) = \log_e \frac{p}{1 - p}.$$

The logit transformation, however, breaks down for proportions of precisely 0 or 1. We can get around this problem by remapping the interval $(0, 1)$ to $(.025, .975)$, for example.

Again, the logit transformation is simple to calculate in S, either from proportions or percentages. The `logit` function in `car` takes care of remapping proportions or percentages when there are 0s or 1s (or 0 or 100 percent) in the data:

```
> logit(seq(0.1, 0.9, 0.1))
[1] -2.19722 -1.38629 -0.84730 -0.40547  0.00000  0.40547
[7]  0.84730  1.38629  2.19722

> logit(seq(0, 1, 0.1))
 [1] -3.66356 -1.99243 -1.29505 -0.80012 -0.38467  0.00000
 [7]  0.38467  0.80012  1.29505  1.99243  3.66356
Warning message:
Proportions remapped to (0.025,0.975) in: logit(seq(0, 1, 0.1))
```

To illustrate the use of the logit transformation, I apply it to the distribution of the gender composition of occupations in the Canadian occupational-prestige data:

```
> detach(SLID)
> attach(Prestige)
> plot(density(women, from=0, to=100))
> plot(density(logit(women), adjust=.75))
Warning message:
Proportions remapped to (0.025,0.975) in: logit(women)
```

The resulting density plots—before and after the logit transformation—are shown in Figure 3.17. The density plot for the untransformed percentages is confined to the domain 0 to 100. The untransformed data, in panel (a), stack up near the boundaries, especially near 0; the transformed data, in panel (b), appear better behaved, and the density plot reveals three apparent concentrations or groups of occupations.

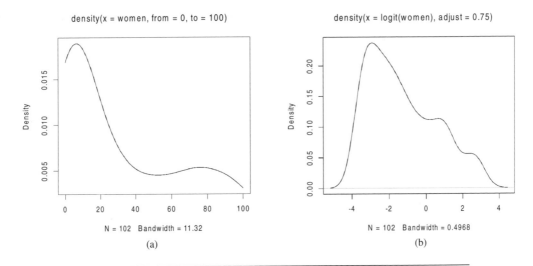

Figure 3.17   Distribution of women in the Canadian occupational-prestige data, (a) before and (b) after logit transformation.

Using `plot` with `density` in S-PLUS

Entering `plot(density(women, from=0, to=100))` in S-PLUS graphs the density estimate as a sequence of points rather than as a line. To plot the density estimate as a line, instead enter `plot(density(women, from=0, to=100), type='l')`. Recall that the `density` function in S-PLUS does not recognize the argument `adjust`.

Transformations for Normality and Symmetry   3.4.1

All the univariate displays discussed in Section 3.1 are useful for examining the distribution of a variable for symmetry, but normal quantile-comparison plots are most appropriate for checking departures from normality. Positive skew can be "corrected" by moving the variable "down the ladder" of powers and roots from $x^{(1)}$ (i.e., no transformation) to $x^{(1/2)}$, $x^{(0)}$, $x^{(-1)}$, etc.; negative skews by moving "up the ladder" to $x^{(2)}$, $x^{(3)}$, etc.

One way to select a transformation to symmetry is by trial and error, replotting the data for different powers and examining the results. The `Ask` function in `car` facilitates the process of trial and error:

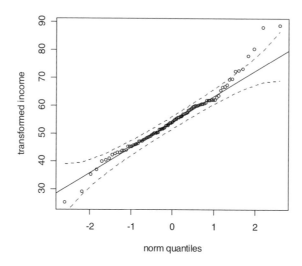

Figure 3.18   Normal quantile-comparison plot for the Box-Cox cube-root transformation of `income` in the Canadian occupational-prestige data.

```
> Ask(p, function(p) qq.plot(box.cox(income, p),
+           ylab='transformed income'))
Enter p : 0
Enter p : 1/2
Enter p : 1/3
Enter p :
>
```

The second argument to `Ask` is the function to be called repeatedly; in this case, the function is "defined on the fly" and takes a single argument, the power p for the Box-Cox transformation of `income` in the `Prestige` data set; I then simply call the `qq.plot` function for the transformed data. The first argument to `Ask` is the argument to be modified, in this case the power p. (If the function called by `Ask` takes additional, non-varying, arguments, then these are specified by name as subsequent arguments to `Ask`.) When you enter a value in response to the prompt from `Ask`, make sure that the *R Console* (or S-PLUS *Commands* window) has the focus, by clicking in its window, if necessary, or selecting its window from the **Window** menu. Enter an empty line to exit from `Ask`.

Recall that the distribution of `income` is positively skewed, so we should transform the variable *down* the ladder of powers and roots; I successively try the powers $p = 0$, $p = 1/2$, and $p = 1/3$. Both the log ($p = 0$) and cube-root ($p = 1/3$) transformations work reasonably well here. The normal quantile-comparison plot produced by $p = 1/3$ is shown in Figure 3.18: The transformed distribution of `income` is quite symmetric now, but heavy tailed relative to the normal distribution.

Another, if less interactive, approach to finding a transformation to symmetry is to generate a sequence of plots in a `for` loop[9]:

```
> for (p in c(1/2, 1/3, 0, -1/3, -1/2, -1))
+     qq.plot(box.cox(income, p),
+     ylab=paste('transformed income, p =',p))
>
```

The `qq.plot` function is called once for each of six values of p. Here, `paste` is used to compose the label for the vertical axis. This approach works in the Windows version of R, where we can record a sequence of plots, by selecting **Recording** in the **History** menu, which appears when a graphics window has the focus. Use the *Page Up* and *Page Down* keys to move through the recorded plots.[10]

*Maximum-Likelihood Estimation of Normalizing Powers**

An alternative to trial and error is to estimate the normalizing transformation parameter λ in $x^{(\lambda)}$. The `box.cox.powers` function in `car` finds normalizing transformations for individual variables or multinormalizing transformations for several variables, by the method of maximum likelihood. For example, for `income` in the Canadian occupational-prestige data:

```
> summary(box.cox.powers(income))
Box-Cox Transformation to Normality

 Est.Power Std.Err. Wald(Power=0) Wald(Power=1)
    0.1793   0.1108        1.6179       -7.4062

 L.R. test, power = 0:  2.7103   df = 1   p = 0.0997
 L.R. test, power = 1:  47.261   df = 1   p = 0
```

The function `box.cox.powers` returns an object. Simply printing the object produces just the estimated power(s); the `summary` method for the object, however, prints a more complete report.

In this case, the maximum-likelihood estimate of the normalizing power is $\hat{\lambda} = 0.18$; we have strong evidence that λ is not equal to 1; and we cannot reject the hypothesis that $\lambda = 0$ (the log transformation). We know from our previous work that $\hat{\lambda} = 0.18$ will make the distribution of `income` symmetric, but it still will have heavier tails than the normal distribution.

---

9. Loops and other S programming constructs are described in Chapter 8.

10. Alternatively, we may place all six plots on the same page, for example, in a 2 × 3 array; this can be accomplished in S by specifying `par(mfrow=c(2,3))` prior to the `for` loop that draws the plots.

Likewise, to find transformations of income and education that make their joint distribution as close to bivariate normal as possible:

```
> summary(box.cox.powers(cbind(income,education)))
Box-Cox Transformations to Multinormality

          Est.Power Std.Err. Wald(Power=0) Wald(Power=1)
income       0.2617   0.1014        2.5799       -7.2800
education    0.4242   0.4033        1.0517       -1.4278

L.R. test, all powers = 0:  7.694    df = 2   p = 0.0213
L.R. test, all powers = 1:  48.8727  df = 2   p = 0
```

That is $\hat{\lambda}_1 = 0.26 \simeq 1/4$ and $\hat{\lambda}_2 = 0.42 \simeq 1/2$. According to the Wald tests (which under the stated hypotheses follow an asymptotic standard normal distribution), the transformation of income is statistically significant but that of education is not. Applying these transformations to each variable produces the scatterplot in Figure 3.19:

```
> scatterplot(income^.25, education^.5, span=.75, lwd=3)
>
```

It is apparent from the scatterplot that while the univariate distributions of transformed income and education are quite symmetric, their joint distribution does not appear to be bivariate normal.

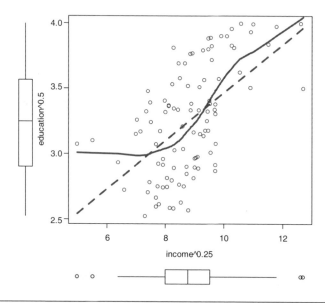

Figure 3.19   Scatterplot of education$^{.5}$ by income$^{.25}$.

Transformations to Equalize Spread   3.4.2

We previously examined the relationship between number of interlocks and nation of control among the 248 large Canadian corporations in Ornstein's interlocking-directorate data set (Figure 3.13). As is often the case, there is an association between *level* and *spread* in these data: Nations with a relatively high level of interlocks (Canada, Other) show more variation than nations with fewer interlocks on average (U.K., U.S.). A *spread-level plot* (Tukey, 1977) is a scatterplot of log-interquartile-range versus log-median and may be constructed directly from the data by the spread.level.plot function in car:

```
> detach(Prestige)
> attach(Ornstein)
> spread.level.plot(interlocks + 1 ~ nation)
     LowerHinge Median UpperHinge Hinge-Spread
US            2    6.0         13           11
UK            4    9.0         14           10
CAN           6   13.0         30           24
OTH           4   15.5         24           20

Suggested power transformation:  0.15345
>
```

The graph produced by spread.level.plot is shown in Figure 3.20. When, as here, there is a positive association between spread and level,

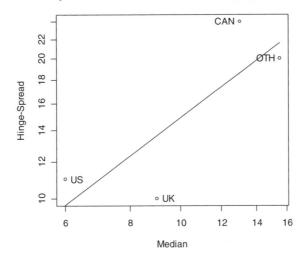

Spread-Level Plot for interlocks + 1 by nation

Figure 3.20   Spread-level plot for the relationship between number of interlocks and nation of control in Ornstein's interlocking-directorate data.

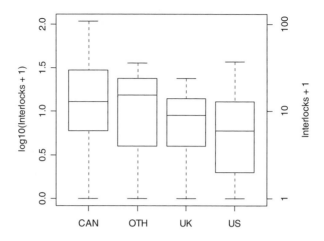

Figure 3.21   Parallel boxplots for $\log_{10}$(interlocks+1) by nation of control.

we can make the spreads more nearly equal by transforming the variable down the ladder of powers and roots. Suppose a line is fit to the spread-level plot and that the slope of the line is b; a spread stabilizing power transformation is then given by $p = 1 - b$.

The expression `interlocks + 1` appears on the left-hand side of the formula passed to `spread.level.plot`. I used the start of 1 because some firms have 0 interlocks. The function returns a table giving the first quartile ("lower hinge"), median, third quartile ("upper hinge"), and interquartile range ("hinge-spread"), along with the suggested power transformation of `interlocks + 1`. The suggested power, $p = 0.15$, is close to the log transformation. Figure 3.21 shows parallel boxplots for the log-transformed data:

```
> old.margins <- par(mar=c(5.1, 4.1, 4.1, 4.1))
> boxplot(log(interlocks+1,10) ~ nation,
+     ylab='log10(Interlocks + 1)')
> power.axis(power=0, base=10, at=c(1,10,100),
+     axis.title='Interlocks + 1')
> par(mar=old.margins)
> remove(old.margins)
>
```

The spreads in the transformed data for the four groups are much less different than those in the untransformed data (Figure 3.13).

The production of the boxplot is very simple, taking just one command; I use logs to the base 10 for interpretability. The remaining S statements leave space for, and then plot, the right-side axis, which translates the log scale back to the number of interlocks (plus 1). The `car` function `power.axis` draws the additional axis (treating the log transformation as the zero power). After making the plot, I restore the original margins

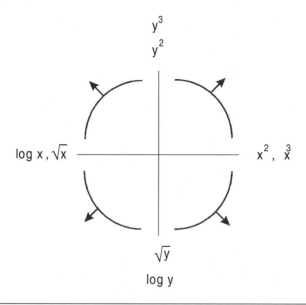

Figure 3.22   Mosteller and Tukey's bulging rule for finding linearizing transformations: When the bulge points *down*, transform *y down* the
ladder of powers and roots; when the bulge points *up*, transform *y up*; when the bulge points *left*, transform *x down*; when
the bulge points *right*, transform *x up*.

of the plot window.[11] The functions `box.cox.axis` and `prob.axis` in
`car` may be used similarly to produce axes on the untransformed scale
corresponding to Box-Cox and logit transformations.

Transformations to Linearity   3.4.3

Another common application of power transformations is to linearize
nonlinear relationships. An analytic approach to linearizing transformations is discussed in Chapter 6; here I consider trial and error, guided
by Mosteller and Tukey's (1977) *bulging rule,* which is illustrated in
Figure 3.22.

An example appears in Figure 3.23. Panel (a) of this figure shows the
relationship between infant-mortality rate (infant deaths per 1000 live
births) and GDP per capita (in U.S. dollars) for 193 nations of the world;
the data are from the United Nations (1998). Because the relationship is

---

11. Many global graphics parameters in S are set or queried with the par function. The `mar` setting
is for the plot margins; see `help(par)` for details. Graphics parameters are discussed in Chapter 7.

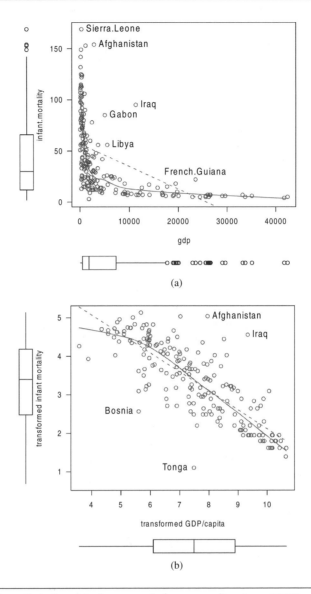

Figure 3.23   Relationship between infant morality (per 1000) and GDP per capita (U.S. dollars) for 193 nations: (a) original scatterplot; (b) with both variables log-transformed.

monotone (infant mortality decreases with GDP, though at a declining rate) and simple (the direction of curvature of the relationship does not change), power transformation of one or both variables is a promising strategy. The graph is produced by the following S commands:

```
> detach(Ornstein)
> data(UN)
```

```
> UN[1:5,]  # first 5 obs.
               infant.mortality  gdp
Afghanistan               154 2848
Albania                    32  863
Algeria                    44 1531
American-Samoa             11   NA
Andorra                    NA   NA

> attach(UN)
> scatterplot(gdp, infant.mortality, labels=row.names(UN))
[1]    1  63  65  87 107 166
```

There are 207 nations in all, but some data are missing. Using the mouse, I identified a few observations in the scatterplot.

To search for linearizing transformations by trial and error, I invoke the Ask function:

```
> Ask(p, function(p) scatterplot(box.cox(gdp,p[1]),
+       box.cox(infant.mortality, p[2]),
+       xlab='transformed GDP/capita',
+       ylab='transformed infant mortality',
+       labels=row.names(UN)))
Enter p : c(0,1)
Enter p : c(0,0)
Enter p :
>
```

Because Ask expects only one changing argument, I specify this argument, p, as a two-element vector; the first element, p[1], is used for a Box-Cox power transformation of gdp, the second element, p[2], for the transformation of infant.mortality. The bulge in the original scatterplot [Figure 3.23(a)] points *down* and to the *left*, and I therefore try transforming both infant morality and GDP per capita *down* the ladder of powers and roots. My second attempt, specifying "0" powers (i.e., log transformations) for both variables, produces Figure 3.23(b). These transformations serve not only substantially to straighten the relationship between the variables, but also to make each variable more symmetric, rendering the scatterplot much easier to examine.

CHAPTER 4

Fitting Linear Models

S provides excellent facilities for specifying and fitting linear and related statistical models. The basic S function for fitting linear models by least squares is lm. The model is specified by a *formula*—a special notation in which the arithmetic operators +, -, *, /, and ^ take on meanings different from their ordinary ones. I augment these facilities in car with functions for testing hypotheses, as described in this chapter, and for regression "diagnostics," discussed in Chapter 6.

The current chapter begins with linear regression models, the specification of which is very simple, and gradually introduces more complex linear models. The chapter concludes with a general discussion of lm. I take up the closely related topic of generalized linear models in the next chapter; other regression models are described in the Web appendix to the text.

LINEAR LEAST SQUARES REGRESSION 4.1

Simple Regression 4.1.1

The data frame Davis in car contains data on the measured and reported heights and weights of 200 men and women engaged in regular exercise[1]:

```
> library(car)
  . . .
```

---

1. Some of the data values are missing, however: There are 182 complete observations for the regression reported below.

119

```
> data(Davis)
> names(Davis)
[1] "sex"    "weight" "height" "repwt"   "repht"

> Davis[1:5,]
  sex weight height repwt repht
1   M     77    182    77   180
2   F     58    161    51   159
3   F     53    161    54   158
4   M     68    177    70   175
5   F     59    157    59   155
```

Here, weight and repwt are in kilograms, and height and repht are in centimeters. One of the objects of the researcher who collected these data (Davis, 1990) was to determine whether reports of height and weight are sufficiently accurate to replace the actual measurements, which suggests regressing each measurement on the corresponding report; I focus here on weight.

Let y = weight and x = repwt; then the simple linear regression model

$$y_i = \alpha + \beta x_i + \varepsilon_i$$

is fit in S in the following manner:

```
> attach(Davis)
> davis.mod <- lm(weight ~ repwt)
> davis.mod

Call:
lm(formula = weight ~ repwt)

Coefficients:
(Intercept)         repwt
      5.336         0.928
```

The formula weight ~ repwt, with the response variable on the left-hand side of the tilde (~) and the predictor on the right, specifies the regression of weight on repwt.

As is my usual practice, I attach the Davis data frame to make the variables in it visible on the search path. An alternative is to supply a data argument to lm, as in lm(weight ~ repwt, data=Davis). This approach has the advantage of associating the model explicitly with a data frame—which may avoid problems, for example, if the model is updated when the data frame is no longer attached. It is my experience, however, that new users of S find it simpler to attach a data frame to the search path.

The lm function returns a linear-model object, which I save in davis.mod. Printing the object produces a brief report. The summary method for linear models yields more information:

```
> summary(davis.mod)

Call:
lm(formula = weight ~ repwt)

Residuals:
    Min      1Q  Median      3Q     Max
 -7.048  -1.868  -0.728   0.601 108.705

Coefficients:
            Estimate Std. Error t value Pr(>|t|)
(Intercept)   5.3363     3.0369    1.76     0.08
repwt         0.9278     0.0453   20.48   <2e-16

Residual standard error: 8.42 on 181 degrees of freedom
Multiple R-Squared: 0.699,       Adjusted R-squared: 0.697
F-statistic:   420 on 1 and 181 degrees of freedom,
        p-value:    0
```

Handling Missing Data with `lm` in S-PLUS

Recall that the default `na.action` for `lm` in S-PLUS is `na.fail`. There is missing data in Davis's data set, and so it is necessary to set `na.action=na.omit` or `na.exclude` to make this example work. An alternative is to filter the data set for missing data prior to attaching it; for example, `Davis.good <- na.omit(Davis)`.

If individuals are unbiased reporters of their weight, then the regression intercept should be 0 and the slope 1; the least squares regression coefficients are close to 0 and 1, although the intercept is nearly significantly different from 0, as the t test for the intercept demonstrates. The t test for the slope shows that it is highly significantly different from 0; as well, the slope estimate is almost two standard errors from 1, and so it is nearly significantly different from 1. The squared correlation, $R^2 = .699$, is by most standards quite large, but it is not large in the current context, where we are contemplating replacing a measurement by a report. The residual standard deviation is 8.42 kg, a large average error of prediction.

I should have started (of course!) by plotting the data, and I now do so belatedly:

```
> plot(repwt, weight)
> abline(davis.mod)
> abline(0, 1, lty=2)
>
```

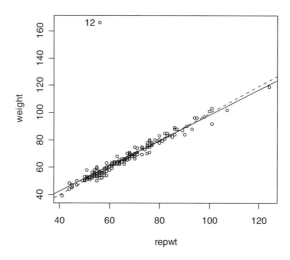

Figure 4.1   Scatterplot of measured weight (`weight`) by reported weight (`repwt`) for Davis's data.

The function `abline` plots a line on the graph given its intercept and slope—either directly, as in `abline(0, 1, lty=2)`, which plots a broken line (line type 2) with intercept 0 and slope 1, or by extracting the regression coefficients from an `lm` object, as in `abline(davis.mod)`. The resulting graph, which appears in Figure 4.1, reveals an extreme outlier, interactively identified as observation 12:

```
> identify(repwt, weight)
[1] 12
>
```

Recall that to identify a point, place the mouse cursor near the point and press the left mouse button; to exit from `identify`, press the right mouse button.

Because the outlier is at a relatively low-leverage point, the regression line is not greatly affected, and the least squares line is quite close to the line of unbiased reporting. Nevertheless, the outlier appears to increase the intercept of the regression line slightly and to decrease its slope slightly; moreover, the outlier inflates the residual standard error and substantially decreases the correlation.

It seems bizarre that an individual who weighs more than 160 kg would report her weight as less than 60 kg, but there is a simple explanation: On data entry, subject 12's height in centimeters and weight in kilograms were inadvertently exchanged. The proper course of action would be to correct the data, but to extend the example, I instead will use the update function to refit the model removing the 12th observation:

```
> davis.mod.2 <- update(davis.mod, subset=-12)
> summary(davis.mod.2)

Call:
lm(formula = weight ~ repwt, subset = -12)

Residuals:
   Min      1Q Median      3Q     Max
-7.530  -1.101 -0.132   1.129   6.389

Coefficients:
             Estimate Std. Error t value Pr(>|t|)
(Intercept)    2.7338     0.8148    3.36  0.00097
repwt          0.9584     0.0121   78.93  < 2e-16

Residual standard error: 2.25 on 180 degrees of freedom
Multiple R-Squared: 0.972,      Adjusted R-squared: 0.972
F-statistic: 6.23e+003 on 1 and 180 degrees of freedom,
        p-value:   0
```

Equivalently, I could have used lm to fit a new model, specifying the subset argument, but update generally is a more convenient way to make small changes to a model. As expected, the intercept is now even closer to 0 and the slope closer to 1; the squared correlation is much larger; and the standard deviation of the residuals is much smaller (if not wholly negligible). Paradoxically (because of the smaller error variance), the intercept and slope are now significantly different from the respective values of 0 and 1.

Multiple Regression 4.1.2

Fitting a multiple linear regression is equally simple. To provide an illustration, let us return to the Canadian occupational-prestige data, introduced in Chapter 2:

```
> detach(Davis)
> data(Prestige)
> attach(Prestige)
> names(Prestige)
[1] "education" "income"   "women"     "prestige" "census"
[6] "type"
```

Then let us regress occupational prestige, y, on the average number of years of education of occupational incumbents, x_1; their average level of income, x_2; and the percentage of women in the occupation, x_3—fitting the model

$$y_i = \alpha + \beta_1 x_{i1} + \beta_2 x_{i2} + \beta_3 x_{i3} + \varepsilon_i.$$

```
> prestige.mod <- lm(prestige ~ income + education + women)
> summary(prestige.mod)

Call:
lm(formula = prestige ~ income + education + women)

Residuals:
    Min      1Q  Median      3Q     Max
-19.825  -5.333  -0.136   5.159  17.504

Coefficients:
             Estimate Std. Error t value Pr(>|t|)
(Intercept) -6.794334   3.239089   -2.10    0.039
income       0.001314   0.000278    4.73 7.6e-06
education    4.186637   0.388701   10.77  < 2e-16
women       -0.008905   0.030407   -0.29    0.770

Residual standard error: 7.85 on 98 degrees of freedom
Multiple R-Squared: 0.798,      Adjusted R-squared: 0.792
F-statistic:  129 on 3 and 98 degrees of freedom,
        p-value:   0
```

There is, therefore, strong evidence that occupational prestige is related to the income and education levels of the occupations, but not to their gender composition. We will revisit this model in Chapter 6 on regression diagnostics.

4.1.3   Standardized Regression Coefficients

I am not terribly enamoured of standardized regression coefficients, but obtaining them in S is not hard: One way to proceed is by standardizing all of the variables to mean 0 and standard deviation 1, using the scale function:

```
> Prestige.scaled <- data.frame(scale(
+     Prestige[,c('prestige', 'income', 'education', 'women')]))

> Prestige.scaled[1:5,]
                    prestige  income education    women
GOV.ADMINISTRATORS   1.27680 1.30787   0.86935 -0.56167
GENERAL.MANAGERS     1.29424 4.49398   0.55781 -0.78673
ACCOUNTANTS          0.96293 0.58246   0.74473 -0.41857
PURCHASING.OFFICERS  0.57931 0.48684   0.24994 -0.62629
CHEMISTS             1.54998 0.37803   1.42277 -0.54528
```

```
> summary(lm(prestige ~ income + education + women,
+    data=Prestige.scaled))

Call:
lm(formula = prestige ~ income + education + women,
   data = Prestige.scaled)
. . .
Coefficients:
              Estimate Std. Error  t value Pr(>|t|)
(Intercept) -2.66e-16   4.52e-02  -5.9e-15     1.00
income       3.24e-01   6.86e-02     4.73  7.6e-06
education    6.64e-01   6.16e-02    10.77  < 2e-16
women       -1.64e-02   5.61e-02    -0.29     0.77

Residual standard error: 0.456 on 98 degrees of freedom
. . .
```

As an alternative to attaching the Prestige.scaled data frame, I have instead specified a data argument to lm (as explained previously). In this manner, I avoid detaching the Prestige data frame, which I intend to use below: Having *both* Prestige and Prestige.scaled attached simultaneously is not useful, because the variables in the more recently attached Prestige.scaled would shadow those in Prestige.

The intercept of the standardized regression model is necessarily 0 (within rounding error). We can suppress the intercept by specifying −1 in the model formula, but doing so changes the residual degrees of freedom and, hence, the residual standard error, coefficient standard errors, and t values[2]:

```
> summary(lm(prestige ~ income + education + women - 1,
+    data=Prestige.scaled))

Call:
lm(formula = prestige ~ income + education + women - 1,
   data = Prestige.scaled)
. . .

Coefficients:
          Estimate Std. Error t value Pr(>|t|)
income      0.3242     0.0682    4.75  6.8e-06
education   0.6640     0.0613   10.83  < 2e-16
women      -0.0164     0.0558   -0.29     0.77

Residual standard error: 0.454 on 99 degrees of freedom
. . .
```

---

2. In any event, the standard errors of the standardized regression coefficients are not strictly correct: Computing standardized coefficients requires estimates of the standard deviations of the variables, which are also subject to sampling variation.

4.2   DUMMY-VARIABLE REGRESSION

4.2.1   Factors

In *dummy-variable regression* (also called *analysis of covariance*), there are both quantitative and categorical predictors. In S, categorical predictors are most naturally treated as *factors*. Recall that the read.table function by default makes factors of character data.

Consider, for example, the variable type (type of occupation) in the currently attached Prestige data frame:

```
> type
 [1] prof prof prof prof prof prof prof prof prof prof prof prof
[13] prof prof prof prof prof prof prof prof prof prof prof prof
[25] prof prof prof bc   prof prof wc   prof wc   NA   wc   wc
 . . .
[97] bc   bc   bc   bc   bc   bc
Levels:  bc prof wc
```

We can tell that type is a factor (1) because its values are printed unquoted and (2) because (in R) the *levels* (i.e., categories) of the factor are printed below the values. The three levels represent blue-collar (bc), professional and managerial (prof), and white-collar (wc) occupations. The levels were automatically alphabetized when the factor was created; more about this later.

Some of the occupations have missing type; because I intend to fit several models to these data, it will be safest to ensure that all models use the same subset of valid observations. A simple way to make sure that this is the case is to create, and then attach, a new version of the data frame consisting only of complete observations:

```
> detach(Prestige)
> Prestige.2 <- na.omit(Prestige)
> attach(Prestige.2)
> type
 [1] prof prof prof prof prof prof prof prof prof prof prof prof
[13] prof prof prof prof prof prof prof prof prof prof prof prof
[25] prof prof prof bc   prof prof wc   prof wc   wc   wc   wc
 . . .
[97] bc   bc
Levels:  bc prof wc
```

Factors are vectors of class factor; they encode level membership numerically, with information about the levels of the factor saved in a levels attribute:

```
> class(type)
[1] "factor"

> unclass(type)
 [1] 2 2 2 2 2 2 2 2 2 2 2 2 2 2 2 2 2 2 2 2 2 2 2 2 2 2 2 2 1 2 2
[31] 3 2 3 3 3 3 3 3 3 3 3 3 3 3 3 3 3 3 3 3 3 3 1 3 3 3 1 1 1 1 1
[61] 1 1 1 1 1 1 1 1 1 1 1 1 1 1 1 1 1 1 1 1 1 1 1 1 1 1 1 1 1 1 1
[91] 1 2 1 1 1 1 1 1
attr(,"levels")
[1] "bc" "prof" "wc"
```

The unclass function removes the class attribute of its argument, in this instance causing type to be printed by the default print method rather than by the print method for factors. This allows us to see the internal structure of the object.

Contrasts   4.2.2

Because a factor is intrinsically categorical, it would be entirely meaningless to treat its numeric levels as a quantitative predictor in a linear model. Instead, we need to code *dummy regressors* or *contrasts* to represent the levels of the factor. We could do this manually, but S will code contrasts for us automatically. I assume that the notion of coding dummy regressors, and the particular coding schemes that are described here, are at least somewhat familiar.

How S codes dummy regressors is controlled by the contrasts option:

```
> options('contrasts')
$contrasts
          unordered            ordered
  "contr.treatment"       "contr.poly"
```

Two values are provided by this option: one for unordered factors (the current context), and the other for ordered factors (to be described later in this section). Each value corresponds to a function that converts a factor into an appropriate set of contrasts.

Default Contrasts in S-PLUS

In S-PLUS, the default contrast type for unordered factors is contr.helmert, which is described later in this section.

We can see how the contrasts for a factor are coded by using the contrasts function:

```
> contrasts(type)
     prof wc
bc      0  0
prof    1  0
wc      0  1
```

The 0/1 coding scheme employed by contr.treatment is often termed *dummy coding* or *indicator coding*. The first level of the factor is taken as the "reference" or "baseline" category. The choice of reference category is essentially arbitrary, and we can modify it, if we wish, in the following manner:

```
> contrasts(type) <- contr.treatment(levels(type), base=2)
> contrasts(type)
     bc wc
bc    1  0
prof  0  0
wc    0  1
```

Dummy coding produces easy-to-interpret regression coefficients, but other choices are available in S.

Helmert Coding

```
> contrasts(type) <- 'contr.helmert'
> contrasts(type)
     [,1] [,2]
bc     -1   -1
prof    1   -1
wc      0    2
```

Helmert coding produces orthogonal (i.e., uncorrelated) contrasts when there are equal numbers of observations at the different levels of the factor; whether or not there are equal observations at the different levels, the coefficients for the Helmert regressors compare each level with the average of the "preceding" ones.

Deviation Coding

```
> contrasts(type) <- 'contr.sum'
> contrasts(type)
     [,1] [,2]
bc      1    0
prof    0    1
wc     -1   -1
```

```
> contrasts(type) <- NULL
>
```

Deviation coding results from so-called "sigma" or "sum-to-zero" constraints on the coefficients of the over-parametrized model: The coefficient
for the last level (here wc) is implicitly constrained equal to the sum of the
coefficients for the other levels, and the redundant last coefficient is omitted from the model. Each coefficient compares the corresponding level of
the factor to the average of the other levels. [Entering contrasts(type)
<- NULL ensures that the contrasts option applies once more to type.]

An alternative to changing the contrasts of individual factors is to reset
the global contrasts option. For example:

```
> options(contrasts = c('contr.helmert', 'contr.poly'))
>
```

Finally, as explained in Section 4.7, contrasts may be assigned to factors in the call to lm.

Before proceeding, I return the contrasts option to its default value:

```
> options(contrasts = c('contr.treatment', 'contr.poly')
>
```

Changing the Contrast Type in S-PLUS

In S-PLUS, you cannot change the contrast type for a factor simply by
specifying a character string with the name of the contrast function.
Instead, you may take the following approach:

```
> contrasts(type) <- contr.treatment(c("bc", "wc", "prof"))
```

```
> contrasts(type) <- contr.helmert(levels(type))
```

```
> contrasts(type) <- contr.sum(levels(type))
```

Notice that to specify the baseline level for contr.treatment, it is
necessary to give the levels explicitly, with the baseline listed first.

There is an additional complication in S4: You must explicitly copy the
factor (here, type) from the attached data frame into the working data
before making a change to it, by entering type <- type. This operation
takes place automatically in S3 (and R).

4.2.3   Ordered Factors

An ordered factor may be created in the following manner:

```
> type.ord <- ordered(type, levels=c('bc', 'wc', 'prof'))
> type.ord
 [1] prof prof prof prof prof prof prof prof prof prof prof prof
. . .
[97] bc   bc
Levels:  bc < wc < prof

> round(contrasts(type.ord), 3)
          .L     .Q
bc    -0.707  0.408
wc     0.000 -0.816
prof   0.707  0.408
```

I specified the levels of the factor explicitly to avoid ordering them alphabetically, which would be inappropriate here: The *conventional* order of these levels is bc (blue-collar occupations), wc (white-collar occupations), prof (professional and managerial occupations).

Because type.ord is an ordered factor, contrasts are created by default using contr.poly, which codes orthogonal polynomials when the factor levels are equally spaced and there are equal numbers of observations at the different levels. The first term (labeled .L) represents a linear trend; the second (.Q), a quadratic trend. In general, the order of the polynomial (two, in this example) is one less than the number of levels (three). Polynomial contrasts are most compelling when the ordered factor is a quantitative discrete variable—for example, number of surviving grandparents—but they are also useful for ordinal predictors such as type.ord. Helmert contrasts may also be of interest for an ordered factor.

4.2.4   Fitting Additive Dummy-Regression Models

Suppose that we want to regress prestige on income, education, and type of occupation. The *additive* dummy-regression model takes the form

$$y_i = \alpha + \beta_1 x_{i1} + \beta_2 x_{i2} + \gamma_1 d_{i1} + \gamma_2 d_{i2} + \varepsilon_i,$$

where y = prestige, x_1 = income, x_2 = education, and the specific form of the ds depends on the coding scheme used for the three categories of type—say, "treatment" contrasts.

To fit this model, we simply need to add the factor type to the right-hand side of the model formula:

```
> prestige.mod.1 <- lm(prestige ~ income + education + type)
> summary(prestige.mod.1)

Call:
lm(formula = prestige ~ income + education + type)

Residuals:
    Min      1Q  Median      3Q     Max
-14.953  -4.449   0.168   5.057  18.632

Coefficients:
             Estimate Std. Error t value Pr(>|t|)
(Intercept) -0.622929   5.227525   -0.12     0.91
income       0.001013   0.000221    4.59  1.4e-05
education    3.673166   0.640502    5.73  1.2e-07
typeprof     6.038971   3.866855    1.56     0.12
typewc      -2.737231   2.513932   -1.09     0.28

Residual standard error: 7.09 on 93 degrees of freedom
Multiple R-Squared: 0.835,      Adjusted R-squared: 0.828
F-statistic:  118 on 4 and 93 degrees of freedom,
        p-value:   0
```

Because the first level of type (i.e., bc) is the baseline level, we obtain coefficients for the levels prof and wc, along with the regression constant (the "Intercept") and coefficients for income and education.

The t values in the regression summary are adequate for testing one-degree-of-freedom effects, such as those of income and education in this model, but because the choice of coding and baseline category is essentially arbitrary, we usually want to test the two coefficients for type simultaneously. S provides the anova function to test terms in a linear model:

```
> anova(prestige.mod.1)
Analysis of Variance Table

Response: prestige
          Df Sum Sq Mean Sq F value Pr(>F)
income     1  14022   14022  278.56 <2e-16
education  1   9053    9053  179.85 <2e-16
type       2    591     296    5.87  0.004
Residuals 93   4681      50
```

The sums of squares reported by the anova function are, however, "sequential" sums of squares: for income *ignoring* education and type; for education *after* income but *ignoring* type; and for type *after* income and education.[3] For nonorthogonal data (i.e., when regressors for different terms in the model are correlated), sequential sums of squares do not, in general, correspond to meaningful hypotheses about parameters in the model. Here, however, the last test, for type, gives us what we want, and we already have t values for the single-df effects, income and education.

The anova function may also be used to calculate an incremental (or "extra-sum-of-squares") F test contrasting two nested linear models. For example, we may omit type from the model, and contrast the result with the full model, obtaining the same F statistic for type as before:

```
> prestige.mod.0 <- lm(prestige ~ income + education)
> anova(prestige.mod.0, prestige.mod.1)
Analysis of Variance Table

Model 1: prestige ~ income + education
Model 2: prestige ~ income + education + type
  Res.Df Res.Sum Sq Df Sum Sq F value Pr(>F)
1     95       5272
2     93       4681  2    591    5.87  0.004
```

The Anova function in car (note the uppercase A, to distinguish it from anova) calculates a proper test for *each* of the terms in the linear model[4]; in the case of one-df effects, these F tests are simply t^2:

```
> Anova(prestige.mod.1)
Anova Table (Type II tests)

Response: prestige
          Sum Sq Df F value  Pr(>F)
income      1059  1   21.03 1.4e-05
education   1655  1   32.89 1.2e-07
type         591  2    5.87   0.004
Residuals   4681 93
```

A last point on the additive dummy-regression model: By omitting the regression constant from the model, we can force S to fit a different intercept for each group. This practice is potentially confusing, however, because the hypothesis that the resulting three coefficients for type are all 0 is no longer equivalent to the hypothesis of no type effects. Moreover, in models without a constant, R^2 loses its usual interpretation, as does

---

3. Following popular terminology introduced by the SAS statistical computer package, sequential sums of squares are often called Type I sums of squares. The anova function in S-PLUS (but not R) can also calculate so-called Type III sums of squares, which would give us the result that we are looking for here, but which introduce additional considerations in models with interactions. I discuss Type II and Type III sums of squares later in this chapter.

4. By default, the Anova function calculates Type II sums of squares, but it can calculate Type III sums of squares as well. For this additive model, Type II and Type III sums of squares are identical. See footnote 3.

the omnibus F test for the model. I suggest that you generally avoid this kind of specification.

The constant is suppressed by including -1 on the right-hand side of the model formula:

```
> prestige.mod.2 <- lm(prestige ~ income + education + type - 1)
> summary(prestige.mod.2)
. . .

Coefficients:
            Estimate Std. Error t value Pr(>|t|)
income      0.001013   0.000221    4.59  1.4e-05
education   3.673166   0.640502    5.73  1.2e-07
typebc     -0.622929   5.227525   -0.12     0.91
typeprof    5.416041   8.692156    0.62     0.53
typewc     -3.360160   6.960162   -0.48     0.63

Residual standard error: 7.09 on 93 degrees of freedom
Multiple R-Squared: 0.981,       Adjusted R-squared: 0.98
F-statistic:  966 on 5 and 93 degrees of freedom,
       p-value:    0

> Anova(prestige.mod.2)
Anova Table (Type II tests)

Response: prestige
            Sum Sq Df F value  Pr(>F)
income        1059  1   21.03 1.4e-05
education     1655  1   32.89 1.2e-07
type           923  3    6.11 0.00077
Residuals     4681 93
```

The F tests for income and education are the same as before, but, as explained, the F for type now tests a different, and uninteresting, hypothesis.

Dummy Regression with Interactions   4.2.5

The additive dummy-regression model fits identical slopes in all the levels of a factor. Building interactions into the model permits different slopes at different levels ("different slopes for different folks").

Interactions are specified by colons (:) in the model formula; for example, I use update to add interactions to the dummy-regression model for the prestige data (as explained below):

```
> prestige.mod.3 <- update(prestige.mod.1,
+                          . ~ . + income:type + education:type)

> summary(prestige.mod.3)

Call:
lm(formula = prestige ~ income + education + type + income:type +
    education:type)

Residuals:
   Min     1Q Median    3Q    Max
-13.46  -4.23   1.35  3.83  19.63

Coefficients:
                    Estimate Std. Error t value Pr(>|t|)
(Intercept)         2.28e+00   7.06e+00    0.32    0.748
income              3.52e-03   5.56e-04    6.33  9.6e-09
education           1.71e+00   9.57e-01    1.79    0.077
typeprof            1.54e+01   1.37e+01    1.12    0.266
typewc             -3.35e+01   1.77e+01   -1.90    0.061
income:typeprof    -2.90e-03   5.99e-04   -4.85  5.3e-06
income:typewc      -2.07e-03   8.94e-04   -2.32    0.023
education:typeprof  1.39e+00   1.29e+00    1.08    0.284
education:typewc    4.29e+00   1.76e+00    2.44    0.017

Residual standard error: 6.32 on 89 degrees of freedom
Multiple R-Squared: 0.875,      Adjusted R-squared: 0.863
F-statistic: 77.6 on 8 and 89 degrees of freedom,
      p-value:    0

> Anova(prestige.mod.3)
Anova Table (Type II tests)

Response: prestige
               Sum Sq Df F value  Pr(>F)
income           1132  1   28.35 7.5e-07
education        1068  1   26.75 1.4e-06
type              591  2    7.40  0.0011
income:type       952  2   11.92 2.6e-05
education:type    238  2    2.99  0.0556
Residuals        3553 89
```

This specification fits the model

$$y_i = \alpha + \beta_1 x_{i1} + \beta_2 x_{i2} + \gamma_1 d_{i1} + \gamma_2 d_{i2}$$
$$+ \delta_{11} x_{i1} d_{i1} + \delta_{12} x_{i1} d_{i2} + \delta_{21} x_{i2} d_{i1} + \delta_{22} x_{i2} d_{i2} + \varepsilon_i.$$

Rather than specifying the model from scratch, I have *updated* the previously fit additive model (prestige.mod.1). In the formula argument (i.e., the second argument) to update, the periods (.) are to be read as "the previous value," and so lm reuses the previous left-hand side of the model, and adds interactions between income and type and between education and type to the previous right-hand side.

The Type II tests computed by Anova obey the *principle of marginality*, and are summarized in the following table; for example, the "main-effect" test for income ignores the interactions between income and type, to which income is marginal (but not between education and type):

Sum of Squares for	after...	ignoring...
income	education, type, education:type	income:type
education	income, type, income:type	education:type
type	income, education	income:type, education:type
income:type	income, education, type, education:type	
education:type	income, education, type, income:type	

The "ignoring/after" terminology is a shorthand: For example, the sum of squares for income *ignoring* income:type and *after* education and type is calculated by contrasting the residual sums of squares for two (nested) models: the model including income, education, type, and education:type; and the model including education, type, and education:type (but omitting income). The denominator for the F-test is taken from the estimated error variance for the full model. The Anova function calculates the various sums of squares without actually refitting the model.

In writing the formula for a linear model, it is not necessary to separately specify interactions and their lower-order relatives, such as main effects; using asterisks (*) generates an interaction and all of the terms marginal to it. Thus, the previous model (prestige.mod.3) could have been fit as:

```
> lm(prestige ~ income*type + education*type)
```

S linear-model formulas also make provision for nested effects: The term A %in% B is interpreted as "A nested within B." In the current dummy-regression context, we can use nesting to fit separate education and income slopes at each level of occupational type:

```
> lm(prestige ~ type + (income + education) %in% type)
```

Parentheses in model formulas are expanded in the usual manner: Thus, (income + education) %in% type is equivalent to income %in% type + education %in% type.

Nesting Effects in S-PLUS

In S-PLUS, (income + education) %in% type does not expand to income %in% type + education %in% type. If we desire the second specification, we need to enter it directly.

Suppressing the regression constant fits a separate intercept for each type, as well as separate slopes:

```
> lm(prestige ~ type + (income + education) %in% type - 1)

Call:
lm(formula = prestige ~ type + (income + education) %in% type - 1)

Coefficients:
          typebc           typeprof              typewc
          2.27575           17.62765           -31.26090
   typebc:income     typeprof:income       typewc:income
         0.00352            0.00062             0.00145
typebc:education  typeprof:education  typewc:education
         1.71327            3.10108             6.00415
```

This kind of parametrization, however, makes it relatively difficult to test for type effects and interactions with type. In particular, a properly formulated analysis of variance for the nested model tests the hypotheses (1) that all the intercepts are *zero*, (2) that all the income slopes are *zero*, and (3) that all the education slopes are *zero*—not, for example, that the education slopes are *equal to each other*.

4.3   ANALYSIS OF VARIANCE MODELS

It is, from one point of view, unnecessary to consider analysis of variance models separately from the general class of linear models, but doing so helps to clarify how interactions among factors are handled in S.

Let us begin by detaching the Prestige data frame and accessing data from an experiment on conformity reported by Moore and Krupat (1971):

```
> detach(Prestige.2)
> data(Moore)
> attach(Moore)
> Moore
  partner.status conformity fcategory fscore
1            low          8       low     37
2            low          4      high     57
```

3	low	8	high	65
. . .				
44	high	10	high	52
45	high	15	medium	44

The 45 subjects in the experiment interacted with a partner who was of either relatively low or relatively high status (as recorded in the factor partner.status). In the course of the experiment, the subjects made intrinsically ambiguous judgments, exchanging these judgments with their partners; the partners' judgments were manipulated so that they disagreed with the subjects on 40 critical trials. After exchanging initial judgments, the subjects were given the opportunity to change their judgments. The variable conformity records the number of times in these 40 trials that each subject deferred to his or her partner's judgment. The variable fscore is a measure of "authoritarianism," and fcategory is a categorized version of this variable, dissecting fscore into thirds, labeled low, medium, and high.

Employing partner.status and fcategory as factors, Moore and Krupat performed a two-way analysis of variance of conformity.[5] To replicate their analysis, I start by re-ordering the levels of the factor fcategory, because the alphabetical order is not what we want. (I could treat fcategory as an ordered factor, but do not do so.)

```
> fcategory <- factor(fcategory, levels=c('low','medium','high'))
> fcategory
 [1] low     high    high    low     low     low     medium medium
 . . .
[41] medium high    low     high    medium
Levels:  low medium high
```

Next, I use the tapply (table-apply) function to find the mean and standard deviation of conformity, along with the frequency count of observations, for all combinations of levels (cells) of the two factors[6]:

```
> means <- tapply(conformity, list(fcategory, partner.status), mean)
> means
          high    low
low     17.400  8.900
medium  14.273  7.250
high    11.857 12.625
```

---

5. Actually, Moore and Krupat categorized authoritarianism *separately* within each level of partner's status. The results I present here are similar to theirs, but my procedure is more defensible.

The reader may want to consider variations on the analysis: Using fscore, the quantitative version of authoritarianism, in place of the factor fcategory, produces a dummy regression. Because conformity is a disguised proportion (conforming responses out of 40), a logit transformation of conformity/40 might be tried.

6. The tapply function, and other functions in the "apply" family, are described in Chapter 8.

```
> tapply(conformity, list(fcategory, partner.status),
+       function(x) sqrt(var(x)))
         high    low
low      4.5056 2.6437
medium   3.9520 3.9476
high     3.9340 7.3473

> tapply(conformity, list(fcategory, partner.status), length)
       high low
low       5  10
medium   11   4
high      7   8
```

The first argument to `tapply` is the variable to be summarized; the second argument is a list of factors; and the third argument is the function to be applied. Note how I define a function for the standard deviation "on the fly," as the square root of the variance: It would be simpler to use `sd` (in R) or `stdev` (in S-PLUS), but the example illustrates how to employ an anonymous function as an argument to `tapply`. I assign the means to a variable so that I can conveniently plot them, along with the data (Figure 4.2):

```
> Fcat <- as.numeric(fcategory)
> plot(c(0.5, 3.5), range(conformity), xlab='F category',
+       ylab='Conformity', type='n', axes=F)
> axis(1, at=1:3, labels=c('low', 'medium', 'high'))  # x-axis
> axis(2)  # y-axis
> box()
> points(jitter(Fcat[partner.status == 'low']),
+       conformity[partner.status == 'low'], pch='L')
> points(jitter(Fcat[partner.status == 'high']),
+       conformity[partner.status == 'high'], pch='H')
> lines(1:3, means[,1], lty=1, lwd=3, type='b', pch=19, cex=2)
> lines(1:3, means[,2], lty=3, lwd=3, type='b', pch=1, cex=2)
> legend(locator(1), c('high','low'), lty=c(1,3),
+    lwd=c(3,3), pch=c(19,1))
>
```

Here is a brief explanation of the commands used to draw this graph[7]:

■ The function `as.numeric` "coerces" the factor `fcategory` to numbers, which are used for horizontal coordinates in the graph.

■ Specifying `type='n'` in the call to `plot` sets up the coordinate space for the graph without plotting the data.

■ The `axis` function draws tick marks and tick labels, while `box` places a frame around the graph.

---

7. Chapter 7 describes S graphics in greater detail, including a general strategy for building up complex graphs.

- The `points` function adds the data, using the plotting character `'L'` for low partner's status and `'H'` for high partner's status. Jittering the points horizontally helps to separate them visually.

- The `lines` function plots the profiles of means, providing different symbols (pch=19 and pch=1) and line types (lty=1 and lty=3) for the two levels of `partner.status`.

- Finally, `legend` adds a legend to the graph, positioning it with the mouse via the `locator` function, as explained in the preceding chapter. (Click the left mouse button to set the upper-left corner of the legend.)

`legend` in S-PLUS

In the S-PLUS version of `legend`, the argument `marks` is used in place of `pch` to specify plotting characters.

The standard deviation in the low-status, high-authoritarian condition is substantially larger than in the other conditions, and the plot reveals that two of the eight observations in this condition have especially large conformity scores; I label these observations interactively with the mouse:

```
> identify(Fcat, conformity)
[1] 16 19
```

Because the profiles of means in Figure 4.2 are not parallel, `fcategory` and `partner.status` appear to interact in affecting `conformity`, much

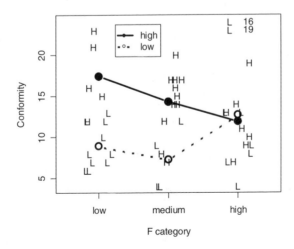

Figure 4.2   Conformity by partner's status and authoritarianism for Moore and Krupat's experiment. The points are jittered horizontally to avoid overplotting.

in the manner that Moore and Krupat anticipated. I invite the reader to redo the analysis described immediately below, removing observations 16 and 19.

How to formulate hypotheses, contrasts, and sums of squares in two-way and higher-way analysis of variance is the subject of a great deal of controversy and confusion. This is not the place to disentangle the issue (see, for example, the discussion in Fox, 1997, Section 8.2), but I will make the following brief points:

■ The essential goal in analysis of variance is to test meaningful hypotheses about differences among cell means and their averages. Contrast coding and sums of squares should follow from the hypotheses.

■ Issues only arise in so-called "unbalanced" data—that is, when the numbers of observations in different cells are unequal, as is the case for Moore and Krupat's experiment.

■ It is difficult to go wrong if you construct tests that conform to the principle of marginality, always ignoring higher-order relatives (e.g., the interaction A:B) when testing lower-order terms (e.g., the main effect A). This approach produces what are sometimes termed Type II sums of squares.

■ If you are careful, however, you can test lower-order terms *after* their higher-order relatives—for example the main effect of A after the B main effect *and* the A:B interaction. The main effect of A, in this construction, represents the effect of A averaged over the categories of B. Whether or not this effect really is of interest is another matter, which depends on context. The incremental sum of squares for a term after everything else in the model is sometimes called a Type III sum of squares. In S, to get properly formulated Type III sums of squares, you should use contr.sum or contr.helmert to code factors; in particular, using contr.treatment with Type III sums of squares will produce tests of generally meaningless hypotheses.

■ Analogous issues arise in other linear models: Consider a dummy-regression model with one factor (A) and one quantitative predictor (or *covariate*, X). Suppose that we test the hypothesis that the "main effect" of A is 0 in the model that includes interactions between A and X. This tests that the intercepts for the different levels of A are the same; but if the slopes vary across the levels of A, then the separation among the levels varies with the value of X, and assessing this separation at X = 0 is probably not meaningful. To justify Type III sums of squares, we could express X as deviations from its mean, making the test for differences in intercepts a test for differences among levels of A at the average score of X. Proceeding in this manner produces a meaningful, but not necessarily interesting, test.

In light of these considerations, I fit an analysis of variance model to Moore and Krupat's data employing sum-to-zero contrasts and calculating both Type II and Type III tests:

```
> options(contrasts=c('contr.sum', 'contr.poly'))
> moore.mod <- lm(conformity ~ fcategory * partner.status)
> summary(moore.mod)

Call:
lm(formula = conformity ~ fcategory * partner.status)

Residuals:
   Min    1Q Median    3Q    Max
-8.625 -2.900 -0.273  2.727 11.375

Coefficients:
                           Estimate Std. Error t value Pr(>|t|)
(Intercept)                  12.051      0.728   16.56   <2e-16
fcategory1                    1.099      1.026    1.07   0.2908
fcategory2                   -1.289      1.061   -1.22   0.2314
partner.status1               2.459      0.728    3.38   0.0017
fcategory1:partner.status1    1.791      1.026    1.74   0.0889
fcategory2:partner.status1    1.052      1.061    0.99   0.3273

Residual standard error: 4.58 on 39 degrees of freedom
Multiple R-Squared: 0.324,      Adjusted R-squared: 0.237
F-statistic: 3.73 on 5 and 39 degrees of freedom, p-value: 0.0074

> Anova(moore.mod)
Anova Table (Type II tests)

Response: conformity
                        Sum Sq Df F value Pr(>F)
fcategory                   12  2    0.28 0.7596
partner.status             212  1   10.12 0.0029
fcategory:partner.status   175  2    4.18 0.0226
Residuals                  818 39

> Anova(moore.mod, type='III')
Anova Table (Type III tests)

Response: conformity
                        Sum Sq Df F value Pr(>F)
(Intercept)               5753  1  274.36 <2e-16
fcategory                   36  2    0.86 0.4315
partner.status             240  1   11.42 0.0017
fcategory:partner.status   175  2    4.18 0.0226
Residuals                  818 39
```

Notice that when sum-to-zero contrasts are employed (in this case, by resetting the global contrasts option), the coefficients for the factor are numbered, rather than named for the factor levels. Here, for example, the two coefficients for `fcategory`, which has levels `low`, `medium`, and `high`, are called `fcategory1` and `fcategory2`, rather than (as I would prefer) `fcategorylow` and `fcategorymedium`. If you do not remember the categories for a factor, or their order, you can recover this information by specifying, for example, `levels(fcategory)`.

In this instance, the Type II and Type III tests produce similar results. You may wish to repeat the analysis with Helmert (`contr.helmert`) and indicator (`contr.treatment`) contrasts.

4.4   USER-SPECIFIED CONTRASTS*

There are times when we are interested in testing finer-grain, single-degree-of-freedom hypotheses about differences among the levels of a factor. Suppose that the vector μ represents the population factor-level means in a one-way analysis of variance (or the raveled cell means for a two-way or higher-way classification). If there are p means, then there are $p - 1$ degrees of freedom for differences among them.

Let the contrast matrix C be a $p \times (p - 1)$ matrix of rank $p - 1$, each of the columns of which sums to 0. Then

$$\mu = [1, C] \begin{bmatrix} \alpha \\ \gamma \end{bmatrix}$$

is a linear model for the cell means (where 1 is a $p \times 1$ vector of 1's). The trick is to formulate C so that the $(p - 1) \times 1$ parameter vector γ represents interesting contrasts among the level means. Because $[1, C]$ is nonsingular (reader: why?), we can solve for the parameters as a linear transformation of the means:

$$\begin{bmatrix} \alpha \\ \gamma \end{bmatrix} = [1, C]^{-1} \mu.$$

A particularly simple way to proceed (though not the only way) is to make the columns of C mutually orthogonal. Then, the rows of $[1, C]^{-1}$ are proportional to the corresponding columns of $[1, C]$, and we can directly code the contrasts of interest among the means in the columns of C.

None of this requires that the factor have equal numbers of observations at its several levels, but if these frequencies are equal, then not only are the columns of C orthogonal, but the columns of the model matrix X constructed from C are orthogonal as well. Under these circumstances, we can partition the regression sum of squares for the model into one-degree-of-freedom components due to each contrast.

Baumann and Jones (as reported in Moore & McCabe, 1993) conducted an experiment in which each of 66 children was assigned at random to one of three experimental groups, 22 subjects to a group. The groups represent different methods of teaching reading: a standard method (called "Basal") and two new methods (called "DRTA" and "Strat"). The researchers conducted two pretests and three posttests of reading comprehension. I focus here on the third posttest. The data for the study reside in the data frame Baumann:

```
> detach(Moore)
> data(Baumann)
> attach(Baumann)
> Baumann
   group pretest.1 pretest.2 post.test.1 post.test.2 post.test.3
1  Basal     4         3           5            4          41
2  Basal     6         5           9            5          41
.  .  .
23  DRTA     7         2           7            6          31
24  DRTA     7         6           5            6          40
.  .  .
65 Strat     5         3           6            8          45
66 Strat     8         3           4            6          42
```

The researchers were interested in whether the new methods produce better results than the standard method and whether the new methods differ in their effectiveness:

```
> tapply(post.test.3, group, mean)
 Basal   DRTA   Strat
41.045 46.727 44.273

> tapply(post.test.3, group, function(x) sqrt(var(x)))
 Basal   DRTA   Strat
5.6356 7.3884 5.7668

> plot(group, post.test.3, xlab='Group', ylab='Reading Score')
>
```

Plotting scores against a factor produces parallel boxplots (Figure 4.3). The means and boxplots suggest that there may be differences among the groups—specifically, between the new methods and the standard one.

It appears natural here to define two contrasts: (1) Basal versus the average of DRTA and Strat and (2) DRTA versus Strat:

```
> contrasts(group) <- matrix(c(1,-0.5,-0.5,  0,1,-1), 3, 2)
```

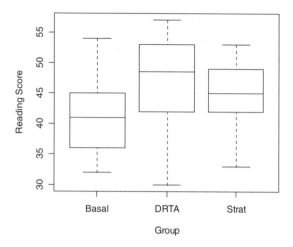

Figure 4.3   Posttest reading score by condition for Baumann and Jones's data.

```
> contrasts(group)
      [,1] [,2]
Basal  1.0   0
DRTA  -0.5   1
Strat -0.5  -1


> summary(lm(post.test.3 ~ group))

Call:
lm(formula = post.test.3 ~ group)

Residuals:
   Min    1Q Median    3Q    Max
-16.73 -3.61   1.11  3.95  12.95

Coefficients:
            Estimate Std. Error t value Pr(>|t|)
(Intercept)   44.015      0.777   56.63   <2e-16
group1        -2.970      1.099   -2.70   0.0088
group2         1.227      0.952    1.29   0.2020

Residual standard error: 6.31 on 63 degrees of freedom
Multiple R-Squared: 0.125,      Adjusted R-squared: 0.0967
F-statistic: 4.48 on 2 and 63 degrees of freedom,
        p-value: 0.0152
```

The *t* statistics for group1 and group2 test the two hypotheses of interest, and so we have strong evidence that the new methods are superior to the old, but little evidence of a difference in efficacy between the two new methods.

User-specified contrasts may also be used for factors in more complex linear models, including multifactor models with interactions.

GENERAL LINEAR HYPOTHESES*   4.5

A general matrix formulation of the linear models considered in this chapter is

$$y = X\beta + \varepsilon,$$

where y is an $n \times 1$ vector containing the response; X is an $n \times p$ model matrix, the first column of which usually contains 1s; β is a $p \times 1$ vector of model parameters; and ε is an $n \times 1$ vector of errors. Assuming that X is of full-column rank, the least squares regression coefficients are

$$b = (X'X)^{-1}X'y.$$

All the hypotheses described in this chapter, and others that I have not discussed, can be tested as general linear hypotheses, of the form $H_0: L\beta = c$, where L is a $q \times p$ hypothesis matrix (of rank q), containing prespecified constants, and c is a prespecified $q \times 1$ vector, most often containing 0s. Under H_0, the test statistic

$$F_0 = \frac{(Lb - c)'[L(X'X)^{-1}L']^{-1}(Lb - c)}{qs^2}$$

follows an F distribution with q and $n - p$ degrees of freedom; s^2 is the estimated error variance for the model.

Here are two nonstandard examples:

Duncan's occupational-prestige regression. Suppose that we want to test that the coefficients of income and education are the same. Because both income and education in the Duncan data set are percentages (of relatively high-income earners and of high-school graduates, respectively), this hypothesis arguably makes some sense. Using the linear.hypothesis function in car:

```
> detach(Baumann)
> data(Duncan)
> attach(Duncan)
> duncan.mod <- lm(prestige ~ income + education)
> summary(duncan.mod)
. . .
Coefficients:
            Estimate Std. Error t value Pr(>|t|)
(Intercept)  -6.0647     4.2719   -1.42     0.16
income        0.5987     0.1197    5.00  1.1e-05
education     0.5458     0.0983    5.56  1.7e-06
. . .
```

```
> linear.hypothesis(duncan.mod, c(0, 1, -1))
F-Test
SS = 12.195      SSE = 7506.7      F = 0.068233  Df = 1 and 42
       p = 0.7952
```

In this case, the hypothesis matrix consists of a single row, $\mathbf{L} = (0, 1, -1)$, contrasting the income and education coefficients; the right-hand-side vector for the hypothesis is implicitly $\mathbf{c} = (0)$. The test shows that the difference between the two coefficients is not statistically significant.

Davis's regression of measured on reported weight.   I previously fit two models to Davis's data: davis.mod includes a bad observation, while davis.mod.2 deletes the bad (12th) observation:

```
> detach(Duncan)
> davis.mod

Call:
lm(formula = weight ~ repwt)

Coefficients:
(Intercept)        repwt
      5.336        0.928

> davis.mod.2

Call:
lm(formula = weight ~ repwt, subset = -12)

Coefficients:
(Intercept)        repwt
      2.734        0.958
```

If individuals are unbiased reporters of their weight, then the intercept should be 0 and the slope 1; we can test these values simultaneously as a linear hypothesis:

```
> diag(2)  # order-2 identify matrix
     [,1] [,2]
[1,]    1    0
[2,]    0    1

> linear.hypothesis(davis.mod, diag(2), c(0,1))
F-Test
SS = 245.97      SSE = 12828      F = 1.7353  Df = 2 and 181
       p = 0.17927

> linear.hypothesis(davis.mod.2, diag(2), c(0,1))
F-Test
SS = 59.691      SSE = 914.3      F = 5.8757  Df = 2 and 180
       p = 0.0033733
```

Here, the hypothesis matrix $\mathbf{L}$ is just an order-2 identify matrix, constructed in S by diag(2), while the right-hand-side vector is $\mathbf{c} = (0, 1)'$.

Even though the regression coefficients are closer to 0 and 1 when observation 12 is omitted, the hypothesis of unbiased reporting is acceptable for the original data set but not for the corrected data (because the error sum of squares is much smaller when observation 12 is deleted).

DATA AND CONFIDENCE ELLIPSES   4.6

Data ellipses and ellipsoids (i.e., the generalization of ellipses beyond two dimensions) provide a visual interpretation of correlation. Moreover, when variables are bivariately or multivariately normally distributed, data ellipses and ellipsoids represent estimated probability contours, containing expected fractions of the data (see, for example, Monette, 1990).

The data.ellipse function in car draws data ellipses for a pair of variables. Illustrating with income and education in Duncan's occupational-prestige data [Figure 4.4(a)]:

```
> data.ellipse(income, education, levels=c(.5,.75,.9,.95))
> identify(income, education, row.names(Duncan))
[1]   6 16 27
```

The contours are set to enclose 50, 75, 90, and 95 percent of bivarate-normal data. Three observations identified with the mouse—representing ministers, railroad conductors, and railroad engineers—are outside of the 95 percent normal contour.

Earlier in this chapter, I regressed prestige on income and education, placing the resulting lm object in duncan.mod. The following command draws a 95 percent joint-confidence region for the coefficients of income and education in this regression:

```
> confidence.ellipse(duncan.mod)
>
```

The 95 percent confidence ellipse in Figure 4.4(b) is the rescaled 90 degree rotation of the 95 percent data ellipse in Figure 4.4(a) (see, e.g., Fox, 1997, Section 9.4.4; Monette, 1990). Thus, the positively correlated predictors income and education produce negatively correlated coefficients.[8]

---

8. The confidence.ellipse function also draws approximate confidence ellipses for the coefficients of generalized linear models, discussed in the next chapter. The scatterplot.matrix function in car has facilities for drawing data ellipses as well. Similar functions are provided by the ellipse library for R.

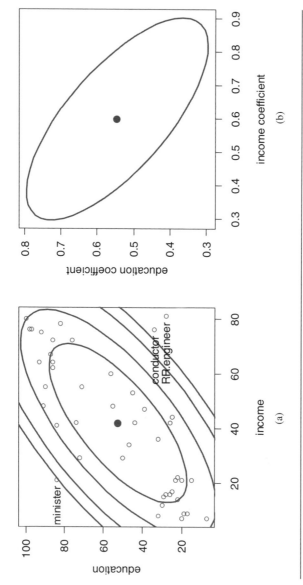

Figure 4.4   (a) 50, 75, 90, and 95 percent data ellipses for income and education in Duncan's occupational-prestige data. (b) 95 percent joint-confidence ellipse for the coefficients of income and education in the regression of prestige on these predictors. In (a), three observations were identified interactively with the mouse.

MORE ON 1m AND MODEL FORMULAS 4.7

The 1m function has several additional useful arguments, and some of the arguments that I discussed have uses that were not mentioned. The args function prints out the arguments to 1m (as it will for any function):

```
> args(lm)
function (formula, data = list(), subset, weights, na.action,
    method = "qr", model = TRUE, x = FALSE, y = FALSE, qr = TRUE,
    singular.ok = TRUE, contrasts = NULL, offset = NULL, ...)
NULL
```

These are the arguments for the R implementation of 1m; the arguments for the S-PLUS implementation are nearly the same.

Here is some additional information about the arguments to 1m; for further details, you can type help(1m) to access the on-line documentation.

formula 4.7.1

As we have seen, a model formula for 1m consists of a left-hand side, specifying the response variable, and a right-hand side, specifying the terms in the model; the two sides of the formula are separated by a tilde (~). We read the formula a ~ b as "a is modeled as b," or "a is regressed on b."

The left-hand side of the formula can be any valid S expression that evaluates to a numeric vector of the appropriate length. On the left side of the formula, the arithmetic operators -, +, *, /, and ^ have their usual meanings, and we can call whatever functions are appropriate to our purpose. For example, with reference to Moore and Krupat's data, we could replace the number of conforming responses with the percentage of conforming responses:

```
> lm(100*conformity/40 ~ partner.status*fcategory, data=Moore)
```

or (using the logit function in car) with the log-odds of conformity:

```
> lm(logit(conformity/40) ~ partner.status*fcategory, data=Moore)
```

The right-hand side of the model formula may include factors and expressions that evaluate to numeric vectors and matrices. Because several operators have special meaning in formulas, arithmetic expressions that use them have to be "protected." Expressions are protected automatically when they are inside function calls: For example, the + in the term log(a + b) has its usual arithmetic meaning on the right-hand side of a model formula, even though a + b does not when it is unprotected.

The *identity function* I() may be used to protect otherwise unprotected arithmetic expressions in model formulas. For example, to regress prestige on the sum of education and income in Duncan's data set (thus implicitly forcing the coefficients of these two predictors to be equal), we may write:

```
> lm(prestige ~ I(income + education), data=Duncan)
```

I have already described most of the special operators that appear on the right of linear-model formulas. In the following table (adapted from Chambers & Hastie, 1992, p. 29), A and B represent elements in a linear model: numeric vectors, matrices, factors, or expressions (such as d + e or d*e) composed from these:

Expression	Interpretation	Example
A + B	include both A and B	income + education
A – B	exclude B from A	a*b*d – a:b:d
A:B	all interactions of A and B	type:education
A*B	A + B + A:B	type*education
B %in% A	B nested within A	education %in% type
A/B	A + B %in% A	type/education
A^k	all effects crossed up to order k	(a + b + d)^2

The last two operators, / and ^, are new to us: / is a shorthand for nesting, in the same sense as * is a shorthand for crossing; and ^ builds crossed effects up to the order given in the "exponent." Thus, the example in the table, (a + b + d)^2, expands to all main effects and pairwise interactions among a, b, and d: that is, a + b + d + a:b + a:d + b:d. Note that this is equivalent to another example in the table, a*b*d – a:b:d. The intercept, represented by 1 in model formulas, is included in the model unless it is explicitly excluded, by specifying –1 in the formula.

4.7.2   data

When lm is called from the command line, the data argument defaults to the "global environment," and so objects will be found in the normal manner along the search path, such as in an attached data frame. The data argument can also be set to a list structure with named components, typically a data frame.

subset   **4.7.3**

As the term implies, the subset argument may be used to fit a model to a subset of observations. Several forms are possible:

■ A logical vector, as in

```
> lm(weight ~ repwt, data=Davis,
+     subset = sex == 'F')  # fit only to women
```

■ A numeric vector of observation indices:

```
> lm(weight ~ repwt, data=Davis,
+     subset=1:100)  # use only obs. 1 to 100
```

■ A numeric vector with negative entries, indicating observations to be omitted from the fit:

```
> lm(prestige ~ income + education, data=Duncan,
+     subset=-c(6,16)) # exclude obs. 6, 16
```

■ A character vector containing the row names of the observations to be included (an option for which it is hard to provide a compelling example).

weights   **4.7.4**

If it is specified, the weights argument takes a numeric vector of length equal to the number of observations, and produces a weighted least squares fit. Letting w_i represent the weight attached to observation i and e_i the residual for observation i, coefficients are computed to minimize the weighted residual sum of squares, $\sum w_i e_i^2$. Weighted least squares regression is appropriate when the error variance is different for different observations, but is known up to a constant of proportionality (see Section 6.3).

na.action   **4.7.5**

In R, the default na.action is given by the na.action option, which is initially set to 'na.omit', deleting observations with missing data. In S-PLUS, there is no preset missing-data default option, and na.action in lm defaults to na.fail, which produces an error when it encounters missing data. The function na.exclude is similar to na.omit, but saves information about the deleted observations: This information may be used by functions, such as `residuals`, that do computations on linear-model objects. Although I will not pursue the possibility here, you can handle missing data in other ways by writing suitable missing-data functions and using these in place of `na.omit`, `na.fail`, or `na.exclude`.

Because we usually fit more than one model to the data, it is generally advantageous to handle missing data outside of `lm`, to ensure that all models are fit to the same subset of valid observations. To do otherwise is to invite inconsistency. This is true, incidentally, not only in S but in other statistical software as well.

4.7.6   `method, model, x, y, qr`*

These are technical arguments, relating to how the computations are performed and what information is stored in the returned linear-model object.

4.7.7   `singular.ok`*

Under normal circumstances, S builds a full-rank model matrix, removing redundant dummy regressors, for example. Under some circumstances, however—perfect collinearity, for example, or when there is an empty cell in an analysis of variance—the model matrix may be of deficient rank, and not all the coefficients in the linear model will be estimable. If `singular.ok` is TRUE, then S will fit the model anyway, automatically omitting the redundant (or "aliased") parameters. In S-PLUS, `singular.ok` defaults to FALSE; in R, only `singular.ok = TRUE` is currently supported.

4.7.8   `contrasts`

This argument allows you to specify contrasts for factors in a linear model, in the form of a list with named elements. For example:

```
> lm(conformity ~ partner.status * fcategory,
+   contrasts=list(partner.status=contr.sum, fcategory=contr.poly))
```

offset (R only)   4.7.9

An *offset* is a term added to the right-hand side of a model with no associated parameter to be estimated—it implicitly has a fixed coefficient of 1. In a linear model, specifying a variable as an offset is equivalent to subtracting the variable from the response. Offsets are of more use in generalized linear models (discussed in Chapter 5) than in linear models.

CHAPTER 5

Fitting Generalized Linear Models

A synthesis due to Nelder and Wedderburn (1972), generalized linear models (GLMs) substantially extend the range of application of linear statistical models by accommodating response variables with nonnormal conditional distributions. Except for the error, the right-hand side of a generalized linear model is essentially the same as for a linear model, and thus the formulas used to specify the right-hand side of GLMs in S are the same as those described in the preceding chapter. Despite the diversity and broad applicability of generalized linear models, the extension of the procedures for fitting linear models in S to GLMs is largely straightforward.

Section 5.1 summarizes the general structure of GLMs, and introduces the glm function in S. The most commonly used GLMs in social research (beyond models with normal errors) are models for categorical data and for count data, which are described in Sections 5.2 and 5.3, respectively. Section 5.4 briefly takes up the less frequently employed gamma and inverse-Gaussian GLMs, and summarizes the arguments to the glm function in S.

THE STRUCTURE OF GENERALIZED LINEAR MODELS 5.1

A generalized linear model consists of three components:

1. A *random component*, specifying the conditional distribution of the response variable, y_i, given the predictors. Traditionally,

the random component is an exponential family—the normal (Gaussian), binomial, Poisson, gamma, or inverse-Gaussian family of distributions—but, as I will explain, the implementation of generalized linear models in S is somewhat broader.

2. A linear function of the regressors, called the *linear predictor*,

$$\eta_i = \alpha + \beta_1 x_{i1} + \cdots + \beta_k x_{ik}$$

on which the expected value μ_i of y_i depends. The xs may include quantitative predictors, but they may also include transformations of predictors, polynomial terms, contrasts generated from factors, interaction regressors, and so on. That is, the linear predictor is as general as in the linear model of the previous chapter.

3. An invertible *link function* $g(\mu_i) = \eta_i$, which transforms the expectation of the response to the linear predictor. The inverse of the link function is sometimes called the *mean function*: $g^{-1}(\eta_i) = \mu_i$. Standard link functions and their inverses are shown in Table 5.1. The logit, probit, and complementary log-log links are for *binomial data*, where y_i represents the observed proportion and μ_i the expected proportion of "successes" in n_i binomial trials—that is, μ_i is the probability of a success. For the probit link, Φ is the standard-normal cumulative distribution function, and Φ^{-1} is the standard-normal quantile function. An important special case is *binary data*, where all the binomial trials are 1, and therefore all the observed proportions y_i are either 0 or 1.

Generalized linear models in S are fit with the `glm` function. Most of the arguments of `glm` are similar to those of `lm`: For example, the response variable and regressors are given in a model `formula`, and `data`, `subset`, and `na.action` arguments determine the data on which the model is fit. In addition, the `family` argument to `glm` is used to specify

Table 5.1 Standard link functions and their inverses: μ_i is the expected value of the response; η_i is the linear predictor.

Link	$\eta_i = g(\mu_i)$	$\mu_i = g^{-1}(\eta_i)$
Identity	μ_i	η_i
Log	$\log_e \mu_i$	e^{η_i}
Inverse	μ_i^{-1}	η_i^{-1}
Inverse square	μ_i^{-2}	$\eta_i^{-1/2}$
Square root	$\sqrt{\mu_i}$	η_i^2
Logit	$\log_e \frac{\mu_i}{1-\mu_i}$	$\frac{1}{1+e^{-\eta_i}}$
Probit	$\Phi^{-1}(\eta_i)$	$\Phi(\mu_i)$
Complementary log-log	$\log_e[-\log_e(1-\mu_i)]$	$1 - \exp[-\exp(\eta_i)]$

Table 5.2   Default (canonical) link, response range, and conditional variance
function for generalized linear model families; ϕ is the dispersion
parameter, η_i is the linear predictor, and μ_i is the expectation of y_i
(the response). In the binomial family, n_i is the number of trials.

Family	Default Link	Range of y_i	$V(y_i|\eta_i)$
gaussian	identity	$(-\infty, +\infty)$	ϕ
binomial	logit	$\frac{0,1,\ldots,n_i}{n_i}$	$\mu_i(1 - \mu_i)$
poisson	log	$0, 1, 2, \ldots$	μ_i
Gamma	inverse	$(0, \infty)$	$\phi\mu_i^2$
inverse.gaussian	1/mu^2	$(0, \infty)$	$\phi\mu_i^3$

a family-generator function, which may itself take additional arguments, such as a link function.

The names of the generator functions for the five standard exponential families are given in Table 5.2, along with the default (or *canonical*) link, the range of the response variable, and the conditional variance of the response for each family. All family names start with lowercase letters, except for the Gamma family (to avoid confusion with the gamma function in S). Canonical links are not only the ones most commonly used, but they also arise naturally from the general formula for distributions in the exponential families. Nevertheless, other links may be more appropriate for the specific problem at hand, and, indeed, one of the strengths of the GLM paradigm—in contrast, for example, with transformation of the response variable in a linear model (as described in Chapter 6)—is the separation of the link function from the conditional distribution of the response.

For distributions in the exponential families, the variance is a function of the mean together with a dispersion parameter ϕ. For the binomial and Poisson distributions, the dispersion parameter is fixed to 1; for the Gaussian distribution, the dispersion parameter is the usual error variance, often symbolized by σ^2, as in Chapter 4.

Table 5.3 shows the links available for each family-generator function. Note that these differ somewhat in R and S-PLUS. Nondefault links are selected via a link argument to the family generator functions: for example, binomial(link=probit). The quasi, quasibinomial, and quasipoisson family generators do not correspond to exponential families; these family generators are described in Section 5.4. If no family argument is supplied to glm, then the gaussian family, with identity link, is assumed, resulting in a fit identical to that of lm, albeit computed less efficiently—like using a sledge hammer to set a tack.

GLMs are typically fit to data by the method of maximum likelihood. Denote the maximum-likelihood estimates of the regression parameters

Table 5.3   Family generators and link functions for `glm`: S, available in S-PLUS; R, available in R. In each case, the default link is shown in boldface.

family	link identity	inverse	log	logit	probit	cloglog	sqrt	1/mu^2
gaussian	**S,R**	R	R					
binomial			R	**S,R**	S,R	S,R		
poisson	S,R		**S,R**				S,R	
Gamma	S,R	**S,R**	S,R					
inverse.gaussian	R	R	R					**R**
quasi	**S,R**	S,R	S,R	S,R	S,R	S,R	S,R	S,R
quasibinomial				**R**	R	R		
quasipoisson	R		**R**				R	

as $\hat{\alpha}, \hat{\beta}_1, \ldots, \hat{\beta}_k$. These imply an estimate of the mean of the response, $\hat{\mu}_i = g^{-1}(\hat{\alpha} + \hat{\beta}_1 x_{i1} + \cdots + \hat{\beta}_k x_{ik})$.

The log-likelihood for the model, maximized over the regression coefficients, is

$$\log_e L_0 = \sum_{i=1}^{n} \log_e p(\hat{\mu}_i, \phi; y_i),$$

where $p(\cdot)$ is the probability or probability-density function corresponding to the family employed. A "saturated" model, which dedicates one parameter to each observation, and hence fits the data perfectly, has log-likelihood

$$\log_e L_1 = \sum_{i=1}^{n} \log_e p(y_i, \phi; y_i).$$

Twice the difference between these log-likelihoods defines the *residual deviance* under the model, a generalization of the residual sum of squares for linear models:

$$D(\mathbf{y}; \hat{\boldsymbol{\mu}}) = 2(\log_e L_1 - \log_e L_0).$$

Dividing the deviance by the estimated dispersion produces the *scaled deviance*: $D(\mathbf{y}; \hat{\boldsymbol{\mu}})/\hat{\phi}$.

5.2   MODELS FOR CATEGORICAL RESPONSES

5.2.1   Dichotomous Data

As I explained, three link functions are provided for the binomial family: the logit, probit, and complementary log-log links. The logit and probit

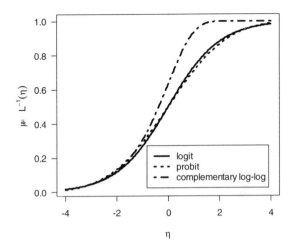

Figure 5.1   Comparison of logit, probit, and complementary log-log links. The probit link is rescaled to match the variance of the logistic distribution, $\pi^2/3$.

links approach probabilities of 0 and 1 symmetrically and—once their variances are equated—are very similar. The complementary log-log link is asymmetric and may therefore be useful when the logit and probit links are inappropriate. The logit, probit, and complementary log-log links are compared in Figure 5.1.

The response for a binomial GLM may be specified in several forms:

■ For binary data, the response may be a variable or an S expression that evaluates to 0s ("failure") and 1s ("success"); a logical variable or expression (with TRUE representing success and FALSE failure); or a factor (in which case the first category is taken to represent failure and the others success).

■ For binomial data, the response may be a two-column matrix, with the first column giving the count of successes and the second the count of failures for each binomial observation.

■ Also for binomial data, the response may be a vector giving the *proportion* of successes, while the binomial denominators (total counts or numbers of trials) are given by the `weights` argument to `glm`.

Binary Data

To illustrate fitting a binomial GLM, let us turn to a logistic regression (linear logit model) from Long's (1997) text on categorical data analysis. This example draws on data from the 1976 U.S. Panel Study of Income Dynamics, originally employed in a different context by Mroz (1987).

The same data are used by Berndt (1991) as an exercise in linear logistic regression. The data are in the data frame Mroz; printing 10 of the $n = 753$ observations at random:

```
> library(car)
. . .
> data(Mroz)
> Mroz[sort(sample(753,10)),]   # sample 10 obs.
     lfp k5 k618 age  wc  hc     lwg    inc
46   yes  0    2  34  no  no 1.24479  5.000
57   yes  0    0  55 yes yes 2.26545 14.000
151  yes  0    2  42 yes yes 1.49503 27.500
197  yes  0    1  36  no  no 1.88442 11.100
288  yes  0    2  34  no  no 0.98727  3.900
365  yes  0    2  46  no  no 0.91629 12.400
489   no  0    0  44  no  no 0.51422 18.900
516   no  1    2  36  no yes 0.87148 17.045
617   no  2    1  30  no  no 0.48838 16.200
655   no  1    3  35  no  no 0.90876 24.000
```

The variables in this data frame are defined as follows (using the variable names employed by Long):

Variable	Description	Remarks
lfp	Wife's labor-force participation	Factor: no, yes
k5	Number of children aged 5 and younger	0–3, few 3s
k618	Number of children aged 6 to 18	0–8, few > 5
age	Wife's age in years	30–60, single years
wc	Wife's college attendance	Factor: no, yes
hc	Husband's college attendance	Factor, no, yes
lwg	Log of wife's estimated wage rate	See text
inc	Family income excluding wife's income	$1000s

With the exception of lwg, the definition of these variables is straightforward. The log of the woman's estimated wage rate is based on her actual earnings if she is in the labor force; if the woman is not in the labor force, then this variable is based on the predicted value from a regression of log wages on the other predictors in the model (for women in the labor force, of course). As I will explain in Chapter 6 (on regression diagnostics), this definition of expected earnings creates a problem for the logistic regression.

Because the default contrast type in R is "treatment" contrasts, the factors will generate 0/1 dummy regressors, with no as the baseline category (see Section 4.2). Fitting a linear logit model to Mroz's data is simple:

```
> attach(Mroz)
> mod.mroz <- glm(lfp ~ k5 + k618 + age + wc + hc + lwg + inc,
+   family=binomial)
> summary(mod.mroz)

Call:
glm(formula = lfp ~ k5 + k618 + age + wc + hc + lwg + inc,
    family = binomial)

Deviance Residuals:
   Min      1Q  Median      3Q     Max
-2.106  -1.090   0.598   0.971   2.189

Coefficients:
              Estimate Std. Error z value Pr(>|z|)
(Intercept)    3.18214    0.64432    4.94  7.9e-07
k5            -1.46291    0.19697   -7.43  1.1e-13
k618          -0.06457    0.06800   -0.95  0.34231
age           -0.06287    0.01278   -4.92  8.7e-07
wcyes          0.80727    0.22997    3.51  0.00045
hcyes          0.11173    0.20603    0.54  0.58760
lwg            0.60469    0.15081    4.01  6.1e-05
inc           -0.03445    0.00821   -4.20  2.7e-05

(Dispersion parameter for binomial family taken to be 1)

    Null deviance: 1029.75  on 752  degrees of freedom
Residual deviance:  905.27  on 745  degrees of freedom
AIC: 921.3

Number of Fisher Scoring iterations: 3
```

Reminder: Default Contrasts in S-PLUS

Recall that, in S-PLUS, the default contrast type for unordered factors is Helmert contrasts—which for dichtomous factors, such as in Mroz's data, produces the coding −1 and +1 for the levels no and yes, respectively. To produce the results reported here, change the default contrasts to contr.treatment, or change the contrasts for the individual factors in the model.

The printout produced by summary is very similar to the printout for a linear model. The ratios of the coefficients to their standard errors are Wald statistics for testing the hypothesis that the corresponding regression parameters are 0; these are asymptotically normally distributed under the null hypothesis (but can be problematic in binomial GLMs). In addition, the summary includes the deviance and degrees of freedom for a model with only an intercept (the null deviance), the residual deviance and degrees of freedom for the fitted model, and the Akaike information criterion (AIC). I discuss residuals for GLMs in Chapter 6.

The AIC is an index of fit that takes account of the parsimony of the model by penalizing for the number of parameters; it is defined as

$$\text{AIC} = -2 \times (\text{maximized log-likelihood}) + 2 \times (\text{number of parameters}),$$

and thus smaller values are indicative of a better fit to the data. In the current context, the AIC is just the residual deviance plus twice the number of regression coefficients (including the intercept). The AIC is used to compare the fit of alternative (and not necessarily nested) models with different numbers of parameters, and is typically employed for model selection.

The anova function may be used to compute a likelihood-ratio test or *F* test for nested GLMs. The type of test is selected via an optional test argument, set either to 'Chisq' (for the likelihood-ratio test) or to 'F'; the default is to report sequential differences in the deviance but no test statistic. Because anova uses the estimated dispersion parameter in calculating the denominator of *F* statistics, there is no sense in specifying *F* tests when the dispersion parameter is fixed, as in a binomial model (but see the discussion of the quasibinomial and quasipoisson families in Section 5.4).

For example, to compute a likelihood-ratio test for the coefficient of k5 in the logistic regression for Mroz's data:

```
> anova(update(mod.mroz, . ~ . - k5), mod.mroz, test='Chisq')
Analysis of Deviance Table

Model 1: lfp ~ k618 + age + wc + hc + lwg + inc
Model 2: lfp ~ k5 + k618 + age + wc + hc + lwg + inc
  Resid. Df Resid. Dev  Df Deviance P(>|Chi|)
1       746        972
2       745        905   1       66   3.5e-16
```

The generic Anova function in car will also handle GLMs, calculating likelihood-ratio, Wald, or *F* tests, specified via the test argument (with 'LR' as the default, and 'Wald' and 'F' as options). Likelihood-ratio tests and *F* tests require refitting the model, while Wald tests do not. Moreover, the *F* tests computed by Anova base the estimated dispersion on the Pearson statistic (by default), and therefore are not the same as likelihood-ratio tests even when, as in the binomial and Poisson models, the dispersion is fixed.

As in the case of linear models, Anova will compute either Type II or Type-III tests (selected via the type argument). For the Mroz regression, there is no distinction between the two types of tests, because there are no higher-order terms in the model; as well, because in this case each term in the model has only 1 degree of freedom, the Wald chi-square statistics provided by Anova are simply the squares of the zs printed out by the summary function.

For example, to obtain a likelihood-ratio test for each term in the model fit to Mroz's data:

```
> Anova(mod.mroz)
Anova Table (Type II tests)

Response: lfp
      LR Chisq Df Pr(>Chisq)
k5        66.5  1    3.3e-16
k618       0.9  1    0.34204
age       25.6  1    4.2e-07
wc        12.7  1    0.00036
hc         0.3  1    0.58749
lwg       17.0  1    3.7e-05
inc       19.5  1    1.0e-05
```

In analogy to the analysis of variance for a linear model, this table is termed an *analysis of deviance*.

Binomial Data

Fitting a GLM with binomial denominators greater than 1 is especially useful in analyzing a contingency table that includes a dichotomous response variable. Consider, for example, the data given in Table 5.4, from Campbell, Converse, Miller, and Stokes's (1960) classic study of voting in the 1956 U.S. presidential election. The body of the table gives frequency counts for combinations of categories of the predictors (perceived

Table 5.4   Voter turnout by perceived closeness of the election and intensity of partisan preference for the 1956 U.S. presidential election. Frequency counts are shown in the body of the table. *Source of data:* Campbell et al. (1960, Table 5-3).

Perceived Closeness	Intensity of Preference	Turnout		Logit
		Voted	Did Not Vote	$\log_e \frac{\text{Voted}}{\text{Did Not Vote}}$
One-sided	Weak	91	39	0.847
	Medium	121	49	0.904
	Strong	64	24	0.981
Close	Weak	214	87	0.900
	Medium	284	76	1.318
	Strong	201	25	2.084

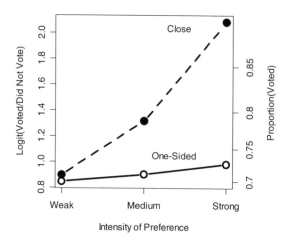

Figure 5.2   Voter turnout by perceived closeness of the election and intensity of partisan preference.

closeness of the election and intensity of partisan preference) and the response (whether or not the respondent reported voting in the election).

The final column of Table 5.4 shows the sample logit for each combination of categories of the predictors, computed as the log-odds of voting. These logits are graphed in Figure 5.2, much as one would graph cell means in an analysis of variance when the response variable is quantitative. Voter turnout appears to increase with intensity of preference, but much more dramatically when the election is perceived close than when it is perceived one sided.

To analyze the data with a binomial logit model, we may define variables containing the predictors (as factors) and the cell counts of successes and failures. I enter `preference`, which has three categories, as an ordered factor; because the alphabetical ordering of the levels of `closeness` and `preference` is not what we want, I specify the levels explicitly:

```
> closeness <- factor(rep(c('one.sided', 'close'), c(3,3)),
+     levels=c('one.sided', 'close'))

> preference <- ordered(rep(c('weak', 'medium', 'strong'), 2),
+     levels=c('weak', 'medium', 'strong'))

> voted <- c(91, 121, 64, 214, 284, 201)
> did.not.vote <- c(39, 49, 24, 87, 76, 25)
>
```

Then, to check the data (and reproduce Table 5.4):

```
> logit.turnout <- log(voted/did.not.vote)
> data.frame(closeness, preference, voted, did.not.vote,
+     logit=logit.turnout)
```

	closeness	preference	voted	did.not.vote	logit
1	one.sided	weak	91	39	0.84730
2	one.sided	medium	121	49	0.90397
3	one.sided	strong	64	24	0.98083
4	close	weak	214	87	0.90007
5	close	medium	284	76	1.31824
6	close	strong	201	25	2.08443

Figure 5.2 is constructed as follows:

```
> par(mar=c(5.1, 4.1, 4.1, 4.1))  # leave room for right axis
> plot(rep(1:3, 2), logit.turnout, type='n', axes=F,
+     xlab='Intensity of Preference',
+     ylab='Logit(Voted/Did Not Vote)')
> axis(1, at=1:3, labels=c('Weak', 'Medium', 'Strong'))  # x-axis
> axis(2)  # y-axis
> prob.axis(side='right', at=seq(.7, .85, by=.05),
+     axis.title='Proportion(Voted)')  # right y-axis
> box()
> points(1:3, logit.turnout[1:3], pch=1, type='b',
+     lty=1, lwd=3, cex=2)  # one-sided
> points(1:3, logit.turnout[4:6], pch=16, type='b',
+     lty=2, lwd=3, cex=2)  # close
> text(locator(2), c('Close', 'One-Sided'))  # position the labels
>
```

Note the use of the prob.axis function from car to draw a right-side probability axis, preceded by setting the mar (margins) graphics parameter to leave enough room at the right for the axis title. The text function is used along with locator to place the labels 'Close' and 'One-Sided' on the graph: Click the left mouse button to position each label.[1]

We want to fit the logit-model analog of a two-way analysis of variance to the data of Campbell et al. (1960):

```
> options(contrasts=c('contr.sum', 'contr.poly'))
> mod.campbell <- glm(cbind(voted, did.not.vote) ~
+     closeness * preference, family=binomial)
> summary(mod.campbell)

Call:
glm(formula = cbind(voted, did.not.vote) ~ closeness * preference,
    family = binomial)

Deviance Residuals:
[1]  0  0  0  0  0  0
```

---

1. Chapter 7 describes a general strategy for constructing graphs in S.

```
Coefficients:
                        Estimate Std. Error z value Pr(>|z|)
(Intercept)               1.1725     0.0746   15.71  < 2e-16
closeness1               -0.2618     0.0746   -3.51  0.00045
preference.L              0.4659     0.1392    3.35  0.00082
preference.Q              0.0752     0.1184    0.63  0.52558
closeness1:preference.L  -0.3715     0.1392   -2.67  0.00762
closeness1:preference.Q  -0.0669     0.1184   -0.57  0.57196

(Dispersion parameter for binomial family taken to be 1)

    Null deviance:  3.4832e+01  on 5  degrees of freedom
Residual deviance: -3.7914e-14  on 0  degrees of freedom
AIC: 44.09

Number of Fisher Scoring iterations: 2
```

The residuals for this model are all 0, and, consequently, the residual deviance is 0 as well ($-3.79 \times 10^{-14} \simeq 0$, within rounding error): The model, which has six independent parameters, necessarily fits the six binomial proportions perfectly. A model of this type is called a *saturated model*. Had we fit an equivalent *binary* logit model to the 1275 individual observations comprising Campbell et al.'s data set, we would have obtained exactly the same estimated coefficients and standard errors, but a nonzero deviance for the six-coefficient model. *Differences* in deviance between alternative models (and, consequently, likelihood-ratio tests), however, would be unchanged.

Examining the Wald tests for the coefficients of the model, there is strong evidence ($p < .01$) for an interaction between perceived closeness of the election and the linear trend over intensity of preference. An analysis of deviance table, produced by the Anova function, combines the 2 degrees of freedom for preference:

```
> Anova(mod.campbell)
Anova Table (Type II tests)

Response: cbind(voted, did.not.vote)
                    LR Chisq Df Pr(>Chisq)
closeness               8.29  1      0.004
preference             19.11  2    7.1e-05
closeness:preference    7.12  2      0.028
```

As in an analysis of variance, the Type II tests for the "main effects" should not be interpreted here in the presence of the significant interaction between closeness and preference. Had we specified Type III tests, we could have interpreted each of the main-effects tests as an average over the levels of the other factor. (These tests, however, would be of dubious interest in light of the interaction.)

Polytomous Data   5.2.2

There are several procedures for analyzing polytomous (multiple-category) responses. One approach is to resolve an m-category polytomy into a set of $m - 1$ nested dichotomies. Another approach is to generalize the binomial GLM to a multinomial logit or probit model. Finally, specialized logit and probit models have been introduced for ordered categorical responses.

Nested Dichotomies

Nested dichotomies are based on successive binary divisions of the category set of a polytomous response. They are, perhaps, best explained by an example: The data frame `Womenlf` contains data drawn from a social survey of the Canadian population conducted in 1977; the data are for $n = 263$ married women between the ages of 21 and 30.

```
> data(Womenlf)
> Womenlf[sort(sample(263, 10)),]  # sample 10 obs.
      partic hincome children   region
16  not.work      15  present Atlantic
43  parttime      28   absent  Ontario
86  fulltime      27   absent       BC
99  fulltime      15   absent  Ontario
102 not.work      23  present Atlantic
108 not.work      19  present  Ontario
173 not.work       7  present  Ontario
184 fulltime      18   absent  Ontario
185 not.work      13   absent  Ontario
240 not.work      13  present   Quebec
```

The following variables are included in this data set[2]:

- `partic`: labor-force participation, a factor with levels `not.work`, `parttime`, and `fulltime`.

- `hincome`: husband's income, in thousands of dollars.

- `children`: presence of children in the household, a factor with levels `absent` and `present`.

- `region`: a factor with levels `Atlantic`, `Quebec`, `Ontario`, `Prairie`, and `BC`.

---

2. I have listed the levels of `partic` in their natural order, and of `region` from east to west, but the levels are in alphabetical order in the data frame.

Using the `recode` function from `car`, I define two nested dichotomies to represent the three categories of labor-force participation—working versus not working outside the home and part-time versus full-time work:

```
> attach(Womenlf)
> working <- recode(partic, " 'not.work' = 'no'; else = 'yes' ")

> fulltime <- recode (partic,
+     " 'fulltime' = 'yes'; 'parttime' = 'no'; 'not.work' = NA ")

> working
  [1] no  no  no  no  no  no  no  yes no  no  no  yes no  no  no
 [16] no  no  no  no  no  yes no  yes yes no  no  no  no  no  yes
 . . .
[256] no  yes no  no  no  no  no  no
Levels:  no yes

> fulltime
  [1] NA  NA  NA  NA  NA  NA  NA  yes NA  NA  NA  yes NA  NA  NA
 [16] NA  NA  NA  NA  NA  no  NA  yes yes NA  NA  NA  NA  NA  yes
 [31] NA  NA  NA  NA  NA  NA  NA  yes NA  no  NA  no  no  NA  no
 . . .
[256] NA  yes NA  NA  NA  NA  NA  NA
Levels:  no yes
```

■ In forming a set of nested dichotomies, each compound category is subdivided until there are only elementary categories left. Thus, the yes category for the `working` dichotomy, which comprises women working part time and full time, is subdivided into the two categories, yes and no, of the `fulltime` dichotomy.

■ Even when, as here, there are only three categories in the polytomy, there is more than one way of forming nested dichotomies. For example, we could alternatively define the dichotomies {full time vs. part time or not working} and {part time vs. not working}. Models for alternative sets of nested dichotomies are not equivalent, and so this approach should only be used when there is a substantively compelling resolution of the polytomy into a *specific* set of nested dichotomies. For example, in work on education, it is common to employ so-called *continuation dichotomies*: {less than high school vs. some high school or more}, {incomplete high school vs. high-school graduate or more}, {high-school graduate vs. some postsecondary or more}, and so forth.

■ Except for the highest-level dichotomy (working, in the example), other dichotomies are defined only for subsets of observations. For example, women who are not working outside the home are NA for the `fulltime` dichotomy.

I proceed by fitting a binomial GLM separately to each nested dichotomy. By the mode of formation of nested dichotomies, models fit to different dichotomies are statistically independent. This means, for example, that we can sum chi-square test statistics and degrees of freedom over the models and can combine the models to get fitted probabilities for the several categories of the polytomy (see below).

For the women's labor-force participation data:

```
> options(contrasts=c('contr.treatment', 'contr.poly'))
> mod.working <- glm(working ~ hincome + children + region,
+    family=binomial)
> summary(mod.working)
. . .
Coefficients:
                Estimate Std. Error z value Pr(>|z|)
(Intercept)       1.2677     0.5527    2.29    0.022
hincome          -0.0453     0.0206   -2.20    0.027
childrenpresent  -1.6043     0.3018   -5.32  1.1e-07
regionBC          0.3420     0.5848    0.58    0.559
regionOntario     0.1878     0.4675    0.40    0.688
regionPrairie     0.4719     0.5566    0.85    0.397
regionQuebec     -0.1731     0.4994   -0.35    0.729
. . .

> mod.fulltime <- glm(fulltime ~ hincome + children + region,
+    family=binomial)
> summary(mod.fulltime)
. . .
Coefficients:
                Estimate Std. Error z value Pr(>|z|)
(Intercept)       3.7616     1.0568    3.56  0.00037
hincome          -0.1048     0.0403   -2.60  0.00936
childrenpresent  -2.7478     0.5687   -4.83  1.4e-06
regionBC         -1.1825     1.0274   -1.15  0.24977
regionOntario    -0.1488     0.8469   -0.18  0.86057
regionPrairie    -0.3917     0.9630   -0.41  0.68417
regionQuebec      0.1484     0.9328    0.16  0.87359
. . .

> Anova(mod.working)
Anova Table (Type II tests)

Response: working
          LR Chisq Df Pr(>Chisq)
hincome       5.13  1      0.024
children     30.55  1    3.3e-08
region        2.43  4      0.657

> Anova(mod.fulltime)
Anova Table (Type II tests)
```

```
Response: fulltime
          LR Chisq Df Pr(>Chisq)
hincome        7.8  1      0.0051
children      31.9  1    1.6e-08
region         2.7  4      0.6176
```

In this example, the results are broadly similar for the two dichotomies: Working outside the home, and working full time among those working outside the home, both decline with husband's income and presence of children. In both cases, there is no evidence of `region` effects. We could, if we wished, manually add the corresponding likelihood-ratio chi-square statistics and degrees of freedom (e.g., for the `region` effects) across the two analysis of deviance tables.

Reminder: Handling Missing Data in S-PLUS

Remember that, unlike R, S-PLUS does not have an `na.action` option. The default `na.action` for `glm` (as for `lm`) is `na.fail`. Because the `fulltime` dichotomy has NAs for women who are not in the labor force, it is necessary to include the argument `na.action=na.omit` or `na.action=na.exclude` in the call to `glm`.

To graph the results, I begin by refitting the models, eliminating region:

```
> mod.working.1 <- update(mod.working, . ~ . - region)
> mod.fulltime.1 <- update(mod.fulltime, . ~ . - region)
>
```

Then, using the `expand.grid` function, I construct an artificial data frame for all combinations of values of the predictors, letting hincome and children range over their values (1 to 45, and absent, present, respectively)[3]:

```
> predictors <- expand.grid(hincome=1:45,
+     children=c('absent', 'present'))
> predictors
   hincome children
1        1   absent
2        2   absent
3        3   absent
. . .
44      44   absent
45      45   absent
46       1  present
47       2  present
. . .
89      44  present
90      45  present
```

---

3. Here husband's income is discrete, but we can take the same approach for a continuous predictor, using enough values along its range to suggest a smooth curve.

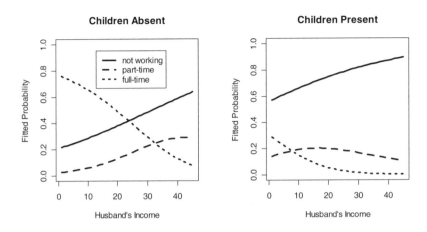

Figure 5.3   Fitted probabilities for the women's labor-force participation data from binary logit models fit to the `working` and `fulltime` dichotomies.

The `predict` function returns fitted values for the two models:

```
> p.work <- predict(mod.working.1, predictors, type='response')
> p.fulltime <- predict(mod.fulltime.1, predictors,
+      type='response')
> p.full <- p.work * p.fulltime
> p.part <- p.work * (1 - p.fulltime)
> p.not <- 1 - p.work
>
```

Specifying the argument `type='response'` to `predict` yields fitted values on the probability scale; the default, `type='link'`, produces fitted values on the logit scale. The fitted values for the `fulltime` dichotomy are *conditional* on working outside the home; I multiply by the probability of working to produce *unconditional* fitted probabilities of working full time. The unconditional probability of working part time is found similarly, and the probability of not working outside the home is calculated as the complement of the probability of working.

So as not to clutter the graph unduly, I use the `mfrow` plot parameter to create two panels: one for children absent and the other for children present. The result is shown in Figure 5.3[4]:

```
> par(mfrow=c(1,2))  # 1 row and 2 columns of plots

> plot(c(1,45), c(0,1),
+      type='n', xlab="Husband's Income", ylab='Fitted Probability',
+      main='Children Absent')
> lines(1:45, p.not[1:45], lty=1, lwd=3)   # not working
```

---

4. General strategies for constructing complex graphs are described in Chapter 7.

```
> lines(1:45, p.part[1:45], lty=2, lwd=3)  # part-time
> lines(1:45, p.full[1:45], lty=3, lwd=3)  # full-time
> legend(locator(1), lty=1:3, lwd=3,
+     legend=c('not working', 'part-time', 'full-time'))

> plot(c(1,45), c(0,1),
+     type='n', xlab="Husband's Income", ylab='Fitted Probability',
+     main='Children Present')
> lines(1:45, p.not[46:90], lty=1, lwd=3)
> lines(1:45, p.part[46:90], lty=2, lwd=3)
> lines(1:45, p.full[46:90], lty=3, lwd=3)
>
```

Note that the horizontal axis label (the xlab argument to plot) is enclosed in double quotes because a single quote (in the form of the apostrophe in Husband's) appears in the label. The legend for the graph is positioned with the mouse using the locator function.

Multinomial Logit Model

The multinomial logit model is an alternative to nested dichotomies for a polytomous response. Aside from treating one of the categories— say, the first—as an arbitrary baseline (to impose the constraint that the fitted probabilities across the m categories of the response sum to 1), the multinomial logit model treats the categories of the response symmetrically. Letting μ_{ij} denote the probability that observation i falls in response category j, the model is given by the equations[5]

$$\mu_{ij} = \frac{\exp(\alpha_j + \beta_{1j}x_{i1} + \cdots + \beta_{kj}x_{ik})}{1 + \sum_{\ell=2}^{m} \exp(\alpha_\ell + \beta_{1\ell}x_{i1} + \cdots + \beta_{k\ell}x_{ik})} \quad \text{for } j = 2, \dots, m,$$

$$\mu_{i1} = 1 - \sum_{j=2}^{m} \pi_{ij} \quad \text{(for category 1)}.$$

The αs and βs are then logistic-regression coefficients for log-odds of membership in each category relative to the first:

$$\log_e \frac{\mu_{ij}}{\mu_{i1}} = \alpha_j + \beta_{1j}x_{i1} + \cdots + \beta_{kj}x_{ik} \quad \text{for } j = 2, \dots, m.$$

When $m = 2$, this is just the usual binomial logit model. Moreover, for the log-odds between *any* pair of response categories j and $j' \neq 1$,

$$\log_e \frac{\mu_{ij}}{\mu_{ij'}} = \log_e \left(\frac{\mu_{ij}/\mu_{i1}}{\mu_{ij'}/\mu_{i1}} \right)$$

$$= \log_e \frac{\mu_{ij}}{\mu_{i1}} - \log_e \frac{\mu_{ij'}}{\mu_{i1}}$$

$$= (\alpha_j - \alpha_{j'}) + (\beta_{1j} - \beta_{1j'})x_{i1} + \cdots + (\beta_{kj} - \beta_{kj'})x_{ik}.$$

---

5. I assume here that the model has constant terms—the α_js—but this is not a requirement.

Thus, the logistic-regression coefficients for the log-odds of membership in category j versus j' are given by *differences* in the corresponding parameters of the multinomial logit model.

The multinomial logit model cannot be fit by glm, but the multinom function in the nnet library (one of the R and S-PLUS libraries associated with Venables & Ripley, 1999) will do the trick; some functions in nnet require the MASS library, so I load that as well:

```
> library(nnet)
> library(MASS)
> mod.multinom <- multinom(participation ~ hincome + children)
# weights:  12 (6 variable)
initial  value 288.935032
iter  10 value 211.454772
final  value 211.440964
converged

> summary(mod.multinom, cor=F, Wald=T)

Re-fitting to get Hessian

Call:
multinom(formula = participation ~ hincome + children)

Coefficients:
         (Intercept)      hincome childrenpresent
parttime     -1.4323    0.0068926        0.021456
fulltime      1.9828   -0.0972300       -2.558605

Std. Errors:
         (Intercept)   hincome childrenpresent
parttime     0.59247  0.023455         0.46904
fulltime     0.48418  0.028096         0.36220

Value/SE (Wald statistics):
         (Intercept)   hincome childrenpresent
parttime     -2.4175   0.29387        0.045744
fulltime      4.0953  -3.46067       -7.064106

Residual Deviance: 422.88
AIC: 434.88
```

Specifying cor=F as an argument to summary suppresses printing the correlation matrix of the coefficient estimates, while Wald=T prints out the Wald statistic for each coefficient. Examining the Wald statistics, the coefficients for the logit of parttime versus the baseline not.work are, apart from the regression constant, small and nonsignificant, while the coefficients for the logit of fulltime versus not.work are much larger and highly statistically significant. Apparently, husband's income and presence of children primarily affect the decision to work full time, as opposed to part time or not to work outside the home.

Taking an approach similar to the one I employed for nested binomial logit models, we can obtain and plot fitted probabilities for the three categories of the response as a function of the two predictors:

```
> p.fit <- predict(mod.multinom, predictors, type='probs')
>
```

Specifying type='probs' returns fitted probabilities for each category of the response. The default, type='class', applies the so-called "Bayes prediction rule" to assign each observation to the highest-probability category. Printing out the first few fitted probabilities:

```
> data.frame(predictors, p.fit)[1:5,]  # first 5 rows
  hincome children not.work parttime fulltime
1      1   absent  0.12770 0.030700  0.84160
2      2   absent  0.13847 0.033519  0.82801
3      3   absent  0.14994 0.036546  0.81352
4      4   absent  0.16212 0.039788  0.79810
5      5   absent  0.17501 0.043249  0.78174
```

Plots of the fitted values are shown in Figure 5.4. The S statements to produce these graphs are similar to those employed for Figure 5.3, and so I omit the details. Comparing the fits from Figures 5.3 and 5.4, we can see that the two models produce similar, but not identical results. In particular, for the nested-dichotomies model, the probability of working part time turns down at high levels of husband's income when children are present, while, for the multinomial logit model, this probability continues to rise gradually. Because high husband's income is a region of the predictor space where data are sparse, we should not overinterpret this difference, and the two models have similar degrees of overall fit to the

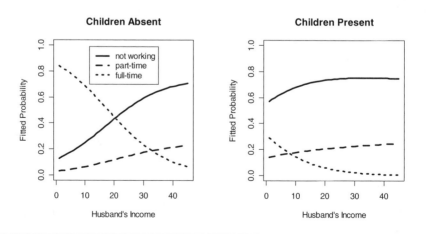

Figure 5.4   Fitted probabilities from the multinomial logit model fit to the women's labor-force participation data.

data: Both models use six parameters, and the deviance for the multinomial logit model is 422.9, while that for the combined nested logit models is 424.3 (only slightly worse). In this example, however, the multinomial logit model draws our attention more clearly to the fact that the two predictors primarily serve to differentiate full-time work from the other two response categories.

Proportional-Odds Model

There are several statistical models for ordinal responses, developed, for example, in Agresti (1984), Clogg and Shihadeh (1994), and Powers and Xie (2000). Using continuation dichotomies, as described previously, is one approach that is sometimes applicable. Another common approach is the proportional-odds logistic regression model.

Suppose that there is a continuous, but unobservable, response variable, ξ, that is a linear function of k predictors plus a random error:

$$\xi_i = \alpha + \beta_1 x_{i1} + \cdots + \beta_k x_{ik} + \varepsilon_i.$$

We cannot observe ξ directly, but instead implicitly dissect its range into m class intervals at the (unknown) cut points $\alpha_1 < \alpha_2 < \cdots < \alpha_{m-1}$, producing the observed ordinal response variable y. That is,

$$y_i = \begin{cases} 1 & \text{if } \xi_i \leq \alpha_1, \\ 2 & \text{if } \alpha_1 < \xi_i \leq \alpha_2, \\ \vdots & \\ m-1 & \text{if } \alpha_{m-2} < \xi_i \leq \alpha_{m-1}, \\ m & \text{if } \alpha_{m-1} < \xi_i. \end{cases}$$

The cumulative probability distribution of y is given by

$$\begin{aligned} \Pr(Y_i \leq j) &= \Pr(\xi_i \leq \alpha_j) \\ &= \Pr(\alpha + \beta_1 x_{i1} + \cdots + \beta_k x_{ik} + \varepsilon_i \leq \alpha_j) \\ &= \Pr(\varepsilon_i \leq \alpha_j - \alpha - \beta_1 x_{i1} - \cdots - \beta_k x_{ik}) \end{aligned}$$

for $j = 1, 2, \ldots, m - 1$. If the errors ε_i are independently distributed according to the standard logistic distribution, then we get the ordered logit model[6]:

$$\begin{aligned} \text{logit}[\Pr(Y_i > j)] &= \log_e \frac{\Pr(Y_i > j)}{\Pr(Y_i \leq j)} \\ &= (\alpha - \alpha_j) + \beta_1 x_{i1} + \cdots + \beta_k x_{ik} \end{aligned}$$

for $j = 1, 2, \ldots, m - 1$.

---

6. Alternatively, if the errors are normally distributed, then we obtain the ordered probit model. Because the normal and logistic distributions are very similar, so are the ordered logit and probit models.

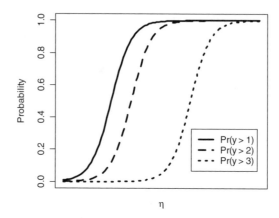

Figure 5.5 The proportional-odds model: Cumulative probabilities, $\Pr(y > j)$, plotted against the linear predictor, η, for a four-category ordered response.

Because the equations for $\text{logit}[\Pr(Y_i > j)]$ for different values of j differ only in their intercepts, the regression curves for the cumulative probabilities $\Pr(Y_i > j)$ are horizontally parallel, as illustrated in Figure 5.5; in this figure, the cumulative probabilities are plotted for a four-category response against an imagined linear predictor $\eta = \alpha + \beta_1 x_1 + \cdots + \beta_k x_k$. The designation "proportional odds" follows from the constant difference between the cumulative log-odds (logits) for different categories, which translates into a constant ratio of odds.

Assuming that the errors follow a standard logistic distribution fixes the scale of the latent response ξ but not its origin; a consequence is that the general intercept α is not identified independently of the cut points α_j. Setting $\alpha = 0$ to fix the origin of ξ, the negatives of the category boundaries (i.e., the $-\alpha_j$) become the intercepts for the logistic regression equations.

Compared with logit models for nested dichotomies, or with the multinomial logit model, both of which use $(m-1)(k+1)$ parameters, the proportional-odds model is relatively parsimonious, with only $m + k - 1$ independent parameters. A corollary is that the proportional-odds model is more restrictive than these other models and may not fit the data well. The models are not properly nested to perform a likelihood-test—that is, the proportional-odds model is not a specialization of either the nested-dichotomies model or the multinomial logit model—but comparison of the relative fit of the models (e.g., via the AIC) can be informative. There is also a score test (as far as I know, unavailable in S) of the proportional-odds assumption. An "informal" likelihood-ratio test, comparing the deviances for the proportional-odds and multinomial logit models, usually produces results similar to the score test for proportional odds.

The proportional-odds model may be fit in S using the `polr` function in the MASS library, which was loaded previously (Venables & Ripley, 1999). For the women's labor-force data, we may proceed as follows:

```
> mod.polr <- polr(participation ~ hincome + children)
> summary(mod.polr)

Re-fitting to get Hessian

Call:
polr(formula = participation ~ hincome + children)

Coefficients:
                   Value Std. Error t value
hincome        -0.053901    0.01949 -2.7655
childrenpresent -1.971957    0.28695 -6.8722

Intercepts:
                    Value  Std. Error  t value
not.work|parttime  -1.852    0.386     -4.794
parttime|fulltime  -0.941    0.370     -2.544

Residual Deviance: 441.66
AIC: 449.66
```

The AIC for the proportional-odds model (449.7) is substantially larger than that for the multinomial logit model fit earlier (434.9), casting doubt on the assumption of proportional odds. A rough analysis of deviance yields a p value of .00008, suggesting the inadequacy of the proportional-odds model:

```
> 1 - pchisq(441.66 - 422.88, df = 6 - 4)
[1] 8.3555e-05
```

The fit of the proportional-odds model, shown in Figure 5.6, is also quite different from that of the multinomial logit model (Figure 5.4) and the nested-dichotomies model (Figure 5.3). Fitted values to produce Figure 5.6 are obtained much as for the multinomial logit model:

```
> p.fit <- predict(mod.polr, predictors, type='probs')
>
```

POISSON GENERALIZED LINEAR MODELS FOR COUNT DATA   5.3

Poisson generalized linear models arise in two common formally identical but substantively distinguishable contexts: when the response variable in a regression model takes on nonnegative integer values, such as a count,

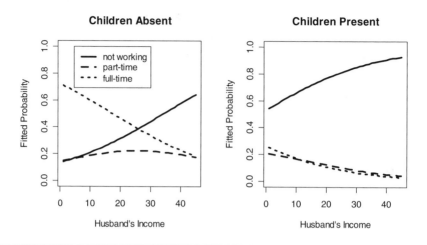

Figure 5.6   Fitted probabilities from the proportional-odds model fit to the women's labor-force participation data.

and to analyze associations among categorical variables in a contingency table of counts. The default link for the `poisson` family generator is the log link.

5.3.1   Poisson Regression

Recall Ornstein's (1976) data on interlocking-directorate and top executive positions among 248 major Canadian firms, introduced in Chapter 3:

```
> data(Ornstein)
> Ornstein[sort(sample(248,10)),]  # sample 10 obs.
    assets sector nation interlocks
23   14163    AGR    CAN          4
26   12810    TRN    CAN         40
27   12080    MIN     US         29
64    4298    AGR    OTH         15
88    2801    WOD    CAN         18
145    888    WOD    CAN          2
173    590    MAN     US          2
177    566    AGR     US          0
182    540    MAN    CAN          6
212    375    MAN     US          8
```

Ornstein performed a least squares regression of the number of interlocks maintained by each firm on the firm's assets and dummy variables for the firm's nation of control and sector of operation. Because the response

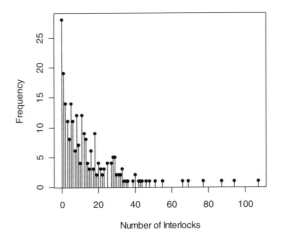

Figure 5.7   Distribution of number of interlocks maintained by 248 large Canadian corporations.

variable (`interlocks`) is a count, a Poisson linear model might be preferable. Indeed, the marginal distribution of number of interlocks, in Figure 5.7, shows many zero counts and a substantial positive skew.

To construct this graph, I first use the `table` function to find the frequency distribution of counts:

```
> attach(Ornstein)
> tab <- table(interlocks)
> tab
interlocks
   0   1   2   3   4   5   6   7   8   9  10  11  12  13  14  15
  28  19  14  11   8  14  11   6  12   7   4  12   9   8   4   3
  . . .
  94 107
   1   1
```

The numbers on top of the frequencies are the different values of `interlocks`: Thus, there are 28 firms with 0 interlocks, 19 with 1 interlock, 14 with 2, and so on. The graph is produced by plotting the ordered unique values of `interlocks` against the counts:

```
> x <- sort(unique(interlocks))
> plot(x, tab, type='h', xlab='Number of Interlocks',
+     ylab='Frequency')
> points(x, tab, pch=16)
>
```

Specifying `type='h'` in the call to `plot` produces the vertical ("histogram-like") lines, while the `points` function adds the filled circles (`pch=16`) at the tops of the lines.

Using glm to fit a Poisson regression model is very simple:

```
> mod.ornstein <- glm(interlocks ~ assets + nation + sector,
+    family=poisson)
> summary(mod.ornstein)

Call:
glm(formula = interlocks ~ assets + nation + sector,
  family = poisson)

Deviance Residuals:
   Min     1Q  Median      3Q     Max
-5.991  -2.477  -0.858   1.347   7.361

Coefficients:
             Estimate Std. Error z value Pr(>|z|)
(Intercept)  2.32e+00   5.18e-02   44.83  < 2e-16
assets       2.09e-05   1.20e-06   17.34  < 2e-16
nationOTH   -1.63e-01   7.35e-02   -2.22   0.0265
nationUK    -5.77e-01   8.90e-02   -6.49  8.7e-11
nationUS    -8.26e-01   4.89e-02  -16.90  < 2e-16
sectorBNK   -4.09e-01   1.56e-01   -2.62   0.0087
sectorCON   -6.20e-01   2.11e-01   -2.93   0.0034
sectorFIN    6.77e-01   6.87e-02    9.85  < 2e-16
sectorHLD    2.08e-01   1.19e-01    1.76   0.0786
sectorMAN    5.27e-02   7.52e-02    0.70   0.4839
sectorMER    1.78e-01   8.65e-02    2.05   0.0399
sectorMIN    6.21e-01   6.68e-02    9.29  < 2e-16
sectorTRN    6.78e-01   7.48e-02    9.07  < 2e-16
sectorWOD    7.12e-01   7.52e-02    9.46  < 2e-16

(Dispersion parameter for poisson family taken to be 1)

    Null deviance: 3737.0  on 247  degrees of freedom
Residual deviance: 1887.4  on 234  degrees of freedom
AIC: 2813

Number of Fisher Scoring iterations: 4

> Anova(mod.ornstein)
Anova Table (Type II tests)

Response: interlocks
       LR Chisq Df Pr(>Chisq)
assets      391  1     <2e-16
nation      329  3     <2e-16
sector      361  9     <2e-16
```

The analysis of deviance, produced by the Anova function from car, shows that all three predictors have highly statistically significant effects.

Log-Linear Models for Contingency Tables   5.3.2

Poisson GLMs may also be used to fit log-linear models to a contingency table of frequency counts, where the object is to model association among the variables in the table (see, e.g., Fienberg, 1980; Agresti, 1990; Powers & Xie, 2000). The variables constituting the classifications of the table are treated as "predictors" in the Poisson model, while the cell count plays the role of the "response."

In Section 5.2.1, I introduced Campbell et al.'s data on voter turnout in the 1956 U.S. presidential election, using a binomial logit model to analyze a three-way contingency table for turnout by perceived closeness of the election and intensity of partisan preference. The binomial logit model treats turnout as the response.

An alternative is to construct a log-linear model for the expected cell count. Let us reenter the data in the following format, raveling the $2 \times 3 \times 2$ table of counts into a 12-element vector and using the expand.grid function to generate a data frame with all combinations of categories of the three variables in the table:

```
> counts <- c(91, 39, 121, 49, 64, 24, 214, 87, 284, 76, 201, 25)

> Campbell <- expand.grid(turnout=c('voted','did.not.vote'),
+     preference=c('weak', 'medium', 'strong'),
+     closeness=c('one.sided', 'close'))

> cbind(Campbell, counts)
        turnout preference closeness counts
1          voted       weak one.sided     91
2   did.not.vote       weak one.sided     39
3          voted     medium one.sided    121
4   did.not.vote     medium one.sided     49
5          voted     strong one.sided     64
6   did.not.vote     strong one.sided     24
7          voted       weak     close    214
8   did.not.vote       weak     close     87
9          voted     medium     close    284
10  did.not.vote     medium     close     76
11         voted     strong     close    201
12  did.not.vote     strong     close     25
```

Notice that the leftmost argument to expand.grid (here turnout) is the one whose values change most quickly.

Log-linear models are usually defined using sum-to-zero contrasts, and so I reset the contrasts option for unordered factors accordingly:

```
> options(contrasts=c('contr.sum', 'contr.poly'))
>
```

I then fit a "saturated" log-linear model to the data by a Poisson regression of the cell counts on all main effects and interactions among the three factors in the contingency table[7]:

```
> attach(Campbell)
> mod.loglin <- glm(counts ~ closeness * preference * turnout,
+    family=poisson)
> summary(mod.loglin)

Call:
glm(formula = counts ~ closeness * preference * turnout,
   family = poisson)

Deviance Residuals:
 [1]  0  0  0  0  0  0  0  0  0  0  0  0

Coefficients:
                                   Estimate Std. Error z value
(Intercept)                          4.3777     0.0373  117.35
closeness1                          -0.3446     0.0373   -9.24
preference1                          0.1238     0.0499    2.48
preference2                          0.2891     0.0483    5.98
turnout1                             0.5862     0.0373   15.71
closeness1:preference1              -0.0698     0.0499   -1.40
closeness1:preference2               0.0215     0.0483    0.45
closeness1:turnout1                 -0.1309     0.0373   -3.51
preference1:turnout1                -0.1494     0.0499   -2.99
preference2:turnout1                -0.0307     0.0483   -0.63
closeness1:preference1:turnout1      0.1177     0.0499    2.36
closeness1:preference2:turnout1      0.0273     0.0483    0.57

 . . .

(Dispersion parameter for poisson family taken to be 1)

    Null deviance:  6.6929e+02  on 11  degrees of freedom
Residual deviance: -4.4415e-16  on  0  degrees of freedom
AIC: 98.62

Number of Fisher Scoring iterations: 2
```

Because the saturated model has as many parameters (12) as there are cells in the table, the deviance under the model is 0. An analysis of deviance reveals that the highest-order term, closeness × preference × turnout, is statistically significant, suggesting that the association between any pair of the variables depends on the level of the

---

7. In structural analogy to terms in an ANOVA model, two-way and higher-order terms in a log-linear model are often called "interactions," but they are more clearly conceptualized as association parameters.

third:

```
> Anova(mod.loglin)
Anova Table (Type II tests)

Response: counts
                             LR Chisq Df Pr(>Chisq)
closeness                         201  1    < 2e-16
preference                         56  2    6.8e-13
turnout                           376  1    < 2e-16
closeness:preference                1  2      0.540
closeness:turnout                   8  1      0.004
preference:turnout                 19  2    7.1e-05
closeness:preference:turnout        7  2      0.028

> detach(Campbell)
>
```

As mentioned, I previously treated turnout as the response variable for a logit model fit to the three-way table. As long as a log-linear model for the table includes the one-way and two-way terms for the predictors, closeness and preference, along with the one-way term for turnout, it is equivalent to a binomial logit model with turnout as the response. Therefore, the likelihood-ratio test for the closeness × preference × turnout association in the log-linear model is identical to the likelihood-ratio test for the closeness × preference interaction in the logit model for turnout.

Preparing Data for Fitting a Log-Linear Model

Contingency tables are more naturally represented as multi-way arrays of counts, rather than as vectors. Indeed, the table function, the xtabs function (in R), and the crosstabs function (in S-PLUS) all take individual observations as input and return contingency tables in the form of arrays.

I do not have the original data set that produced Campbell et al.'s table, but if I did, I could proceed as follows[8]:

```
> campbell <- table(turnout, preference, closeness)
> campbell
, , closeness = one.sided

              preference
turnout       weak medium strong
   voted         91    121     64
   did.not.vote  39     49     24
```

---

8. Because I do not have the data, the input and output shown here are simulated.

```
, , closeness = close

                preference
turnout        weak medium strong
   voted        214    284    201
   did.not.vote  87     76     25
```

In R, applying the `as.data.frame` coercion function to the table object ravels the table into a form suitable for input to `glm`, producing the same results as above (using the automatically generated variable Freq as the response in the Poisson GLM)[9]:

```
> Campbell <- as.data.frame(campbell)
> Campbell
         turnout preference closeness Freq
1          voted       weak one.sided   91
2  did.not.vote       weak one.sided   39
3          voted     medium one.sided  121
4  did.not.vote     medium one.sided   49
5          voted     strong one.sided   64
6  did.not.vote     strong one.sided   24
7          voted       weak     close  214
8  did.not.vote       weak     close   87
9          voted     medium     close  284
10 did.not.vote     medium     close   76
11         voted     strong     close  201
12 did.not.vote     strong     close   25

> mod.loglin <- glm(Freq ~ closeness * preference * turnout,
+     family=poisson, data=Campbell)
>
```

Raveling Tables in S-PLUS

In S-PLUS, applying `as.data.frame` to a table object does not produce a data frame suitable for input to `glm`. (Try it!) You may instead use the following simple function:

```
> ravel.table <- function(table){
+     cbind(expand.grid(dimnames(table)),
+         Freq=as.vector(table)
+     }
>
```

---

9. An alternative is to use the `loglin` function in S (or the `loglm` function in the MASS library, which provides a formula-based front end to `loglin`): `loglin` fits hierarchical log-linear models to tables in the form of multidimensional arrays, using the method of iterative proportional fitting. I see little advantage to this approach, however.

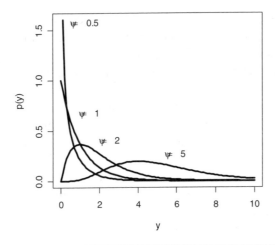

Figure 5.8   Gamma densities for various values of the shape parameter, $\psi = 1/\phi$.

ODDS AND ENDS   5.4

Other Generalized Linear Models   5.4.1

Gamma Models

Though less common than binomial and Poisson GLMs, gamma models are also potentially useful. The gamma distribution requires a nonnegative, continuous response variable.[10] The gamma distribution is appropriate when the conditional standard deviation of the response y is proportional to its mean μ, that is, when the coefficient of variation $\sqrt{V(y|\eta)}/\mu$ is constant. The specific shape of distributions in the gamma family depends on a *shape parameter* ψ, which, in a gamma GLM, is the inverse of the dispersion parameter. Some representative gamma distributions are shown in Figure 5.8.

Quasi-Likelihood Estimation

As you may be aware, GLMs are fit to data by an iterated weighted least squares (IWLS) procedure (see Section 5.5). Aside from its computational advantages, IWLS produces coefficient standard errors and a

---

10. The inverse-Gaussian family is also appropriate for continuous nonnegative data, but although I have seen theoretical discussions of inverse-Gaussian GLMs, I have never encountered an application.

variety of other useful quantities as by-products. For GLMs in the exponential families, IWLS yields maximum-likelihood estimates, but the procedure requires only the link and variance functions. In *quasi-likelihood estimation*, this property of IWLS is exploited to calculate estimates for an arbitrary combination of link and variance functions, in the absence of an explicit conditional distribution for the response.

The resulting estimates share many of the properties of maximum-likelihood estimates, including asymptotic normality, asymptotic unbias, and the usual covariance matrix for the estimates. This is not an unfamiliar idea: When we apply least squares regression to a model with nonnormal errors, for example, the resulting estimates are unbiased, asymptotically normal, and have the usual covariance matrix, as long as the assumptions of linearity, constant error variance, and independence hold. When the errors are nonnormal, moreover, the least squares estimates are not in general maximum-likelihood estimates, but are still maximally efficient among linear unbiased estimators (by the Gauss-Markov theorem), though no longer necessarily among *all* unbiased estimators.

In S, quasi-likelihood estimation for GLMs is achieved by specifying the quasi family generator, with link and variance as arguments. These arguments default to 'identity' and 'constant', respectively, a combination that yields linear least squares estimates. Of course, there would be no reason to compute the least squares estimates in this convoluted manner.

Overdispersed Binomial and Poisson Models

As we have seen, the binomial and Poisson GLMs fix the dispersion parameter ϕ to 1. It is possible, however, to fit versions of these models in which the dispersion is a free parameter, to be estimated along with the coefficients of the linear predictor, although the resulting error distribution is not an exponential family.

It turns out that the regression coefficients are unaffected by allowing dispersion different from 1, but the coefficient standard errors are multiplied by the square root of $\hat{\phi}$. Because the estimated dispersion typically exceeds 1, this inflates the standard errors; put another way, failing to account for "overdispersion" produces misleadingly small standard errors, overstating the precision of the estimated coefficients.

So-called *overdispersed* binomial and Poisson models arise in several different circumstances. For example, in modeling proportions, it is possible that the probability of success μ varies for different individuals who share identical values of the predictors (this is called "unmodeled heterogeneity") or that the individual successes and failures for a "binomial" observation are not independent, as required by the binomial distribution.

The Anova function in car estimates the dispersion parameter when *F* tests are requested, and thus applies a correction for overdispersion in binomial and Poisson GLMs. In R, essentially the same effect can be achieved by employing the quasibinomial and quasipoisson families in fitting the GLM in the first place. The summary of the resulting fitted model provides coefficient standard errors and *t* tests corrected for dispersion.

For example, for Ornstein's interlocking-directorate regression:

```
> mod.ornstein.q <- update(mod.ornstein, family=quasipoisson)
> summary(mod.ornstein.q)

Call:
glm(formula = interlocks ~ assets + nation + sector,
    family = quasipoisson)
. . .
Coefficients:
               Estimate Std. Error t value Pr(>|t|)
(Intercept)   2.325e+00  1.458e-01  15.943  < 2e-16
assets        2.085e-05  3.381e-06   6.167 3.03e-09
nationOTH    -1.632e-01  2.068e-01  -0.789 0.430793
. . .
sectorTRN     6.778e-01  2.102e-01   3.224 0.001444
sectorWOD     7.115e-01  2.116e-01   3.363 0.000902

(Dispersion parameter for quasipoisson family taken to be 7.9079)

    Null deviance: 3737.0  on 247  degrees of freedom
Residual deviance: 1887.4  on 234  degrees of freedom
AIC: NA

Number of Fisher Scoring iterations: 4

> Anova(mod.ornstein.q, test='F')
Anova Table (Type II tests)

Response: interlocks
               SS  Df       F     Pr(>F)
assets     390.90   1 49.4311 2.237e-11
nation     328.94   3 13.8656 2.363e-08
sector     361.46   9  5.0787 2.819e-06
Residuals 1850.45 234
>
```

Note the use of update to change the family argument to glm. In this case, the estimated dispersion, $\hat{\phi} = 7.9079$, is substantially greater than 1, producing much larger standard errors than were obtained from the standard Poisson regression model.

Overdispersed Poisson and Binomial Models in S-PLUS

Although the `quasipoisson` family is not present in S-PLUS, the same result can be achieved using the `quasi` family generator—for example, `update(mod.ornstein, family=quasi(link=log, var='mu'))`. A similar approach can be taken to fit overdispersed binomial GLMs, using `family=quasi(link=logit, var='mu(1-mu)')`, as long as none of the observed y values is 0 or 1—a stipulation that precludes fitting an overdispersed binomial GLM to binary data by this method.

"Rolling Your Own" Generalized Linear Model

In addition to the flexibility provided by the standard and `quasi` family generators, it is also possible to add family generators, link functions, and variance functions to S—assuming, of course, that you have the necessary statistical knowledge and programming prowess. Venables and Ripley's MASS library, for example, includes a family generator for negative-binomial GLMs, an alternative to the Poisson GLM for overdispersed count data.

5.4.2   Arguments to `glm`

The `glm` function in R takes the following arguments (and the arguments to `glm` in S-PLUS are nearly identical):

```
> args(glm)
function (formula, family=gaussian, data=list(), weights=NULL,
    subset=NULL, na.action=na.fail, start=NULL, offset=NULL,
    control=glm.control(...), model=TRUE, method="glm.fit",
    x=FALSE, y=TRUE, contrasts=NULL, ...)
```

I have already discussed in some detail the use of the `formula` and `family` arguments. The `data`, `subset`, `na.action`, and `contrasts` arguments work as in `lm` (see Section 4.7).

Here are a few comments on the other arguments to `glm`:

`weights`

These are so-called "prior" weights, as for `lm`, not to be confused with the weights employed in the IWLS fitting procedure (see Section 5.5).[11]

---

11. In S-PLUS, applying the `weights` function to a fitted `glm` object yields the weights from the final IWLS iteration, not the prior weights.

As mentioned previously, the `weights` argument may be used to specify binomial denominators in a binomial GLM.

start

This argument supplies start values for the coefficients in the linear predictor; it is usually safe to let `glm` find its own start values.

offset *(R only)*

As for a linear model, an offset is included in the linear predictor with a fixed coefficient of 1, but (unlike in a linear model) in a GLM this is not generally the same as simply subtracting the offset from the left-hand side of the model. Equivalently, one may use the `offset` function as part of the specification of the linear predictor in the `glm` model formula.

control

This argument allows the user to set several technical parameters, in the form of a list controlling the IWLS fitting algorithm: `epsilon`, the convergence criterion (which defaults to 0.0001), representing the maximum relative change in the deviance before a solution is declared and iteration stops; `maxit`, the maximum number of iterations (default, 10); and `trace` (default, `FALSE`), which, if `TRUE`, causes a record of the IWLS iterations to be printed. These control parameters can also be specified directly as arguments to `glm`. The ability to control the IWLS fitting process is sometimes useful—for example, when convergence problems are encountered.

model, method, x, y

As for linear models, these are technical options.

FITTING GENERALIZED LINEAR MODELS BY ITERATED WEIGHTED LEAST SQUARES*   5.5

As mentioned, maximum-likelihood estimates for generalized linear models in S are obtained by *iterated weighted least squares (IWLS)*, also called *iteratively reweighted least squares (IRLS)*. It occasionally helps to know some of the details.

IWLS proceeds by forming a quadratic local approximation to the log-likelihood function; maximizing this approximate log-likelihood is a linear weighted least squares problem. Suppose that the vector $\beta^{(t)}$ contains the current estimates of the regression parameters of the GLM. From these estimates, we calculate the current values of the linear predictor, $\eta_i^{(t)} = \mathbf{x}_i'\beta^{(t)}$; the fitted values, $\mu_i^{(t)} = g^{-1}(\eta_i^{(t)})$; the variance function, $v_i^{(t)} = V(\mu_i^{(t)})/\phi$, the *working response*,[12]

$$z_i^{(t)} = \eta_i^{(t)} + \left(y_i - \mu_i^{(t)}\right)\left(\frac{\partial \eta_i}{\partial \mu_i}\right)^{(t)}$$

and the weights

$$w_i^{(t)} = \frac{1}{c_i v_i^{(t)} \left[\left(\partial \eta_i / \partial \mu_i\right)^{(t)}\right]^2},$$

where the c_i are fixed constants (e.g., in the binomial family, $c_i = n_i^{-1}$). Then we perform a weighted least squares regression of $z^{(t)}$ on the xs in the linear predictor, minimizing the weighted sum of squares $\sum_{i=1}^{n} w_i(z_i - \mathbf{x}_i'\beta)^2$, where $\mathbf{x}_i'$ is the ith row of the model matrix, obtaining new estimates of the regression parameters, $\beta^{(t+1)}$. This process is initiated with suitable starting values, $\beta^{(0)}$, and continues until the coefficients stabilize at the maximum-likelihood estimates, $\hat{\beta}$.

The estimated asymptotic covariance matrix of $\hat{\beta}$ is obtained from the last iteration of the IWLS procedure, as

$$\widehat{\mathcal{V}}(\hat{\beta}) = \hat{\phi}(\mathbf{X}'\mathbf{W}\mathbf{X})^{-1},$$

where $\mathbf{W} = \text{diag}\{w_i\}$.

Binomial logistic regression provides a relatively simple illustration; we have (after algebraic manipulation):

$$\mu_i^{(t)} = \left[1 + \exp\left(-\eta_i^{(t)}\right)\right]^{-1},$$

$$v_i^{(t)} = \mu_i^{(t)}\left(1 - \mu_i^{(t)}\right),$$

$$\left(\frac{\partial \eta_i}{\partial \mu_i}\right)^{(t)} = \frac{1}{\mu_i^{(t)}\left(1 - \mu_i^{(t)}\right)},$$

$$z_i^{(t)} = \eta_i^{(t)} + \left(y_i - \mu_i^{(t)}\right)/v_i^{(t)},$$

$$w_i^{(t)} = n_i v_i.$$

---

12. The values

$$z_i^{(t)} - \eta_i^{(t)} = (y_i - \mu_i^{(t)})\left(\frac{\partial \eta_i}{\partial \mu_i}\right)^{(t)}$$

are called *working residuals* and play a role in diagnostics for GLMs (see Section 6.6).

CHAPTER 6

Diagnosing Problems in Linear and Generalized Linear Models

Regression diagnostics are methods for determining whether a fitted regression model adequately represents the data. I construe the term "regression" broadly in this chapter to include methods that are appropriate for linear and generalized linear models. Because most of the methods for diagnosing problems in linear models extend naturally to generalized linear models, I deal at greater length with linear-model diagnostics, briefly introducing the extensions to GLMs.

Linear models fit by least squares make strong, and often unrealistic, assumptions about the structure of the data. When these assumptions are violated, least squares estimates can behave badly and may even completely misrepresent the data. Regression diagnostics can reveal such problems and often point the way toward solutions.

Section 6.1 describes methods for detecting unusual data, including outliers, high-leverage points, and influential observations. Section 6.2 deals with detecting and correcting nonnormally distributed errors, and Section 6.3 with nonconstant error variance. Section 6.4 takes up the problem of nonlinearity. Collinearity and the related topic of variable selection are the subjects of Section 6.5. The final section of the chapter considers the extension of diagnostic methods to generalized linear models, such as logistic and Poisson regression.

Most of the methods discussed in this chapter are programmed in the car library. Many of these methods can also be obtained straightforwardly, but more tediously, by using standard facilities available in S.

For example, added-variable plots (described in Section 6.1.3) are constructed by regressing a particular predictor and the response on all the other predictors, computing the residuals from these auxiliary regressions, and plotting one set of residuals against the other. This is not hard to do in S, although the steps are somewhat more complicated when there are factors, interactions, or polynomial terms in the model. It is my experience, however, that diagnostic methods are much more likely to be employed when their use is *convenient*. Thus, the av.plots function in car makes all the added-variable plots for a linear or generalized linear model available through a menu, and adds such enhancements as a least squares line and point identification.

As well, some of the diagnostic functions in car are more general than similar functions in standard S. For example, cookd in car is a generic function, with methods for linear and generalized linear models, while cooks.distance in R is applicable only to linear models.

6.1   UNUSUAL DATA

Unusual data can wreak havoc with least squares estimates and may prove interesting in their own right. Unusual data in regression include outliers, high-leverage points, and influential observations.

6.1.1   Outliers: Studentized Residuals

Regression outliers are *y* values that are unusual *conditional on* the values of the predictors. The standard statistics for detecting regression outliers are the *studentized residuals* for the model.[1]

There are several equivalent routes to the studentized residuals, but one that is particularly illuminating is via the *mean-shift outlier model*

$$y_i = \alpha + \beta_1 x_{i1} + \cdots + \beta_k x_{ik} + \gamma d_i + \varepsilon_i,$$

where d is a dummy regressor coded 1 for a particular observation (let us say the first) and 0 for all others. If $\gamma \neq 0$, then the conditional expectation of the first observation differs systematically from the others. The t statistic for testing the null hypothesis H_0: $\gamma = 0$ (which has $n - k - 2$ degrees of freedom) is the studentized residual for the first observation.

---

1. Unfortunately, although the terminology that I employ is the most common, it is not universal. What I call "studentized residuals" are sometimes termed "externally studentized residuals" or "deleted studentized residuals."

To obtain a complete set of studentized residuals, we could refit the mean-shift model n times, once for each observation in the data set. In practice, there are much more efficient ways to do the computation that do not require refitting the model.

Generally, our attention is drawn to the largest (absolute) studentized residual, and this presents a problem: Even if the studentized residuals were independent, which they are not, there would be an issue of simultaneous inference involved in picking the largest of n test statistics. The dependence of the studentized residuals complicates the issue. We can deal with this problem (1) by Bonferroni adjustment of the p value for the largest absolute studentized residual, multiplying the usual two-tail p by n, or (2) by constructing a quantile-comparison plot of the studentized residuals with a confidence envelope that takes their dependence into account.

In Chapter 1, I introduced Duncan's occupational-prestige data, regressing `prestige` on occupational `income` and `education` levels:

```
> library(car)

Attaching Package "package:car":

    The following object(s) are masked from package:base :

    dfbetas rstudent

> data(Duncan)
> attach(Duncan)
> mod.duncan <- lm(prestige ~ income + education)
>
```

Note that the `rstudent` function in `car` masks `rstudent` in the R base library: Studentized residuals are standardly available in R via the `rstudent` function; `car` provides a generic version of `rstudent`, with methods for linear and generalized linear models.

The `qq.plot` function in `car` has a method for linear models, plotting studentized residuals against the corresponding quantiles of t with $n - k - 2$ degrees of freedom. Setting the argument `simulate` to `TRUE` generates a 95 percent pointwise confidence envelope for the studentized residuals, using a parametric version of the bootstrap.[2] The method used is from Atkinson (1985).

```
> qq.plot(mod.duncan, simulate=T, labels=row.names(Duncan))
[1] 6
```

The resulting plot is shown in Figure 6.1. The `qq.plot` function returns the index of the observation with the largest studentized residual

---

2. Bootstrap methods in S are described in the Web appendix to the book.

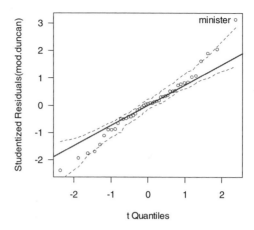

Figure 6.1   Quantile-comparison plot of studentized residuals from Duncan's occupational-prestige regression, showing the pointwise 95 percent simulated confidence envelope. The observation `minister` was identified interactively with the mouse.

(`minister`), which strays outside of the confidence envelope and which I identified interactively with the mouse: Point identification in `qq.plot` is turned on by supplying the `labels` argument; to identify a point, place the mouse cursor near it and press the left button; press the right button to exit from `qq.plot`. The distribution of the studentized residuals looks heavy-tailed compared with the reference t distribution: Perhaps a method of robust regression would be more appropriate for these data.[3]

The generic `outlier.test` function in `car`, which has a method for linear models, performs a Bonferroni t test for the largest absolute studentized residual (3.1345, for `minister`):

```
> outlier.test(mod.duncan, labels=row.names(Duncan))
 max|rstudent| df unadjusted p Bonferroni p
        3.1345 41    0.0031772        0.14297

Observation: minister
```

The Bonferroni-adjusted p value is not statistically significant.

6.1.2   Leverage: Hat Values

Observations that are relatively far from the center of the predictor space, taking account of the correlational pattern among the predictors, have

---

3. S functions for robust and resistant regression are described in the Web appendix to the text.

potentially greater influence on the least squares regression coefficients; such points are said to have "high leverage." The most common measures of leverage are the *hat values*, so called because they arise from the relationship between the fitted values (i.e., $\hat{y}_i$, or "y hat") and the observed response (y_i). The fitted values are linear combinations of the observations, $\hat{y}_j = \sum_{i=1}^{n} h_{ij} y_i$, and so h_{ij} represents the weight attached to y_i in the determination of $\hat{y}_j$. The hat value, $h_i = \sum_{j=1}^{n} h_{ij}^2$, summarizes the weights associated with y_i in the determination of all of the fitted values.[4] The average hat value is $\bar{h} = (k+1)/n$, where $k+1$ is the number of coefficients in the regression model (including the constant). A rough rule is that hat values that exceed $2\bar{h}$ (or, in small samples, $3\bar{h}$) are noteworthy.

The generic function hatvalues in car has methods for linear and generalized linear models. One way of examining the hat values (and other individual-observation diagnostic statistics) is to construct an *index plot*, graphing the hat values against the corresponding observation indices. For example, Figure 6.2 shows an index plot for the hat values from Duncan's occupational-prestige regression:

```
> plot(hatvalues(mod.duncan))
> abline(h=c(2, 3)*3/45, lty=2)  # reference lines
> identify(1:45, hatvalues(mod.duncan), row.names(Duncan))
[1]  6 16 27
```

I used abline to draw horizontal reference lines at $2\bar{h}$ and $3\bar{h}$. The occupations railroad engineer (RR.engineer), conductor, and minister, interactively identified with the mouse, stand out from the rest.

Influence Measures   6.1.3

An observation that combines "outlyingness" with high leverage exerts influence on the regression coefficients, in the sense that if the observation is removed, the coefficients change substantially.

---

4. * The vector of fitted values is given by

$$\hat{y} = Xb$$
$$= X(X'X)^{-1}X'y$$
$$= Hy,$$

where

$$H = \{h_{ij}\} = \{X\}(X'X)^{-1}X',$$

called the *hat matrix*, projects y into the subspace spanned by the columns of the model matrix X. Because $H = H'H$, the hat values h_i are simply the diagonal entries of the hat matrix.

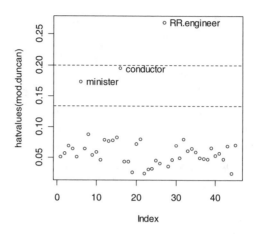

Figure 6.2   Index plot of the hat values from Duncan's occupational-prestige regression. The horizontal lines show twice and three times the average hat value. Three observations were identified with the mouse.

dfbeta and dfbetas

The most direct measure of influence, termed dfbeta$_{ij}$, assesses the impact on the jth coefficient of deleting the ith observation:

$$\text{dfbeta}_{ij} = b_{j(-i)} - b_j,$$

where b_j is the coefficient computed using all of the data and $b_{j(-i)}$ is the same coefficient computed with observation i omitted. The computation of the dfbeta$_{ij}$ can be accomplished without having to refit the model.

The dfbeta$_{ij}$ are expressed in the metric (units of measurement) of the coefficient b_j. A standardized version, dfbetas$_{ij}$, divides dfbeta$_{ij}$ by the standard error of b_j.

The standard `dfbetas` function in R takes a linear model as its argument and returns all of the dfbetas$_{ij}$. The generic `dfbetas` function in car shadows the standard function and provides methods for both linear and generalized linear models. The `car` library also contains the function `dfbeta`.

Let us calculate dfbetas$_{ij}$ for Duncan's regression and display the first few values:

```
> dfbs.duncan <- dfbetas(mod.duncan)
> dfbs.duncan[1:5,]   # first 5 obs.
   (Intercept)     income    education
1 -2.2534e-02  6.6621e-04   0.03594387
2 -2.5435e-02  5.0877e-02  -0.00811827
3 -9.1867e-03  6.4837e-03   0.00561927
4 -4.7204e-05 -6.0177e-05   0.00013975
5 -6.5817e-02  1.7005e-02   0.08677706
```

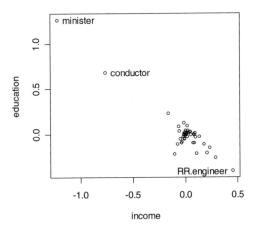

Figure 6.3   dfbetas$_{ij}$ values for the income and education coefficients in Duncan's occupational-prestige regression.

We could examine each column of the dfbetas matrix separately (e.g., via an index plot), but because we are not really interested here in influence on the regression intercept, and because there are just two slope coefficients, I instead plot influence on the income coefficient against influence on the education coefficient (Figure 6.3):

```
> plot(dfbs.duncan[,c(2,3)])  # for b1 and b2
> identify(dfbs.duncan[,2], dfbs.duncan[,3], row.names(Duncan))
[1]  6 16 27
```

The negative relationship between the dfbetas$_{ij}$ values for the two predictors reflects the *positive* correlation of the predictors themselves. Two pairs of values stand out: The observations minister and conductor make the income coefficient smaller and the education coefficient larger. (I also identified the occupation railroad engineer in the plot.)

Cook's Distance

A practical problem with dfbeta$_{ij}$ or dfbetas$_{ij}$ is their large number: These sets of diagnostic statistics contain n values for each of the $k + 1$ regression coefficients—that is, $n \times (k + 1)$ values in all. Several summary measures have been proposed, the most commonly used of which is Cook's D_i, a scale-invariant measure of the distance between the regression coefficients with the ith observation absent and present.

Cook's distance may be expressed as

$$D_i = \frac{e_i^2}{s^2(k+1)} \times \frac{h_i}{1 - h_i},$$

where e_i^2 is the squared residual for the ith observation, s^2 is the variance of the residuals, and h_i is (as above) the hat value for observation i. The

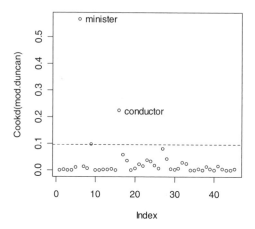

Figure 6.4   Index plot of Cook's distances for Duncan's occupational-prestige regression. The horizontal line is at $4/(n - k - 1)$. Two observations were identified with the mouse.

first factor may be thought of as a measure of outlyingness and the second as a measure of leverage. The value $4/(n - k - 1)$ has been suggested as a rough cutoff for noteworthy values of D_i.

The generic function cookd in car has methods for linear-model and generalized-linear-model objects. Applying this function to Duncan's regression once again draws attention to the occupations minister and conductor (see Figure 6.4):

```
> plot(cookd(mod.duncan))
> abline(h=4/42, lty=2)
> identify(1:45, cookd(mod.duncan), row.names(Duncan))
[1]  6 16
```

The "bubble plot" in Figure 6.5 combines the display of studentized residuals, hat values, and Cook's distances, with the areas of the circles proportional to Cook's D_i[5]:

```
> plot(hatvalues(mod.duncan), rstudent(mod.duncan), type='n')
> cook <- sqrt(cookd(mod.duncan))
> points(hatvalues(mod.duncan), rstudent(mod.duncan),
+    cex=10*cook/max(cook))
> abline(h=c(-2, 0, 2), lty=2)
> abline(v=c(2, 3)*3/45, lty=2)
> identify(hatvalues(mod.duncan), rstudent(mod.duncan),
+    row.names(Duncan))
[1]  6  9 16 27
```

The plot function is used to set up the coordinate space for the graph, without plotting the points (via the argument type='n'). Then points

---

5. In Chapter 8, I describe how to write a function for constructing graphs of this kind.

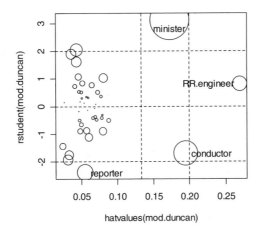

Figure 6.5   Plot of hat values, studentized residuals, and Cook's distances for Duncan's occupational-prestige regression. The size of the circles is proportional to Cook's D_i. Several observations have been identified with the mouse.

is employed to add circles to the graph, with radius proportional to the square root of Cook's D and, consequently, area proportional to Cook's D; this is accomplished (in R) via the cex ("character-expansion") argument to points; the factor 10 scales the circles to a reasonable size and was determined by trial and error. The abline function draws horizontal and vertical lines on the graph. Finally, unusual points are labeled interactively with identify.

Drawing Circles in S-PLUS

Vectorized use of the argument cex is not supported by S-PLUS. An alternative, which works in both S-PLUS and R, is to draw the circles in a for loop:

```
> cook <- sqrt(as.vector(cookd(mod.duncan)))
> max.cook <- max(cook)
> hat <- hatvalues(mod.duncan)
> rstud <- rstudent(mod.duncan)
> for (i in 1:length(cook))
+     points(hat[i], rstud[i], cex=10*cook[i]/max.cook)
>
```

[The odd construction as.vector(cookd(mod.duncan)) is required by S3 to strip away the names attribute of the vector of Cook's distances, which otherwise causes a problem for the cex argument to points.] See Chapter 7 for more information on drawing graphs, and Chapter 8 for a discussion of programming constructs such as for loops.

Added-Variable Plots

A potential defect of single-observation deletion diagnostics is that they can fail to identify influential pairs or subsets of observations, which can mask each other's presence. *Added-variable plots* (also called *partial-regression plots*) reduce the higher-dimensional regression problem to a series of two-dimensional plots and show leverage and influence of the observations on each coefficient of the model.

The added-variable plot for the first predictor, x_1, is formed by regressing both the response variable y and the predictor x_1 on all of the other predictors, $x_2, \ldots, x_k$. The residuals from these regressions (say, $e_{y|2,\ldots,k}$ and $e_{1|2,\ldots,k}$) are then plotted against each other. It turns out that the slope from the simple regression of $e_{y|2,\ldots,k}$ on $e_{1|2,\ldots,k}$ is the multiple regression slope b_1, that the residuals from this simple regression are the multiple-regression residuals, e_i, and that the standard error of the simple regression slope is (except for degrees of freedom) the multiple-regression standard error for b_1. A similar added-variable plot can be constructed for each coefficient of the model, including the constant, and coefficients for dummy regressors and interaction regressors.

The `av.plots` function in `car` works for both linear and generalized linear models, presenting the user with a menu of plots[6]:

```
> av.plots(mod.duncan, labels=row.names(Duncan))

1:(Intercept)
2:income
3:education
Selection: 2

1:(Intercept)
2:income
3:education
Selection: 3

1:(Intercept)
2:income
3:education
Selection: 0
>
```

I have selected the added-variable plots for the `income` and `education` coefficients in Duncan's regression (shown in Figure 6.6); entering 0 exits from the menu. Notice how the occupations `minister` and `conductor` act jointly to depress the `income` coefficient and inflate the `education` coefficient; the occupation railroad engineer has high leverage on both coefficients, but is more or less in line with the rest of the data.

---

6. Alternatively, the argument `ask=F` causes all of the plots to be drawn on a single "page."

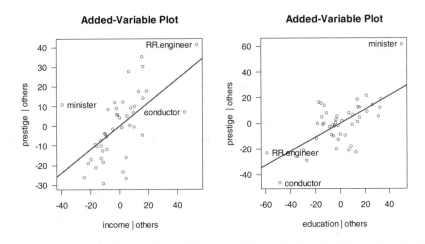

Figure 6.6   Added-variable plots for the income and education coefficients in Duncan's occupational-prestige regression. Several points were interactively identified with the mouse.

Sall (1990) has suggested a generalization of the added-variable plot, termed a *leverage plot*, that constructs a single graph for a multiple-degree-of-freedom term such as a set of dummy regressors. The plot shows leverage and influence on the hypothesis that all of the coefficients in the term are 0. It should be understood that an observation can change the individual coefficients in a term substantially without affecting the F for the hypothesis that the term is 0, and thus leverage plots are potentially less informative than separate added-variable plots for each coefficient. There is a leverage.plots function in car, which works only for linear models.

NONNORMAL ERRORS   6.2

Least squares regression performs best when the errors are normally distributed. Substantially nonnormal errors can compromise the efficiency of least squares (e.g., in the case of heavy-tailed errors) and can cast doubt on the reasonableness of estimating the conditional mean of y given the xs (e.g., when the errors are skewed). The distribution of the regression residuals is the key to discovering the distribution of the errors, although the relationship between the two is not altogether simple: Even if the errors are normally and independently distributed with constant variance, the residuals have different variances and are dependent. Moreover, because they are weighted averages of the data, the residuals tend to look normal even when the errors are not, a phenomenon sometimes termed "supranormality."

A quantile-comparison plot of studentized residuals against the t distribution, as described in Section 6.1.1, is useful in drawing our attention to the tail behavior of the residuals, clearly revealing heavy-tailed or skewed distributions. A nonparametric density estimate, however, does a better job of conveying a general sense of the shape of the distribution of the residuals.

In Chapter 5, I fit a Poisson regression to Ornstein's data on interlocking directorates among Canadian corporations, regressing the number of interlocks maintained by each firm on the firm's assets, nation of control, and sector of operation. Because number of interlocks is a count, the Poisson model is a natural starting point, but the original source employed a least squares regression similar to the following[7]:

```
> detach(Duncan)
> data(Ornstein)
> attach(Ornstein)
> mod.ornstein <- lm(interlocks + 1 ~ assets + nation + sector)
> Anova(mod.ornstein)
Anova Table (Type II tests)

Response: interlocks + 1
          Sum Sq  Df  F value  Pr(>F)
assets     16904   1   175.06  < 2e-16
nation      3449   3    11.91  2.8e-07
sector      3706   9     4.26  3.9e-05
Residuals  22595 234
```

Our interest here is to examine the residuals from this regression, and so I have not printed a summary of the model (as I would do, of course, were we really interested in the results of the analysis). I have also added 1 to the number of interlocks because we will shortly consider power transformations of the response variable and want to avoid values of 0; in a linear model, adding 1 to the response simply increases the regression constant by 1.

Quantile-comparison and density plots of the studentized residuals, in Figure 6.7, are produced by the following S statements:

```
> qq.plot(mod.ornstein, sim=T)
> plot(density(rstudent(mod.ornstein)), main='rstudent')
>
```

The studentized residuals are positively skewed, a condition that often can be corrected by transforming y down the ladder of powers and roots. Trial and error here suggests the square-root transformation of interlocks.

---

7. Ornstein (1976) employed both assets and the log of assets in the regression. No criticism is implied here, by the way: As far as I know, in the 1970s sociologists did not use Poisson regression models for count data.

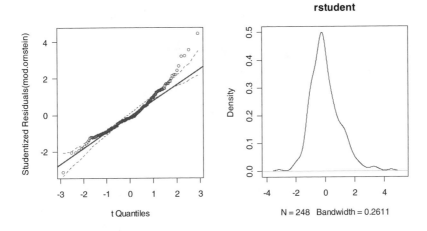

Figure 6.7   Quantile-comparison plot and nonparametric density estimate for the distribution of the studentized residuals from Ornstein's interlocking-directorate regression.

Reminder: Density Plots in S-PLUS

Recall that to make a density plot in S-PLUS, you have to supply the argument type='l' to the plot function:

```
> plot(density(rstudent(mod.ornstein)), type='l')
>
```

Box-Cox Transformation of *y*   6.2.1

The *Box-Cox regression model* (Box & Cox, 1964) is an alternative to guided trial and error for transforming the response:

$$y_i^{(\lambda)} = \alpha + \beta_1 x_{i1} + \cdots + \beta_k x_{ik} + \varepsilon_i,$$

where

$$y_i^{(\lambda)} = \begin{cases} \dfrac{y^\lambda - 1}{\lambda} & \text{for } \lambda \neq 0, \\ \log_e y & \text{for } \lambda = 0. \end{cases}$$

The normalizing power-transformation parameter λ is estimated, along with the regression coefficients and error variance, by the method of maximum likelihood.

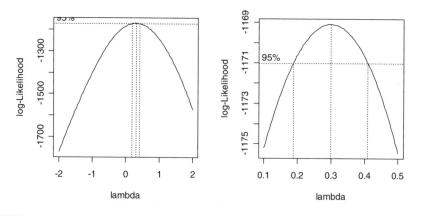

Figure 6.8   Profile log-likelihood for the transformation parameter λ in the Box-Cox model applied to Ornstein's interlocking-directorate regression.

The boxcox function in Venables and Ripley's (1999) MASS library fits the Box-Cox model, producing a plot of the profile log-likelihood against the transformation parameter λ:

```
> library(MASS)
> boxcox(mod.ornstein)
>
```

The resulting plot is shown in the left panel of Figure 6.8. By default, boxcox plots over the range $-2 < \lambda < 2$, but we can focus more closely on the value of λ that maximizes the likelihood, as shown in the right panel of Figure 6.8:

```
> boxcox(mod.ornstein, lambda=seq(.1, .5, by=.01))
>
```

Thus, $\hat{\lambda} \simeq 0.3$, with the 95 percent confidence interval for λ running from just under 0.2 to just over 0.4—quite a sharp estimate.

6.2.2   Constructed-Variable Plot for the Box-Cox Transformation

Atkinson (1985) suggests an approximate score test and diagnostic plot for the Box-Cox transformation of y, based on the *constructed variable*

$$ g_i = y_i \left[\log_e \left(\frac{y_i}{\widetilde{y}} \right) - 1 \right], $$

where $\widetilde{y}$ is the geometric mean of y; that is, $\widetilde{y} = (y_1 \times y_2 \times \cdots \times y_n)^{1/n}$. The constructed variable is added to the regression, and the t statistic for this variable is the approximate score statistic for the transformation. An added-variable plot for the constructed variable in the auxiliary regression—called a *constructed-variable plot*—shows leverage and influence on the decision to transform y.

The box.cox.var function in car facilitates the computation of the constructed variable. Thus, for Ornstein's regression:

```
> mod.ornstein.cv <- update(mod.ornstein,
+     . ~ . + box.cox.var(interlocks + 1))

> summary(mod.ornstein.cv)
. . .
                          Estimate Std. Error  t value Pr(>|t|)
(Intercept)               1.41e+01   1.03e+00    13.66  < 2e-16
assets                   -3.57e-05   6.22e-05    -0.57   0.5673
. . .
box.cox.var(interlocks + 1)  6.94e-01   3.91e-02    17.73  < 2e-16
. . .
> av.plots(mod.ornstein.cv, 'box.cox.var(interlocks + 1)')
>
```

We are only interested in the t test and added-variable plot for the constructed variable, and we can request the latter directly from the av.plots function, bypassing the menu; the constructed-variable plot is shown in Figure 6.9. The t statistic for the constructed variable demonstrates that there is very strong evidence of the need to transform y (cf. the likelihood-ratio test, which may be read roughly off

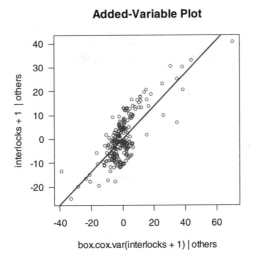

Figure 6.9   Constructed-variable plot for the Box-Cox transformation of y in Ornstein's interlocking-directorate regression.

Figure 6.8[8]). The constructed-variable plot suggests that this evidence is spread through the data, rather than being dependent on a small fraction of the observations.

6.3   NONCONSTANT ERROR VARIANCE

One of the assumptions of the standard linear model is that the conditional variance of y (the error variance) is everywhere the same. Because the regression surface is generally high dimensional, it is not possible to look directly at the distribution of the residuals around the fitted surface. A common pattern of nonconstant error variance, however, is for the spread of y to increase with its level, a pattern that can be detected by plotting residuals against fitted values—projecting the higher-dimensional point cloud onto a two-dimensional surface. It is important to realize that plots of this kind are not infallible: Incorrectly modeling the dependence of the mean of y on the xs can also produce nonconstant spread in a plot of residuals against fitted values (see, e.g., Cook, 1998, Section 1.2.1).

Because the residuals do not have the same variance, even when the error variance is constant, I prefer to plot studentized residuals against fitted values. For example, for Ornstein's interlocking-directorate regression (Figure 6.10):

```
> plot(fitted.values(mod.ornstein), rstudent(mod.ornstein))
> abline(h=0, lty=2)  # zero line
>
```

Although the skewness in the fitted values makes the plot difficult to examine, it appears that the residual spread increases with the level of the fitted values. The diagonal lining up of the points on the lower left reflects the fact that the number of interlocks cannot be less than 0, an observation that suggests that a linear model is not altogether appropriate for these data. Recall the Poisson GLM fit to Ornstein's data in the preceding chapter.

An alternative diagnostic adapts Tukey's (1977) spread-level plot, plotting the log of the absolute studentized residuals against the log of the fitted values. This approach also produces a suggested spread-stabilizing power transformation of y. The spread.level.plot function in car has

---

8. The likelihood-ratio chi-square statistic, on 1 degree of freedom, is twice the difference in the log-likelihood at $\lambda = \hat{\lambda}$ (the maximum-likelihood estimate) and at $\lambda = 1$ (corresponding to no transformation). Here, the test statistic is approximately $2(1250 - 1169) = 162$, which is overwhelmingly statistically significant. The test statistic can be computed more accurately by assigning the (invisible) result of the boxcox function to a variable and examining it. (By default, boxcox plots rather than prints its result when a graphics window is open.) In the current example, the more precise value of the LR test statistic is $2(1243.2 - 1169.1) = 148.2$.

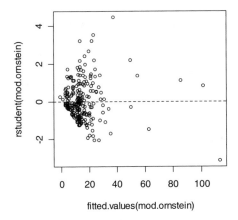

Figure 6.10   Plot of studentized residuals against fitted values for Ornstein's interlocking-directorate regression.

a method for linear models:

```
> spread.level.plot(mod.ornstein)

Suggested power transformation:   0.32222
Warning message:
Start =  2 added to fitted values to avoid 0 or negative values.
   in: spread.level.plot.lm(mod.ornstein)
```

Because there are some negative fitted values, the function adds a start of 2 before taking logs. The spread-level plot, shown in Figure 6.11, has an obvious tilt to it. The suggested transformation, approximately the 1/3 power, is similar to the normalizing transformation estimated previously by the Box-Cox method.

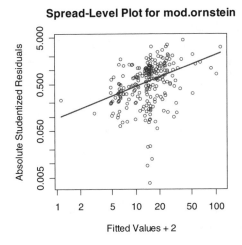

Figure 6.11   Spread-level plot of studentized residuals against fitted values for Ornstein's interlocking-directorate regression.

6.3.1   Score Tests for Nonconstant Error Variance

Breusch and Pagan (1979) and Cook and Weisberg (1983) suggest a score test for nonconstant error variance in a linear model, based on the relationship

$$V(\varepsilon_i) = g(\gamma_0 + \gamma_1 z_{i1} + \cdots + \gamma_p z_{ip}).$$

Here, the z_j are predictors of the error variance, and the function $g(\cdot)$ of the linear predictor $\gamma_0 + \gamma_1 z_{i1} + \cdots + \gamma_p z_{ip}$ need not be known. In typical applications, the zs are the same as the predictors in the linear model (i.e., the xs), or there is just one z, the fitted values $\hat{y}$ from the linear model—in which case we test for a dependence of spread on level.

The ncv.test function in car implements this score test. Let us apply ncv.test to test for the dependence of spread on level (the default) in Ornstein's regression, and for a more general dependence of spread on the predictors in the regression (given in a one-sided formula as the optional second argument to ncv.test):

```
> ncv.test(mod.ornstein)
Non-constant Variance Score Test
Variance formula: ~fitted.values
Chisquare = 46.985    Df = 1      p = 7.1518e-12


> ncv.test(mod.ornstein, ~ assets + nation + sector)
Non-constant Variance Score Test
Variance formula: ~ assets + nation + sector
Chisquare = 74.735    Df = 13     p = 1.0663e-10
```

Both tests are highly statistically significant, and the difference between the two suggests that the relationship of spread to level does not entirely account for the pattern of nonconstant error variance in these data. This conclusion is slightly misleading, however: In addition to nonconstant error variance, the partial relationship between interlocks and assets is nonlinear. Transforming assets to straighten the relationship simplifies the pattern of nonconstant error variance to a more straightforward dependence of spread on level. I invite the reader to examine the data more closely. The more general lesson here is that the problems of nonconstant spread and nonlinearity can be related.

6.3.2   Other Approaches to Nonconstant Error Variance

I have suggested transformation as a strategy for stabilizing error variance, but other approaches are available. In particular, if the pattern of error variance is known up to a constant of proportionality, then weighted least squares (WLS) regression may be employed in preference to ordinary least squares (OLS). WLS fits the regression model by minimizing the weighted sum of squared residuals, $\sum w_i e_i^2$, where the weight w_i attached to observation i is inversely proportional to the variance of the error ε_i.

In S, WLS is performed by specifying the `weights` argument to `lm`, giving the weight w_i for each observation. If, for example, we had reason to believe that the error variance in Ornstein's regression were proportional to `assets`, $V(\varepsilon_i) = \sigma^2 \times$ `assets`$_i$, then we could fit the model weighting each observation inversely in proportion to this variable:

```
> lm(interlocks ~ assets + nation + sector, weights=1/assets)
```

Still another approach, which does not require that we know the form of dependence of $V(\varepsilon_i)$ on the xs, is to correct the estimated covariance matrix of the regression coefficients for nonconstant spread. "Heteroscedasticity-consistent standard errors" were introduced by White (1980).[9] Subsequent work has suggested small modifications to White's procedure (see Long and Ervin, 2000).

White's approach is implemented in the `hccm` ("heteroscedasticity-consistent covariance matrix") function in `car`. The specific form of the correction employed is given by the `type` argument, which defaults to `'hc3'`, the method recommended by Long and Ervin; White's original correction corresponds to `'hc0'`. These corrections may also be employed in the `linear.hypothesis` and `Anova` functions. For example, for Ornstein's regression:

```
> Anova(mod.ornstein, white.adjust="hc3")
Anova Table (Type II tests)

Response: interlocks + 1
          Sum Sq  Df F value  Pr(>F)
assets      4496   1   46.56 7.5e-11
nation      3764   3   12.99 7.0e-08
sector      3377   9    3.89 0.00013
Residuals  22595 234
```

Compare these F tests with the standard tests reported previously in Section 6.2.

---

9. * White proposed estimating the covariance matrix of the regression coefficients **b** by

$$\widetilde{V}(\mathbf{b}) = (\mathbf{X}'\mathbf{X})^{-1}\mathbf{X}'\widehat{\mathbf{\Sigma}}\mathbf{X}(\mathbf{X}'\mathbf{X})^{-1},$$

where $\widehat{\mathbf{\Sigma}} = \text{diag}\{e_i^2\}$, in place of the usual $\widehat{V}(\mathbf{b}) = s^2(\mathbf{X}'\mathbf{X})^{-1}$.

6.4   NONLINEARITY

The standard linear model assumes that the expectation of the error is everywhere 0; nonlinearity, construed broadly, covers any violation of this assumption—that is, any systematic departure from the functional form specified in the model. Because the regression surface is generally high dimensional, one cannot look directly for departures from the model (but see the methods of nonparametric regression described in the Web appendix to the book). Instead, I focus here on nonlinearity in the more conventional sense of a nonlinear partial relationship between the response and a particular predictor.

6.4.1   Component + Residual and CERES Plots

Component + residual plots (also called *partial-residual plots*) are a simple graphical device for detecting nonlinearity in multiple regression. The *partial residuals* for the predictor x_j are formed by adding the fitted linear component in this predictor to the least squares residuals:

$$e_{ij} = e_i + b_j x_{ij}.$$

The partial residuals e_{ij} are then plotted against x_j.[10] Interpretation of component + residual plots is often enhanced by adding a least squares line to the plot (representing the regression surface viewed edge on in the direction of x_j) and a nonparametric-regression smooth.

The cr.plots function in car constructs component + residual plots for linear and generalized linear models, by default via a text menu presented to the user, much in the manner of the av.plots function. Consider, by way of example, the Canadian occupational-prestige regression (discussed in Chapter 4 and refit here):

```
> detach(Ornstein)
> data(Prestige)
> attach(Prestige)
> mod.prestige <- lm(prestige ~ income + education + women)
> cr.plots(mod.prestige)

1:Change span =  0.5
2:income
```

----

10. This sounds similar to the added-variable plot for x_j, but represents a different two-dimensional projection of the $(k + 1)$-dimensional point cloud of the data. Added-variable plots are usually more suitable for detecting leverage and influence on the regression coefficients than they are for revealing nonlinearity. See Cook (1996).

```
3:education
4:women
Selection: 2

1:Change span =  0.5
2:income
3:education
4:women
Selection: 3

1:Change span =  0.5
2:income
3:education
4:women
Selection: 4

1:Change span =  0.5
2:income
3:education
4:women
Selection: 0
>
```

The first selection (Change span) may be used to adjust the span of the local-regression smoother, which initially is set to 0.5. The plots that are produced appear in Figure 6.12. All three component + residual plots show some nonlinearity: prestige appears to increase with income, but at a declining rate; prestige also seems to increase with education, but here the relationship is nearly linear, and the departure from linearity is not simple—with the direction of curvature changing. Finally, the partial relationship between prestige and percentage women is weak but apparently nonmonotone, with higher levels of prestige associated with percentages near 0 and 100, and lower levels in the middle.

Because the relationship of prestige to income is monotone and simple, a power transformation may serve to straighten it; in contrast, we can try to model the relationship of prestige to women as a quadratic, via poly (see below). Using the Ask function facilitates trial-and-error selection of a power transformation for income:

```
> Ask(p, function(p) cr.plots(lm(prestige ~ box.cox(income, p)
+           + education + poly(women, 2)), 'box.cox(income, p)'))
Enter p : 1
Enter p : .5
Enter p : 0
Enter p : -.5
Enter p :
>
```

Specifying 'box.cox(income, p)' as the second argument to cr.plots produces only one component + residual plot each time the model is

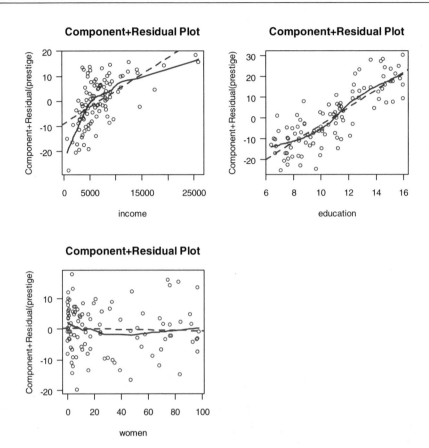

Figure 6.12   Component + residual plots for the Canadian occupational-prestige regression.

refit, bypassing the `cr.plots` menu. The resulting plots (not shown) suggest that a log transformation does a reasonable job of straightening the regression. Fitting and summarizing the resulting model:

```
> mod.prestige.2 <- lm(prestige ~ log(income, 10) + education
+     + poly(women, 2))

> summary(mod.prestige.2)

Call:
lm(formula = prestige ~ log(income, 10) + education
+     + poly(women, 2))

Residuals:
   Min    1Q Median    3Q    Max
-14.82 -5.54   0.63  4.04  18.56

Coefficients:
                Estimate Std. Error t value Pr(>|t|)
(Intercept)     -110.600     13.982   -7.91  4.2e-12
```

```
log(income, 10)    31.094     4.316    7.20  1.3e-10
education                      3.770     0.347   10.85  < 2e-16
poly(women, 2)1    15.088     9.336    1.62   0.109
poly(women, 2)2    15.871     6.970    2.28   0.025

Residual standard error: 6.95 on 97 degrees of freedom
Multiple R-Squared: 0.843,        Adjusted R-squared: 0.837
F-statistic:   131 on 4 and 97 degrees of freedom,
        p-value:    0
```

The term poly(women, 2) in the linear model fits *orthogonal polynomial* regressors of degree 1 (i.e., a linear term) and 2 (i.e., a quadratic term uncorrelated with the linear term). Except for the orthogonality of the linear and quadratic terms, this is equivalent to specifying women + I(women^2) in the model formula. [It is necessary to use the *identity function* I() to "protect" the expression women^2 because exponentiation has special meaning within a model formula, as explained in Section 4.7.] The two specifications are equivalent in the sense that when the linear and quadratic components are combined, they trace out the same partial-regression curve. Therefore, both forms of the model have identical fits to the data. Orthogonal polynomials have computational advantages, however, and they allow us to examine the t statistics for the coefficients to see the statistical significance of each term.

Using Ask in S-PLUS

Using the Ask function to refit the model repeatedly, displaying a component + residual plot for each fit, takes advantage of the "scoping" rules in R (the rules according to which the interpreter resolves references to variables in S expressions). The different scoping rules in S3 and S4 make it more difficult to use Ask in this manner. We can, however, proceed as follows:

```
> Ask(p, function(p) {
+           assign('income.p', box.cox(income, p), frame=1)
+           cr.plots(lm(prestige ~ income.p
+               + education + poly(women,2)), 'income.p')
+           })
Enter p : 1
. . .
```

A general consideration of scoping in S is well beyond the level of this book; see, for example, Venables and Ripley (2000, Section 3.4) and a brief discussion in the Web appendix to the text. A cautionary note is in order, however: Using the assign function with frame = 1 assigns a value to the global variable income.p; if a global variable by this name already exists, its value will be overwritten.

A potential problem with component + residual plots is that they can be fooled by strong nonlinear relationships among the predictors, a phenomenon called "leakage." One way to deal with this problem is to fit a polynomial (typically, quadratic) regression in the focal predictor x_j rather than only a linear term. The cr.plots function accommodates this procedure via its order argument; the default, order = 1, corresponds to a linear fit. A related approach, introduced by Cook (1993), is to use a nonparametric-regression smoother to adjust for nonlinear relationships among the predictors, a method that he terms *CERES* (for *c*ombining conditional *e*xpectations and *res*iduals). The ceres.plots function in car implements Cook's approach. For the Canadian occupational-prestige regression, higher-order component + residual plots and CERES plots are nearly identical to the standard component + residual plots in Figure 6.12.

6.4.2   Box-Tidwell Transformations of the Predictors

As in transforming the response, transformations of the predictors in regression can be estimated by maximum-likelihood. This possibility was suggested by Box and Tidwell (1962), who introduced the model

$$y_i = \alpha + \beta_1 x_{i1}^{\gamma_1} + \cdots + \beta_k x_{ik}^{\gamma_k} + \varepsilon_i,$$

where the usual assumptions are made about the errors: $\varepsilon_i \sim \text{NID}(0, \sigma^2)$. Of course, we do not necessarily want to transform *all* of the predictors, and in some contexts—such as when dummy regressors are present in the model—it does not even make sense to do so.

The Box-Tidwell regression model is a nonlinear model, which, in principle, can be fit by nonlinear least squares.[11] Box and Tidwell describe a more efficient computational approach, which is programmed in the box.tidwell function in car. Let us apply this function to the Canadian occupational-prestige regression, estimating power-transformation parameters for income and education,[12] but specifying a quadratic partial regression for women:

```
> box.tidwell(prestige ~ income + education,
+     other.x= ~poly(women, 2))
                   income education
Initial Power    -0.91030   2.24354
Score Statistic  -5.30129   2.40556
```

---

11. Nonlinear least squares is taken up in the Web appendix to the book.

12. Recall, however, that the curvature of the relationship of prestige to education changes direction, and so a power transformation is not altogether appropriate here.

```
p-value          0.00000    0.01615
MLE of Power    -0.03777    2.19283

iterations =  12
```

The one-sided formula for the argument `other.x` indicates the terms in the model that are *not* to be transformed—here the quadratic in `women`. The score tests for the power transformations of `income` and `education` suggest that both predictors need to be transformed; the maximum-likelihood estimates of the transformation parameters are $\hat{\gamma}_1 = -0.04$ for `income` (effectively, the log transformation of `income`), and $\hat{\gamma}_2 = 2.2$ for `education` (effectively, the square of `education`).

Constructed-Variable Plots for Box-Tidwell Transformations 6.4.3

Constructed variables for the Box-Tidwell transformations of the predictors are given by $x_j \log_e x_j$. These can be easily computed and added to the regression model to produce approximate score tests and constructed-variable plots. Indeed, these constructed variables are the basis for Box and Tidwell's computational approach to fitting the model and yield the score statistics printed by the `box.tidwell` function.

To obtain constructed-variable plots (Figure 6.13) for `income` and `education` in the Canadian occupational-prestige regression:

```
> mod.prestige.cv <- lm(prestige ~ income + education
+      + poly(women, 2) + I(income*log(income))
+      + I(education*log(education)))
> summary(mod.prestige.cv)

 . . .

Coefficients:
                             Estimate Std. Error t value Pr(>|t|)

 . . .

I(income * log(income))      -2.430e-03  4.584e-04  -5.301 7.46e-07
I(education * log(education)) 5.298e+00  2.202e+00   2.406   0.0181

 . . .

> av.plots(mod.prestige.cv)

1:(Intercept)
2:income
3:education
4:poly(women, 2)1
5:poly(women, 2)2
6:I(income * log(income))
7:I(education * log(education))
```

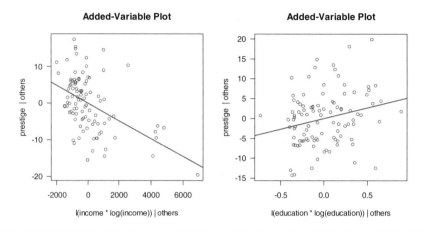

Figure 6.13   Constructed-variable plots for the Box-Tidwell transformation of income and education in the Canadian occupational-prestige regression.

```
Selection: 6

. . .

Selection: 7

. . .

Selection: 0
>
```

Note, once again, the use of the *identity function* I() to "protect" the multiplication operator *, which would otherwise be interpreted specially within a model formula, inappropriately generating "main effects" and an "interaction" (see Section 4.7).

The constructed-variable plot for income reveals some high-leverage points in determining the transformation of this predictor, but even when these points are removed, there is still substantial evidence for the transformation in the rest of the data.

6.5   COLLINEARITY AND VARIABLE SELECTION

6.5.1   Variance-Inflation Factors

When there are strong linear relationships among the predictors in a regression analysis, the precision of the estimated regression coefficients declines. The estimated sampling variance of the jth regression coefficient may be written as

$$\widehat{V}(b_j) = \frac{s^2}{(n-1)s_j^2} \times \frac{1}{1-R_j^2},$$

where s^2 is the estimated error variance, s_j^2 is the sample variance of x_j; and $1/(1-R_j^2)$, called the *variance-inflation factor* (VIF_j) for b_j, is a function of the multiple correlation R_j from the regression of x_j on the other xs. The variance-inflation factor is the simplest and most direct measure of the harm produced by collinearity: The square root of the VIF indicates how much the confidence interval for β_j is expanded relative to similar, uncorrelated data. If we wish to explicate the collinear relationships among the predictors, then we can examine the coefficients from the regression of each predictor with a large VIF on the other predictors.

The variance-inflation factor is not applicable, however, to sets of related regressors for multiple-degree-of-freedom effects, such as contrasts constructed to represent a factor or polynomial regressors. Fox and Monette (1992) generalize the notion of variance inflation by considering the relative size of the joint confidence region for the coefficients associated with a related set of regressors.[13] The resulting measure is called a *generalized variance-inflation factor* (or GVIF). If there are p regressors in a term, then $\text{GVIF}^{1/2p}$ is a one-dimensional expression of the decrease in precision of estimation due to collinearity—analogous to taking the square root of the usual variance-inflation factor. When $p = 1$, the GVIF reduces to the usual VIF.

The `vif` function in `car` calculates variance-inflation factors for the terms in a linear model. When each term has 1 degree of freedom, the usual VIF is returned; otherwise, the GVIF is calculated.

As a first example, consider the data on the 1980 U.S. Census undercount in the data frame `Ericksen` (from work by Ericksen, Kadane, & Tukey, 1989):

```
> detach(Prestige)
> data(Ericksen)
> Ericksen
```

---

13. * Let $\mathbf{R}_{11}$ represent the correlation matrix among the regressors in the set in question, $\mathbf{R}_{22}$ the correlation matrix among the other regressors in the model, and $\mathbf{R}$ the correlation matrix among all of the regressors in the model. Fox and Monette show that the squared area, volume, or hypervolume of the joint confidence region for the coefficients in either set is expanded by the generalized variance-inflation factor

$$\text{GVIF} = \frac{\det \mathbf{R}_{11} \det \mathbf{R}_{22}}{\det \mathbf{R}}$$

relative to similar data in which the two sets of regressors are uncorrelated with each other. This measure is independent of the bases selected to span the subspaces of the two sets of regressors and so, for example, is independent of the contrast-coding scheme employed for a factor.

	minority	crime	poverty	language	highschool
Alabama	26.1	49	18.9	0.2	43.5
Alaska	5.7	62	10.7	1.7	17.5
Arizona	18.9	81	13.2	3.2	27.6
. . .					
San.Francisco	24.8	107	13.7	9.2	26.0
Washington.DC	72.6	102	18.6	1.1	32.9

	housing	city	conventional	undercount
Alabama	7.6	state	0	-0.04
Alaska	23.6	state	100	3.35
Arizona	8.1	state	18	2.48
. . .				
San.Francisco	20.3	city	0	5.18
Washington.DC	21.0	city	0	5.93

These variables describe 66 areas of the United States, including 16 major cities, the 38 states without major cities, and the remainders of the 12 states that contain the 16 major cities. The following variables are included:

- minority: percentage of residents who are black or Hispanic.

- crime: serious crimes per 1000 residents.

- poverty: percentage of residents who are poor.

- language: percentage having difficulty speaking or writing English.

- highschool: percentage of those 25 years of age or older who have not finished high school.

- housing: percentage of dwellings in small, multiunit buildings.

- city: a factor with levels state and city.

- conventional: percentage of households counted by personal enumeration (rather than by mail-back questionnaire with follow-ups).

- undercount: the estimated percentage undercount (with negative numbers indicating an estimated overcount).

Let us regress the Census undercount on the other variables:

```
> mod.census <- lm(undercount ~ ., data=Ericksen)
> summary(mod.census)

Call:
lm(formula = undercount ~ ., data = Ericksen)

Residuals:
    Min     1Q  Median     3Q     Max
-2.8356 -0.8033 -0.0553  0.7050  4.2467
```

```
Coefficients:
              Estimate Std. Error t value Pr(>|t|)
(Intercept)  -0.61141    1.72084   -0.36  0.72368
minority      0.07983    0.02261    3.53  0.00083
crime         0.03012    0.01300    2.32  0.02412
poverty      -0.17837    0.08492   -2.10  0.04012
language      0.21512    0.09221    2.33  0.02320
highschool    0.06129    0.04477    1.37  0.17642
housing      -0.03496    0.02463   -1.42  0.16126
citystate    -1.15998    0.77064   -1.51  0.13779
conventional  0.03699    0.00925    4.00  0.00019

Residual standard error: 1.43 on 57 degrees of freedom
Multiple R-Squared: 0.708,       Adjusted R-squared: 0.667
F-statistic: 17.2 on 8 and 57 degrees of freedom,
   p-value: 1.04e-012
```

Note the compact model formula: When we include the data argument to lm, we may use a dot (·) on the right-hand side of the model formula to represent all the variables in the data frame with the exception of the response (here undercount).

Checking for collinearity, we see that three coefficients (for minority, poverty, and highschool) have variance-inflation factors exceeding 4, indicating that confidence intervals for these coefficients are more than twice as wide as they would be for uncorrelated predictors:

```
> vif(mod.census)
     minority        crime      poverty     language    highschool
       5.0091       3.3436       4.6252       1.6356        4.6192
      housing         city conventional
       1.8717       3.5378       1.6913
```

To illustrate the computation of generalized variance-inflation factors, I return to Ornstein's interlocking-directorate regression, where it turns out that collinearity is relatively slight:

```
> vif(mod.ornstein)
          GVIF Df GVIF^(1/2Df)
assets 2.6748  1       1.6355
nation 1.4347  3       1.0620
sector 3.6538  9       1.0746
```

Other, more complex approaches to collinearity include principal-components analysis of the predictors or standardized predictors and singular-value decomposition of the model matrix or the mean-centered model matrix. These, too, are simple to implement in S. See the princomp and prcomp functions (in the mva library in R) and the svd and eigen functions (discussed in Chapter 8).

6.5.2 Variable Selection

Collinearity is a problem with the data, not (necessarily) with the regression model. That is, it is perfectly possible to have a well-specified regression model for which the data do not contain sufficient information to produce informative coefficient estimates. For this reason, there can be no general solution to the problem of collinearity, and methods that purport to provide a general solution do so at the expense of implicitly changing the questions asked of the data or imposing, often surreptitiously, additional constraints on the model.

The situation is somewhat different, however, when the goal of the regression analysis is to produce a prediction equation, rather than to understand the manner in which the predictors influence the response. As long as the x values for new observations to be predicted are within the configuration of x values on which the prediction equation was developed, we can hope for success.

Perhaps the most common approach in this setting is variable selection, where we seek to reduce the predictors to an optimal subset. Variable selection can also be useful in the absence of collinearity, although selection of noncollinear predictors is relatively straightforward. Finally, by way of preamble, in performing variable selection we should seek to avoid capitalizing on chance—an objective that can be achieved by some form of cross-validation.[14]

There are two general (and many specific) approaches to variable selection: *Stepwise methods* seek good subsets of predictors by adding or subtracting terms one at a time; *optimal subset methods*, in contrast, locate the subset of predictors of a given size that maximizes some measure of fit to the data, perhaps even by enumerating all the subsets of predictors.

Several functions in S may be employed for variable selection. Let us look at step and regsubsets; in R, step is in the base library and regsubsets in the leaps library.

Variable-Selection Functions in S-PLUS

In S-PLUS, the standard step function is somewhat different from the one described here, which instead corresponds more closely to the stepAIC function in the MASS library. As well, there is no regsubsets function, but the leaps function performs the same task, albeit with different syntax. See help(step) and help(leaps) for details.

---

14. In cross-validation, the data are divided into two or more parts; a statistical model fit to part of the data is then tested on the remainder. See, for example, Fox (1997, Chapter 16).

The step function, as the name implies, takes a stepwise approach to variable selection and can perform both forward and backward selection (i.e., adding terms to, and eliminating terms from, the model). An advantage of step is that it is applicable to a broad range of models (e.g., many GLMs) and that it respects multiple-degree-of-freedom terms and relations of marginality among terms: step will not, for example, remove one of a set of contrasts for a factor, nor will it remove a main effect that is marginal to an interaction that is retained in the model. A disadvantage of all stepwise methods is that they may fail to find optimal subsets of predictors. Researchers using these methods are also prone to overinterpret the results: There are often *many* subsets of predictors of a given size that are nearly equally good. This, of course, is not the fault of the step function.

By default, step attempts to maximize the AIC (Akaike information criterion, see Section 5.2) by both adding and subtracting terms. Applying step to the model that I fit to the Census undercount data produces the following result:

```
> census.step <- step(mod.census)
Start:  AIC= 55.21
 undercount ~ minority + crime + poverty + language + highschool +
    housing + city + conventional

                 Df Sum of Sq   RSS    AIC
<none>                         116.0   55.2
- highschool      1      3.8   119.8   55.3
- housing         1      4.1   120.1   55.5
- city            1      4.6   120.6   55.8
- poverty         1      9.0   125.0   58.1
- crime           1     10.9   126.9   59.2
- language        1     11.1   127.1   59.2
- minority        1     25.4   141.4   66.3
- conventional    1     32.5   148.5   69.5
```

Starting with the full model, step has discovered that the AIC *goes up* when any one of the predictors is eliminated, and, consequently, it immediately terminates, returning a linear-model object identical to the original model:

```
> summary(census.step)

Call:
lm(formula = undercount ~ minority + crime + poverty + language +
    highschool + housing + city + conventional, data = Ericksen)
. . .
```

The AIC applies a relatively light penalty for lack of parsimony, adding twice the number of parameters to the deviance for the model. The alternative BIC (Bayes information criterion) applies a heavier penalty, adding $\log_e n$ times the number of parameters to the deviance. The step function accommodates the BIC through the argument k, which specifies the *multiple* of the number of parameters to employ as a penalty. Here, $n = 66$, and so:

```
> census.step.bic <- step(mod.census, k=log(66))
Start:  AIC= 74.92
 undercount ~ minority + crime + poverty + language + highschool +
    housing + city + conventional

                Df Sum of Sq   RSS   AIC
- highschool     1       3.8 119.8  72.9
- housing        1       4.1 120.1  73.0
- city           1       4.6 120.6  73.3
<none>                       116.0  74.9
- poverty        1       9.0 125.0  75.6
- crime          1      10.9 126.9  76.7
- language       1      11.1 127.1  76.7
- minority       1      25.4 141.4  83.8
- conventional   1      32.5 148.5  87.0

Step:  AIC= 72.86
 undercount ~ minority + crime + poverty + language + housing +
    city + conventional

                Df Sum of Sq   RSS   AIC
- housing        1       2.3 122.1  69.9
- city           1       4.2 124.0  71.0
- poverty        1       5.2 125.0  71.5
- crime          1       7.4 127.2  72.6
<none>                       119.8  72.9
- language       1       8.1 127.9  73.0
- minority       1      30.8 150.6  83.8
- conventional   1      31.0 150.8  83.9


 .  .  .


Step:  AIC= 66.33
 undercount ~ minority + crime + language + conventional

                Df Sum of Sq   RSS   AIC
<none>                       131.3  66.3
- language       1      12.5 143.8  68.2
- crime          1      14.7 146.0  69.1
- conventional   1      26.6 157.8  74.3
- minority       1      59.8 191.1  86.9
```

Using the BIC (still labeled AIC in the output), step eventually settles on a subset of four predictors: language, crime, conventional, and minority.

We can start step in a forward direction by beginning with a model including only the regression constant and supplying candidate predictors via the scope argument:

```
> census.step.forward <- step(lm(undercount ~ 1, data=Ericksen),
+     scope= ~ minority + crime + poverty + language
+        + highschool + housing + city + conventional,
+     k=log(66))
Start:  AIC= 122.58
 undercount ~ 1
```

	Df	Sum of Sq	RSS	AIC
+ minority	1	196	201	82
+ city	1	178	219	88
+ crime	1	175	221	88
+ language	1	111	286	105
+ poverty	1	64	333	115
+ housing	1	41	356	120
<none>			397	123
+ highschool	1	8	389	125
+ conventional	1	0.041	397	127

```
Step:  AIC= 81.87
 undercount ~ minority
```

	Df	Sum of Sq	RSS	AIC
+ highschool	1	30	171	75
+ language	1	30	171	76
+ crime	1	29	172	76
+ conventional	1	27	174	77
+ city	1	17	184	80
<none>			201	82
+ poverty	1	12	189	82
+ housing	1	2	199	85
- minority	1	196	397	123

. . .

```
Step:  AIC= 66.33
 undercount ~ minority + conventional + crime + language
```

	Df	Sum of Sq	RSS	AIC
<none>			131.3	66.3
+ poverty	1	6.5	124.8	67.2
- language	1	12.5	143.8	68.2
- crime	1	14.7	146.0	69.1
+ housing	1	2.2	129.1	69.4
+ city	1	1.9	129.3	69.5
+ highschool	1	0.4	130.8	70.3
- conventional	1	26.6	157.8	74.3
- minority	1	59.8	191.1	86.9

In this case, we arrive at the same subset of predictors by both approaches, but starting with the full model is generally more reliable.

Using an efficient computational method, the `regsubsets` function in the `leaps` library finds the optimal subset of predictors of each size. By default, the function returns only optimal subsets and only computes subsets up to size 8; these defaults can be changed using the `nbest` and `nvmax` arguments, respectively.

The `leaps` library includes `plot` and `summary` methods for objects returned by `regsubsets`, but I prefer the `subsets` function in `car`. By default, `subsets` plots the BIC for each model against the number of predictors, automatically generating a code for the predictors in the model:

```
> library(leaps)
> census.subsets <- regsubsets(undercount ~ ., nbest=10,
+    data=Ericksen)
> subsets(census.subsets)
>
```

Alternatively, we could plot the R^2 for each model, the adjusted R^2, the residual sum of squares, or Mallows's C_p statistic. The BIC plot appears in the left-hand panel of Figure 6.14. The `plot.subsets` function positions the legend interactively, with a left-button mouse click indicating the upper-left corner of the legend. This graph clearly conveys the large number of models that are roughly equally effective, but it is impossible to read the individual models. In the right-hand panel, I focus on subsets of three to five predictors, which have the lowest BICs:

```
> subsets(census.subsets, min.size=3, max.size=5, legend=F)
>
```

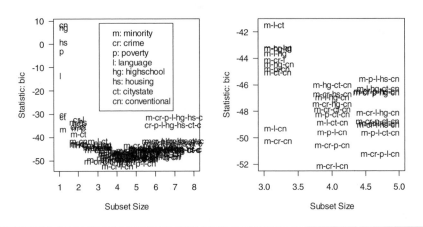

Figure 6.14   Plots of BIC against subset size for up to 10 best subsets of each size. The initial model is for the regression of the Census undercount on 8 predictors.

I could also restrict the vertical axis of the plot, by specifying the ylim argument to subsets.

For this example, the model with the smallest BIC overall (including the predictors minority, crime, language, and conventional) is the same as the one identified by the stepwise approach.

DIAGNOSTICS FOR GENERALIZED LINEAR MODELS   6.6

Most of the diagnostics of the preceding sections extend relatively straightforwardly to generalized linear models. These extensions typically take advantage of the computation of maximum-likelihood estimates for generalized linear models by iterated weighted least squares. The final weighted least squares fit linearizes the model and provides a quadratic approximation to the log-likelihood. Approximate diagnostics are then either based directly on the weighted least squares solution or derived from statistics easily calculated from this solution. Seminal work on the extension of linear least squares diagnostics to generalized linear models was done by Pregibon (1981), Landwehr, Pregibon, and Shoemaker (1984), Wang (1985, 1987), and Williams (1987).

The following functions in car have methods for generalized linear models: rstudent, hatvalues, cookd, dfbeta, dfbetas, outlier.test, av.plots, cr.plots, and ceres.plots. I will illustrate the use of these functions selectively, rather than exhaustively repeating all the topics covered for linear models in the previous sections of the chapter.

Outlier, Leverage, and Influence Diagnostics   6.6.1

Hat Values

Hat values for a generalized linear model can be taken directly from the final iteration of the IWLS procedure for fitting the model, and have the usual interpretation—except that, unlike in a linear model, the hat values in a generalized linear model depend on y as well as on the configuration of the xs.

Residuals

Several kinds of residuals can be defined for generalized linear models:

■ *Response residuals* are simply the differences between the observed response and its estimated expected value: $y_i - \hat{\mu}_i$.

■ *Working residuals* are the residuals from the final WLS fit. These may be used to define partial residuals for component + residual plots (see below).

■ *Pearson residuals* are casewise components of the Pearson goodness-of-fit statistic for the model:

$$\frac{\hat{\phi}^{1/2}(y_i - \hat{\mu}_i)}{\sqrt{\widehat{V}(y_i|\eta_i)}},$$

where ϕ is the dispersion parameter for the model and $V(y_i|\eta_i)$ is the variance of the response given the linear predictor (see Chapter 5).

■ *Standardized Pearson residuals* correct for the conditional response variation and for the leverage of the observations:

$$r_{Pi} = \frac{y_i - \hat{\mu}_i}{\sqrt{\widehat{V}(y_i|\eta_i)(1 - h_i)}}.$$

■ *Deviance residuals*, d_i, are the square roots of the casewise components of the residual deviance, attaching the sign of $y_i - \hat{\mu}_i$.

■ *Standardized deviance residuals* are

$$r_{Di} = \frac{d_i}{\sqrt{\hat{\phi}(1 - h_i)}}.$$

■ Several different approximations to studentized residuals have been suggested. To calculate exact studentized residuals would require literally refitting the model, deleting each observation in turn and noting the decline in the deviance; this procedure, of course, is computationally unattractive. I use Williams's approximation:

$$\text{rstudent}_i = \sqrt{(1 - h_i)r_{Di}^2 + h_i r_{Pi}^2},$$

where, once again, the sign is taken from $y_i - \hat{\mu}_i$. A Bonferroni outlier test using the standard normal distribution may be based on the largest absolute studentized residual.

Influence Measures

An approximation to Cook's distance influence measure is

$$D_i = \frac{r_{Pi}^2}{\hat{\phi}(k + 1)} \times \frac{h_i}{1 - h_i}.$$

This is essentially Williams's definition, except that I divide by the estimated dispersion $\hat{\phi}$ to scale D_i as an F statistic rather than as a chi-square statistic.

Approximate values of dfbeta$_{ij}$ and dfbetas$_{ij}$ may be obtained directly from the final iteration of the IWLS procedure.

I am aware of two extensions of added-variable plots to generalized linear models: Suppose that the focal regressor is x_j. Wang (1985) proceeds by refitting the model with x_j removed, extracting the working residuals from this fit. Then, x_j is regressed on the other xs by WLS, using the weights from the last IWLS step and obtaining residuals. Finally, the two sets of residuals are plotted against each other. The Arc software developed by Cook and Weisberg (1999) employs a similar procedure, except that weights are not used in the least squares regression of x_j on the other xs. The av.plots function in the car library implements both approaches, with Wang's procedure as the default.

To illustrate some of these results, recall from Chapter 5 the binary logistic regression of labor-force participation on husband's income and presence of children for young married Canadian women:

```
> data(Womenlf)
> attach(Womenlf)
> mod.working <- glm(partic != 'not.work' ~ hincome + children,
+     family=binomial)
> summary(mod.working)

Call:
glm(formula = partic != 'not.work' ~ hincome + children,
    family = binomial)

Deviance Residuals:
    Min      1Q  Median      3Q     Max
 -1.677  -0.865  -0.777   0.929   1.997

Coefficients:
                 Estimate Std. Error z value Pr(>|z|)
(Intercept)        1.3358     0.3835    3.48   0.0005
hincome           -0.0423     0.0198   -2.14   0.0323
childrenpresent   -1.5756     0.2921   -5.39  6.9e-08

(Dispersion parameter for binomial family taken to be 1)

    Null deviance: 356.15  on 262  degrees of freedom
Residual deviance: 319.73  on 260  degrees of freedom
AIC: 325.7

Number of Fisher Scoring iterations: 3
```

The expression partic != 'not.work' creates a logical vector, which serves as the binary response variable in the model.

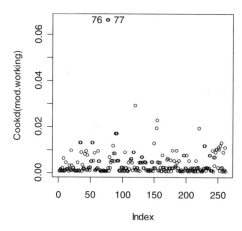

Figure 6.15   Index plot of Cook's distances from the logistic regression of women's labor-force participation on husband's income and presence of children. Two observations were identified interactively with the mouse.

To calculate and plot Cook's distances for this fit (Figure 6.15):

```
> plot(cookd(mod.working))
> identify(1:length(partic), cookd(mod.working))
[1] 76 77
```

The expression `1:length(partic)` generates the observation indices to be used as horizontal coordinates by `identify`.

Note that I have extracted the Cook's distances twice; it would have been more efficient to save the values in a variable, but unless the data set is large, the calculation is nearly instantaneous anyway. Clearly, observations 76 and 77 have much larger Cook's distances than any of the other observations.

Let us follow up by calculating and plotting dfbeta$_{ij}$ (Figure 6.16):

```
> dfb <- dfbeta(mod.working)
> dfb[1:5,]   # first 5 obs.
   (Intercept)     hincome  childrenpresent
1    0.0021293  -0.00014152      -0.0102200
2   -0.0025005   0.00016620      -0.0104562
3    0.0273334  -0.00181673      -0.0057556
4    0.0161297  -0.00107207      -0.0091358
5    0.0099899  -0.00066398      -0.0097021

> plot(dfb[,2], ylab='dfbeta(hincome)')   # for b1
> identify(1:length(partic), dfb[,2])
[1] 76 77

> plot(dfb[,3], ylab='dfbeta(children)')   # for b2
>
```

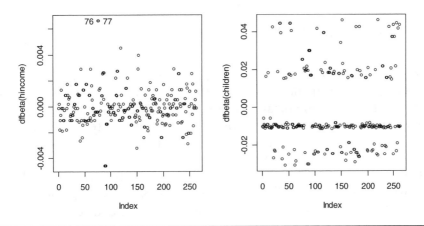

Figure 6.16   Index plots of dfbeta for the coefficients of husband's income and presence of children.

Comparing the dfbeta_{ij} values to the magnitudes of the coefficients in the logistic regression, none of the observations appears terribly influential, although observations 76 and 77 do stand out in their impact on the husband's income coefficient. These two observations are for women who were in the labor force despite having children and high-income husbands. Removing just one of these two observations does not alter the results much (as the approximate dfbeta values suggest, and the reader can confirm), but removing both observations changes the coefficient of husband's income by more than 40 percent:

```
> summary(update(mod.working, subset=-c(76, 77)))

. . .

Coefficients:
                Estimate Std. Error z value Pr(>|z|)
(Intercept)       1.6090     0.4051    3.97  7.1e-05
hincome          -0.0603     0.0212   -2.85   0.0044
childrenpresent  -1.6476     0.2977   -5.53  3.1e-08

. . .
```

Two factors combine to produce this result: (1) The linear approximations involved in calculating deletion diagnostics for GLMs tend to understate the effect of deleting observations, and (2) observations 76 and 77, as an influential pair, partly mask each other's presence.

Notice the banding in the index plot of dfbeta_{ij} for the children coefficient. The four bands are produced by the binary response and the dummy regressor, each of which takes on only two values. When the response is discrete, diagnostic plots for GLMs often show these kinds of effects.

6.6.2 Nonlinearity Diagnostics

Component + residual and CERES plots also extend straightforwardly to generalized linear models. Nonparametric smoothing of the resulting scatterplots can be important to interpretation, especially in models for binary responses, where the discreteness of the response makes the plots difficult to examine. Similar effects can occur for binomial and Poisson data.

Component + residual and CERES plots use the linearized model from the last step of the IWLS fit. For example, the partial residual for x_j adds the working residual to $b_j x_{ij}$; the component + residual plot graphs the partial residual against x_j.

An illustrative component + residual plot, for assets in Ornstein's interlocking-directorate Poisson regression (from Chapter 5), appears in Figure 6.17 and is constructed by the following S commands:

```
> detach(Womenlf)
> attach(Ornstein)
> mod.ornstein.pois <- glm(interlocks ~ assets + nation + sector,
+     family=poisson)
> cr.plots(mod.ornstein.pois)

1:Change span =  0.5
2:assets
3:nation
4:sector
Selection: 2
```

. . .

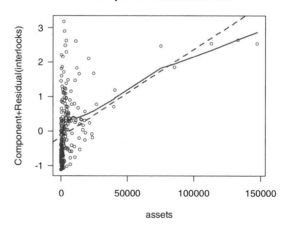

Figure 6.17   Component + residual plot for assets in Ornstein's interlocking-directorate Poisson regression.

Component+Residual Plot

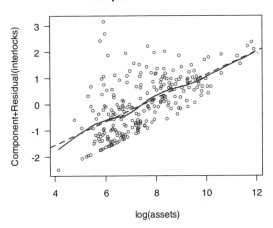

Figure 6.18   Component + residual plot for `log(assets)` in the respecified Poisson regression model for Ornstein's interlocking-directorate data.

This plot is difficult to examine because of the substantial positive skew in assets, but it appears as if the assets slope is a good deal steeper at the left than at the right. I therefore investigated transforming assets down the ladder of powers and roots, eventually arriving at the log transformation, the component + residual plot for which appears quite straight (Figure 6.18):

```
> mod.ornstein.pois.2 <- glm(interlocks ~ log(assets) + nation
+    + sector, family=poisson)
> cr.plots(mod.ornstein.pois.2, 'log(assets)')
>
```

The Box-Tidwell constructed-variable plot for power transformation of an x also extends directly to generalized linear models, augmenting the model with the constructed variable $x_j \log_e x_j$. For example, for Ornstein's interlocking-directorate Poisson regression, we may proceed as follows, fitting an auxiliary model and obtaining an added-variable plot for the constructed variable (Figure 6.19):

```
> mod.ornstein.pois.cv <- update(mod.ornstein.pois,
+    . ~ . + I(assets*log(assets)))

> summary(mod.ornstein.pois.cv)


. . .
```

Coefficients:

	Estimate	Std. Error	z value	Pr(>|z|)
(Intercept)	2.14e+00	5.36e-02	39.89	< 2e-16
assets	2.81e-04	1.69e-05	16.65	< 2e-16

Added-Variable Plot

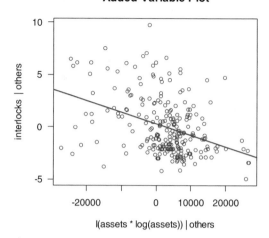

Figure 6.19   Constructed-variable plot for the power transformation of assets in Ornstein's interlocking-directorate Poison regression.

```
. . .
I(assets * log(assets)) -2.18e-05    1.41e-06   -15.42   < 2e-16

. . .

> av.plots(mod.ornstein.pois.cv, 'I(assets * log(assets))')
[1] 1 2
```

The z test statistic for the constructed variable leaves little doubt about the need for transforming assets. The constructed-variable plot supports the transformation.

An estimate of the transformation parameter can be obtained from the coefficient of assets in the *original* Poisson regression (2.09×10^{-5}) and the coefficient of the constructed variable (-2.18×10^{-5}):

$$\tilde{\lambda} = 1 + \frac{-2.18 \times 10^{-5}}{2.09 \times 10^{-5}} = -0.043,$$

that is, essentially the log transformation, $\lambda = 0$.[15]

I conclude with a reexamination of the binary logistic-regression model fit to Mroz's women's labor-force participation data (in Chapter 5). Recall that one of the predictors in this model—the log of the woman's expected wage rate (lwg)—has a peculiar definition: For women in the labor force (for whom the response variable in the regression, lfp, is 1), lwg is the log of the *actual* wage rate; while for women not in the labor force (for whom lfp is 0), lwg is the log of the *predicted* wage rate.

15. Essentially the same calculation is the basis of Box and Tidwell's iterative procedure for finding transformations in linear least squares regression.

Component+Residual Plot

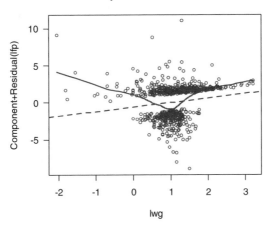

Figure 6.20   Component + residual plot for `lwg` in the binary logistic regression for Mroz's women's labor-force participation data.

To obtain a component + residual plot for `lwg` (Figure 6.20):

```
> detach(Ornstein)
> data(Mroz)
> attach(Mroz)
> mod.mroz <- glm(lfp ~ k5 + k618 + age + wc + hc + lwg + inc,
+     family=binomial)
> cr.plots(mod.mroz, 'lwg')
>
```

The peculiar split in the plot reflects the binary response variable, with the lower cluster of points corresponding to `lfp = 0` and the upper cluster to `lfp = 1`. It is apparent that `lwg` is much less variable when `lfp = 0`, inducing an artifactual curvilinear relationship between `lwg` and `lfp`: We expect fitted values (such as the values of `lwg` when `lfp = 0`) to be more homogeneous than observed values, because fitted values lack a residual component of variation.

I leave it to the reader to construct component + residual or CERES plots for the other predictors in the model.

CHAPTER 7

Drawing Graphs

One of the strengths of S is its ability to produce high-quality statistical graphs. This strength reflects the origin of S at Bell Labs, long a center for innovation in statistical graphics.

From one point of view, standard S graphics are very simple: Making graphs in S is like drawing in ink on a piece of paper. Once an object is drawn, it cannot be erased (except by drawing over it, for example in another color), and if a graph is to be changed in some fundamental way, it is necessary to redraw it. Interaction with S graphs is limited to identifying points and locating coordinates. Graphics windows can also be resized in the normal manner—by dragging a side or corner with the mouse. There is currently a great deal of interest in extending graphics in R and S-PLUS. R, for example, may be linked to the XGobi and GGobi systems for interactive three-dimensional graphics (Swayne et al. 1998), and S-PLUS provides several extensions to the S graphics system. This chapter, however, focuses on standard S graphics.

The simplicity of S graphics is also one of its attractions. First, pursuing the ink-on-paper analogy, the user can build up a complex S graph in a sequence of simple operations. Showing you how to do this is the principal task of the present chapter.

Second, although the graphical model in S is simple, there are *many* useful and sophisticated kinds of graphs that are already programmed in S. Frequently, there is a `plot` method that produces a standard graph or set of graphs for objects of a given class (try plotting a data frame or a linear-model object, for example). Indeed, one of the goals of the car library is to provide functions that make it easy to create graphs—such as added-variable plots and component + residual plots—that are useful in regression analysis (see, in particular, Chapters 3 and 6). In most instances, you will be able to use an existing function to create the graph that you want in a single command; the present chapter shows you how to proceed on those relatively rare occasions when you have to innovate.

This chapter, as well as the following chapter on programming, deals with general matters, and I have employed many of the techniques discussed here in the earlier parts of the book. Rather than introducing this material near the beginning of the book, however, I prefer to regard previous examples of S graphs as background and motivation.

7.1   A GENERAL APPROACH TO S GRAPHICS

It helps to think concretely about drawing graphs. When I want to construct an especially complicated graph, for example, I generally start with a rough paper sketch, showing all the elements of the graph. I can then think more clearly about how to get S to draw what I need.

For the most part, the discussion in this chapter is confined to two-dimensional coordinate plots, and a logical first step in drawing such a graph is to define a coordinate system. Sometimes that first step will include drawing axes and axis labels on the graph, along with a rectangular frame enclosing the plotting region; sometimes, however, these elements will be omitted or added in separate steps, in order to assert greater control over what is plotted. The guts of the graph generally consist of plotted points, lines, text, and, occasionally, shapes and arrows. Such elements are added as required to the plot. The current section describes, in a general way, how to perform these tasks.

7.1.1   Defining a Coordinate System: plot

In S, plot is a generic function, the default method for which can be used to make a variety of point and line graphs; plot can also be used to define a coordinate space, which is my main reason for discussing it here. The list of arguments to the R implementation of plot.default is also a good starting point for understanding how to use the S plotting system[1]:

```
> args(plot.default)
function (x, y = NULL, type = "p", xlim = NULL, ylim = NULL,
    log = "", main = NULL, sub = NULL, xlab = NULL, ylab = NULL,
    ann = par("ann"), axes = TRUE, frame.plot = axes,
```

---

1. The arguments to the S-PLUS version of plot.default are less informative.

```
        panel.first = NULL, panel.last = NULL, col = par("col"),
        bg = NA, pch = par("pch"), cex = 1, lty = par("lty"),
        lab = par("lab"), lwd = par("lwd"), asp = NA, ...)
NULL
```

To see in full detail what the arguments mean, consult the documentation for plot.default[2]; the following points are of immediate interest, however:

■ The first two arguments, x and y, can provide, respectively, the horizontal and vertical coordinates of points or lines to be plotted and also define a data-coordinate system for the graph. The argument x is required. In constructing a complex graph, a good starting point is often to use x and y to establish the range of the axes—which can be as simple as specifying each of these arguments as a two-element vector.

■ type, naturally enough, determines the type of graph to be drawn, of which there are several: The default type, 'p', plots points at the coordinates specified by x and y. The character used to draw the points is given by the argument pch; in R, but not in S-PLUS, pch may designate a vector of characters, which may therefore differ for different points. Specifying type='l' produces a line graph; specifying type='n' sets up the plotting region to accommodate the data but plots nothing. Other types of graphs available in both R and S-PLUS include: 'b', both points and lines; 'o', points and lines overlaid; 'h', "histogram-like" vertical lines; and 's' and 'S', "stairstep-like" lines, starting horizontally and vertically, respectively.

■ The arguments xlim and ylim may be used to define the limits of the horizontal and vertical axes; usually, these arguments are unnecessary, because S will pick reasonable limits from x and y, but they provide an additional measure of control over the graph. For example, extending the limits of an axis can provide room for explanatory text; contracting the limits can cause some data to be omitted from the graph.

■ The log argument makes it easy to define logarithmic axes: log='x' produces a logged horizontal axis, log='y', a logged vertical axis, and log='xy' (or log='yx'), logged axes for both variables.

■ xlab and ylab take character-string arguments, which are used to label the axes; similarly, the argument main may be used to place a title above the plot (or the title function may be called subsequently to add a title). The default axis label, NULL, is potentially misleading, in

---

2. In general, in this chapter, I will not discuss all of the arguments available for the graphics functions that I describe. Details are available in the documentation for R and S-PLUS.

that by default `plot` constructs labels from the arguments x and y. To suppress the axis labels, either specify empty labels—e.g., `xlab=""`—or (in R) set `ann=FALSE`.

■ Setting `axes=FALSE` and (in R) `frame.plot=FALSE`, respectively, suppresses drawing axes and a box around the plotting region.

■ In R, the argument `col` may be used to specify the color (or colors) for the points and lines drawn on the plot; in S-PLUS, `col` gives the color for the plot as a whole. Color selection is described in Section 7.1.3.

■ `cex` (for "character expansion") specifies the relative size of points in the graph; the default size is `cex=1`. In R, `cex` may be a vector, indicating the size of each point individually; in S-PLUS, `cex` is a single value applying to all points (and text) in the graph.

■ The arguments `lty` and `lwd` select the type and width of lines drawn on the graph; see Section 7.1.2 for more information on drawing lines.

For example, the following command sets up the blank plot in Figure 7.1, with axes and frame, but without axis labels:

```
> plot(c(0,1), c(0,1), type='n', xlab="", ylab="")
>
```

Several arguments to `plot`, such as `pch` and `col`, take their defaults from the `par` function. This function is used to set and retrieve a variety of graphics parameters. For instance,

```
> par('col')
[1] "black"
```

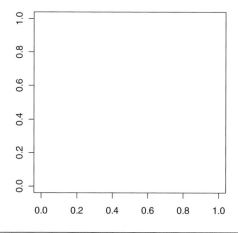

Figure 7.1   Empty plot, produced by `plot(c(0,1), c(0,1), type='n', xlab="", ylab="")`.

To change the general default plotting color to red, for example, we could (in R) enter par(col='red'); in S-PLUS, colors are specified only by number—see Section 7.1.3. To print out the current values of all the plotting parameters, call par with no arguments:

```
> par()
$adj
[1] 0.5

$ann
[1] TRUE

$ask
[1] FALSE

. . .

$yaxs
[1] "r"

$yaxt
[1] "s"

$ylog
[1] FALSE
```

Table 7.1 presents brief descriptions of some of the plotting parameters that can be set by par; many of these can also be used as arguments to plot and other graphics functions. For complete information on the plotting parameters available in R and S-PLUS, see the documentation for par.

Adding Graphical Elements: axis, points, lines, text, and so on   7.1.2

Having defined a coordinate system, we typically want to add graphical elements, such as points and lines, to the plot. Several functions useful for this purpose are described here.

As you might expect, points and lines add points and lines to the current plot; either function can be used to plot points, lines, or both, but their default behavior follows their names. The argument pch is used to select the plotting symbol, as the following example (which produces Figure 7.2) illustrates:

```
> plot(1:25, xlab='Symbol Number', ylab="", type='n')
> for (pch in 1:25) points(pch, pch, pch=pch)
> lines(1:25, type='h', lty=2)
>
```

Table 7.1   Some plotting parameters set by `par`: [R], R only; [S], S-PLUS only.

Parameter	Default Value	Purpose
adj	0.5	Text-string justification: 0 = left, 0.5 = centered, 1 = right
ann [R]	TRUE	Annotate graph
cex	1	Relative character expansion
col	'black' [R], 1 [S]	Default color
las	0	Orientation of axis labels: 0 = parallel to axis
lty	'solid' [R], 1 [S]	Default line type
lwd	1	Default line width
mar	c(5.1, 4.1, 4.1, 2.1)	Plot margins in lines of text: bottom, left, top, right
mfcol, mfrow	c(1,1)	Plot array, filled by columns or rows: number of rows, columns
new	FALSE	If FALSE, next high-level plotting function clears plots
pch	1	Plotting symbol: number or character
pin	Current values	Size of plot in inches: width, height
pty	'm'	Type of plotting region: 'm' maximal; 's' square
srt	0	Rotation of character strings, in degrees
usr	Current values	Range of data ("user") coordinates: x-min, x-max, y-min, y-max

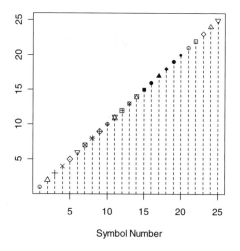

Figure 7.2   Plotting symbols (pch) by number.

The plot function sets up the coordinate system for the graph. A for loop cycles through the plotting symbols, numbered from 1 through 25, and points is used to place each symbol on the plot at the coordinates corresponding to its number. Finally, the lines function draws broken vertical lines (selected by lty=2: see below) up to the symbols; because lines is given only one vector of coordinates, these are interpreted as vertical coordinates, to be plotted against their indices as horizontal coordinates (here, the integers from 1 through 25). Specifying type='h' draws spike-like (or histogram-like) lines up to the points.

As mentioned in the preceding section, in R (but not in S-PLUS) pch can be given a vector of symbol numbers, and line types may be specified by name as well as by number; consequently, a more compact way of producing the plot in Figure 7.2 in R would be:

```
> plot(1:25, pch=1:25, xlab='Symbol Number', ylab="")
> lines(1:25, type='h', lty='dashed')
>
```

One can also plot arbitrary characters, as the following example (shown in Figure 7.3) illustrates:

```
> plot(1:26, xlab='letters', ylab="", type='n', axes=F)
> box()
> for (letter in 1:26)
+     points(letter, 27 - letter, pch=letters[letter])
>
```

Again, a more compact version in R replaces the for loop with a single call to points; and in R, we can replace the separate call to

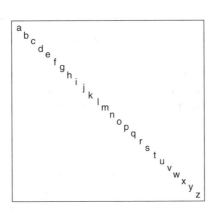

letters

Figure 7.3   Plotting characters—the lower case letters.

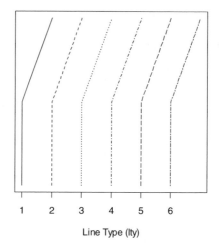

Figure 7.4   Line types (lty), by number.

box, which places a frame around the plotting region, by the argument
frame.plot=T in the initial call to plot.

As shown in Figure 7.4, several different line types are available in S
plots:

```
> plot(c(1,7), c(0,1), type='n', axes=F,
+       xlab='Line Type (lty)', ylab="")
> box()
> axis(1, at=1:6)  # x-axis
> for (lty in 1:6) lines(c(lty, lty, lty + 1),
+                   c(0, 0.5, 1), lty=lty)
>
```

The lines function connects the points whose coordinates are given by
its first two arguments, x and y. If a coordinate is NA, then the line drawn
will be discontinuous. Line type (lty) may be specified by number (as
here) or, in R, by name, such as 'solid', 'dashed', and so on. Line
width is given by the lwd parameter, which defaults to 1. The exact effect
varies according to the graphics device used to display the plot, but the
general unit seems to be pixels: Thus, for example, lwd=2 specifies a line
2 pixels wide.

Note the use of axis in creating Figure 7.4. The first argument to this
function indicates the position of the axis: 1 corresponds to the bottom
of the graph, 2 to the left side, 3 to the top, and 4 to the right side.
The at argument controls the location of tick marks. There are several
other arguments as well. Of particular note is the labels argument: If
labels=T, then numerical labels are used for the tick marks; otherwise,
labels takes a vector of character strings [e.g., c('male', 'female')]
to provide tick labels.

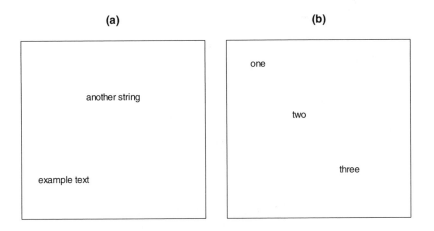

Figure 7.5   Plotting character strings with text.

The text function places character strings on a plot; the function has several arguments that determine the position, size, and font that are employed. For example, the following commands produce Figure 7.5(a):

```
> plot(c(0,1), c(0,1), axes=F, type='n', xlab="", ylab="")
> box()
> text(x=c(.2, .5), y=c(.2, .7),
+     c('example text', 'another string'))
> title('(a)')
>
```

I often find it helpful to use the locator function along with text to position text with the mouse; locator returns a list with vectors of x and y coordinates corresponding to the position of the mouse cursor when the left button is clicked. Figure 7.5(b) was constructed as follows:

```
> plot(c(0,1), c(0,1), axes=F, type='n', xlab="", ylab="")
> box()
> text(locator(3), c('one','two','three'))
> title('(b)')
>
```

To position each of the three text strings, I moved the mouse cursor to a point in the plot and clicked the left button. Called with no arguments, locator() returns pairs of coordinates corresponding to left clicks, until the right mouse button is pressed.

Another useful argument to text, not employed in these examples, is adj, which controls the horizontal justification of text: 0 specifies left justification, 0.5 centering (the initial default, given by par), and 1 right justification. In R, if two values are given, adj=c(x, y), then the second controls vertical justification.

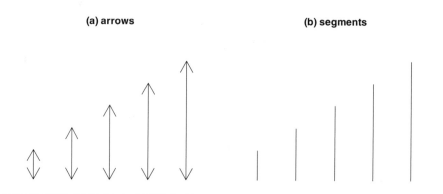

Figure 7.6   The arrows and segments functions.

As their names suggest, the `arrows` and `segments` functions may be used to add arrows and line segments to a plot. For example, the following statements produce Figure 7.6(a) and (b):

```
> plot(c(1,5), c(0,1), axes=F, type='n', xlab="", ylab="")
> arrows(x0=1:5, y0=rep(0.1, 5),
+     x1=1:5, y1=seq(0.3, 0.9, len=5), code=3)
> title('(a) arrows')

> plot(c(1,5), c(0,1), axes=F, type='n', xlab="", ylab="")
> segments(x0=1:5, y0=rep(0.1, 5),
+     x1=1:5, y1=seq(0.3, 0.9, len=5))
> title('(b) segments')
>
```

The argument `code=3` to `arrows` produces double-headed arrows in R.

Arrows and Line Segments in S-PLUS

The S-PLUS implementation of `arrows` does not support the `code` argument and draws only single-headed arrows. As well, the arguments to `arrows` and `segments` in S-PLUS are called `x1`, `y1`, `x2`, and `y2` (rather than `x0`, `y0`, `x1`, and `y1`).

Another self-descriptive function is `polygon`, which takes as its first two arguments vectors defining the *x* and *y* coordinates of the vertices of a closed figure; for example, to produce Figure 7.7:

```
> plot(c(0,1), c(0,1), type='n', xlab="", ylab="")
> polygon(c(.2,.8,.8), c(.2,.2,.8), col=1)
> polygon(c(.2,.2,.8), c(.2,.8,.8))
>
```

The `col` argument, if specified, gives the color to use in filling the polygon (see the discussion of colors in Section 7.1.3).

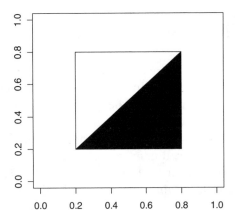

Figure 7.7   Filled and unfilled triangles produced by `polygon`.

The `legend` function may be used to draw a legend on a plot; the function has a number of arguments, and its use differs somewhat in R and S-PLUS. An illustration using R appears in Figure 7.8:

```
> plot(c(1,5), c(0,1), axes=F, type='n', xlab="", ylab="",
+       frame.plot=T)
> legend(locator(1), legend=c('group A', 'group B', 'group C'),
+     lty=1:3, pch=1:3)
>
```

Note the use of `locator` to position the legend: I find that this is often easier than computing where the legend should be placed. In S-PLUS, the `pch` argument would be replaced by `marks`.

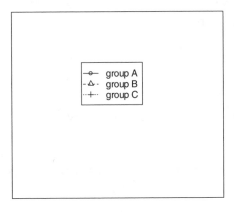

Figure 7.8   Using the `legend` function.

7.1.3   Specifying Colors

Using different colors is often the most effective means of distinguishing graphical elements such as lines or points. Although I am limited to monochrome graphs in this book, the specification of colors in S graphs is nevertheless straightforward to describe.

Plotting functions such as `lines` and `points` specify color via the `col` argument; in R, the `col` argument is vectorized, allowing you to select a separate color for each point. In both R and S-PLUS, colors may be specified by number. The following commands display the numbered colors in R:

```
> piechart(rep(1, length(palette())), col=palette())
```

and in S-PLUS:

```
> piechart(rep(1,16), col=1:16)
```

In R, the numbered colors are given by a *color palette*; calling the `palette` function with no arguments prints out the current palette:

```
> palette()
[1] "black"  "red"     "green3" "blue"    "cyan"    "magenta"
[7] "yellow" "white"
```

This function may also be employed to reset the color palette. Likewise, the numbered colors employed for S-PLUS graphsheet plots may be examined and reset in the Color Schemes dialog box, accessible through the Options menu.

That is the end of the color story for standard S-PLUS graphs, but R is more flexible: First, colors in R may be referenced by name as well as by number. For example, using the default palette, `col='red'` is equivalent to `col=2`. The full set of color definitions appears in the editable file `rgb.txt`, which resides in the R etc subdirectory.

Second, R permits you to specify colors as RGB (red, green, blue) values. For example, the `rainbow` function creates a spectrum of RGB colors:

```
> rainbow(10)
 [1] "#FF0000" "#FF9900" "#CCFF00" "#33FF00" "#00FF66" "#00FFFF"
 [7] "#0066FF" "#3300FF" "#CC00FF" "#FF0099"
```

Similarly, the `gray` function creates gray levels from black [`gray(0)`] to white [`gray(1)`]:

```
> gray(0:8/8)
 [1] "#000000" "#202020" "#404040" "#606060" "#808080" "#9F9F9F"
 [7] "#BFBFBF" "#DFDFDF" "#FFFFFF"
```

The color codes are represented as hexadecimal (base 16) numbers of the form `"#RRGGBB"`, where each pair of hex digits encodes the intensity of one of the three primary colors—from 00 (i.e., 0 in decimal) to FF (i.e., 255 in decimal). To get a sense of how this works, try each of the following commands:

```
> piechart(rep(1,100), col=rainbow(100), labels=rep("", 100))

> piechart(rep(1,100), col=gray(0:100/100), labels=rep("", 100))
```

PUTTING IT TOGETHER: EFFECT DISPLAYS   7.2

As I explained, most of the graphs that you want to create in routine data analysis are easily obtained in S. The aim of this chapter is to show you how to construct the small proportion of graphs that require custom work. By their nature, such graphs are diverse, and it would be futile to try to cover their construction exhaustively. Instead, I will develop an example that is sufficiently rich to demonstrate many of the techniques described in the preceding section.

"Effect displays" are graphical representations of linear or generalized linear models that are most useful for understanding models with inter-actions (see Fox, 1987, for a general description): Briefly, effect displays focus on the high-order terms in a linear model, showing each such term along with its lower-order relatives and setting other terms in the model to typical values.

Effect displays are perhaps best understood through an example, so let us consider a logit model fit by Cowles and Davis (1987) to data on volunteering for psychological experiments. These authors were inter-ested in the personality factors that predispose individuals to volunteer; in particular, they expected that the standard personality dimensions of introversion-extraversion and stability-neuroticism would interact in their effect on volunteering. Both of these personality dimensions were assessed by scales that take on integer values between 0 and 24. Cowles and Davis's data, on 1421 subjects, are in the data frame Cowles in the car library:

```
> library(car)
. . .
> data(Cowles)
> dim(Cowles)
[1] 1421    4

> Cowles[sort(sample(1421, 10)),]   # sample 10 obs.
      neuroticism extraversion    sex volunteer
108            14            8 female        no
283            10           12 female        no
311             5           16   male        no
355            22           13   male        no
```

```
1070            14          12 female        no
1071             4           8 female        no
1205            15          13   male        yes
1222            12           2   male        yes
1304            10           9 female        yes
1416             4          10 female        yes
```

Cowles and Davis fit the following model to their data:

```
> mod.cowles <- glm(volunteer ~ neuroticism * extraversion + sex,
+       data=Cowles, family=binomial)
> summary(mod.cowles)
```

. . .

```
Coefficients:
                         Estimate Std. Error z value Pr(>|z|)
(Intercept)             -2.35820    0.50104   -4.71  2.5e-06
neuroticism              0.11078    0.03763    2.94   0.0032
extraversion             0.16682    0.03770    4.42  9.7e-06
sexmale                 -0.24715    0.11161   -2.21   0.0268
neuroticism:extraversion -0.00855   0.00293   -2.92   0.0035
```

. . .

The anticipated interaction between neuroticism and extraversion proves highly statistically significant, but it is not easy to appreciate the nature of the interaction directly from the coefficients of the model: We can see that volunteering is positively related to each of these predictors when the other predictor is 0 and that the slope for each predictor declines as the value of the other predictor increases. Beyond that, however, we need to make mental calculations to interpret the interaction. The main effect of sex is also statistically significant, with males less inclined to volunteer than females, at fixed levels of neuroticism and extraversion. The sex main effect is much easier to interpret from its coefficient than the interaction is: When the probability of volunteering is near .5, that probability is approximately $-.247/4 = -.062$ lower for males than for females.

Because the structure of the model is relatively simple, with two quantitative predictors (neuroticism and extraversion) and a factor (sex), one approach that works here is to plot the full response surface. I proceed by calculating fitted values under the model for all combinations of the predictors; the $25 \times 25 \times 2 = 1250$ combinations are conveniently generated by the expand.grid function, and predict can then be used to find the fitted values:

```
> neuroticism <- 0:24
> extraversion <- 0:24
> sex <- c('male', 'female')
```

```
> graph.data <- expand.grid(neuroticism=neuroticism,
+                      extraversion=extraversion, sex=sex)
> graph.data$fit <- predict(mod.cowles, newdata=graph.data,
+                      type='response')

> graph.data
     neuroticism extraversion      sex      fit
1              0            0     male 0.068795
2              1            0     male 0.076239
3              2            0     male 0.084416
4              3            0     male 0.093382
5              4            0     male 0.103192
6              5            0     male 0.113904
7              6            0     male 0.125572
8              7            0     male 0.138248
9              8            0     male 0.151982
10             9            0     male 0.166816
. . .
1248          22           24   female 0.393356
1249          23           24   female 0.371051
1250          24           24   female 0.349283
```

Supplying `type='response'` as an argument to `predict` produces fitted values on the probability scale, rather than on the logit scale.

I proceed to construct three-dimensional plots of the logistic-regression surface, using the `persp` function to graph the data for males and females separately; the result is shown in Figure 7.9:

```
> prob <- matrix(graph.data$fit[graph.data$sex=='male'], 25, 25)
> persp(neuroticism, extraversion, prob,
+      phi=30, theta=45, expand=0.65, d=2, shade=0.75,
+      ticktype='detailed', zlab='Probability(Volunteer)',
+      main='Males')

> prob <- matrix(graph.data$fit[graph.data$sex=='female'], 25, 25)
> persp(neuroticism, extraversion, prob,
+      phi=30, theta=45, expand=0.65, d=2, shade=0.75,
+      ticktype='detailed', zlab='Probability(Volunteer)',
+      main='Females')
>
```

To draw these graphs, the fitted probabilities for males, and then for females, are extracted, and each set of fitted values is reshaped into a 25×25 matrix. The first two arguments to `persp` pertain to the variables defining the "floor" of the figure—here the predictors `neuroticism` and `extraversion`, each a vector of values running from 0 to 24; the vertical values, defining the height of the surface at each point on the predictor grid, are given by the matrix of fitted probabilities, in `prob`. The remaining arguments control the orientation and appearance of the graph (see the documentation for `persp`).

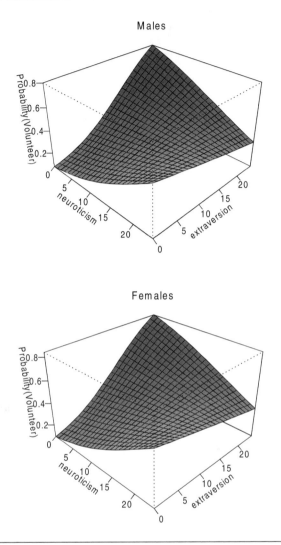

Figure 7.9   Fitted probability of volunteering as a function of `extraversion`, `neuroticism`, and `sex`.

Surface Plots in S-PLUS

The graphs in Figure 7.9 were drawn by the `persp` function in R; the S-PLUS version of `persp` has somewhat different arguments. The `wireframe` function in the S-PLUS `trellis` library (a version of which will likely eventually find its way into the `lattice` library in R) can also draw three-dimensional surface plots of this kind.

A different strategy for plotting the response surface in a two-dimensional graph is employed in Figure 7.10: Here I let one of the

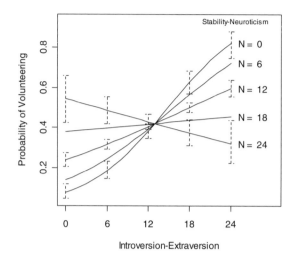

Figure 7.10   Effect display for the interaction between extraversion and neuroticism. Each line represents a different value of neuroticism (N), given at the right of the plot.

predictors, neuroticism, range over its values, setting the other predictor, extraversion, successively to the values 0, 6, 12, 18, and 24. Instead of drawing separate plots for males and females, I take advantage of the fact that sex enters the model additively and simply average over the two categories of this factor (which may be thought of as obtaining fitted values for a group composed half of males and half of females). The vertical bars on the plot give ±1 standard error around the fit at selected points; these error bars are computed on the logit scale and then translated to the probability scale.

Let us consider, step by step, how Figure 7.10 is constructed:

1. The first step is to compute the quantities to be plotted. I could use the predict function, working on the logit scale and subsequently averaging the values obtained for women and men, but I also want standard errors for the averages. Instead, I construct a model matrix at the points in the predictor space where fitted values are desired, using the value 0.5 for the dummy regressor for sex and adding a column of 1s for the constant and a product column for the neuroticism × extraversion interaction:

```
> extraversion <- 0:24
> neuroticism <- seq(0, 24, by=6)
> graph.data <- expand.grid(neuroticism=neuroticism,
+                           extraversion=extraversion)
> X <- cbind(constant=1, as.matrix(graph.data), sex=0.5,
+     neuro.extra=graph.data$neuroticism * graph.data$extraversion)
```

```
> X
     constant neuroticism extraversion sex neuro.extra
1        1            0              0 0.5           0
2        1            6              0 0.5           0
3        1           12              0 0.5           0
4        1           18              0 0.5           0
5        1           24              0 0.5           0
6        1            0              1 0.5           0
7        1            6              1 0.5           6
8        1           12              1 0.5          12
9        1           18              1 0.5          18
10       1           24              1 0.5          24
. . .
121      1            0             24 0.5           0
122      1            6             24 0.5         144
123      1           12             24 0.5         288
124      1           18             24 0.5         432
125      1           24             24 0.5         576
```

2.* Let X_0 represent the model matrix for the predicted values; the predicted values on the logit scale are then simply $X_0 b$, where b is the vector of logistic-regression coefficients. Similarly, the standard errors at the fitted values are the square roots of the diagonal entries of $X_0 V_b X_0'$, where V_b is the covariance matrix of the coefficients; ± 1 standard error around the fitted values represents an approximate pointwise 2/3 confidence interval for the population logistic-regression surface. Finally, both the fitted values and the endpoints of the intervals are translated to the probability scale using the relationship $p = 1/[1 + \exp(-\text{logit})]$:

```
> logit <- X %*% coefficients(mod.cowles)
> se <- sqrt(diag(X %*% Var(mod.cowles) %*% t(X)))
> prob <- matrix(1/(1+exp(-logit)), 5, 25,)
> low <- matrix(1/(1+exp(-(logit - se))), 5, 25)
> high <- matrix(1/(1+exp(-(logit + se))), 5, 25)
> prob
          [,1]      [,2]     [,3]     [,4]     [,5]     [,6]     [,7]
[1,]  0.077146  0.089892  0.10450  0.12118  0.14009  0.16142  0.18529
[2,]  0.139780  0.154254  0.16993  0.18685  0.20504  0.22450  0.24525
[3,]  0.240040  0.251943  0.26423  0.27690  0.28993  0.30332  0.31705
[4,]  0.380411  0.383450  0.38650  0.38955  0.39262  0.39569  0.39878
[5,]  0.544098  0.534548  0.52497  0.51538  0.50577  0.49616  0.48655
. . .
          [,22]    [,23]    [,24]    [,25]
[1,]  0.73524  0.76641  0.79494  0.82080
[2,]  0.64758  0.67347  0.69834  0.72210
[3,]  0.54871  0.56455  0.58026  0.59581
[4,]  0.44584  0.44902  0.45221  0.45540
[5,]  0.34741  0.33875  0.33019  0.32174
```

The 5 rows and 25 columns of the matrices prob, low, and high correspond respectively to the 5 values of neuroticism (0, 6, 12, 18, and 24) and 25 values of extraversion (0, 1, 2, ... , 24) at which the fit is evaluated.

   Although this step is a bit more difficult, the aim is simple: to produce fitted values on the logit scale (logit) and their standard errors (se) for each combination of values of the predictors. The fitted values on the logit scale are then translated to the probability scale (prob). The standard errors are used to calculate ±1-standard-error intervals around the fitted values on the logit scale, and these limits are also translated to the probability scale (low and high).

   3. Next, I set up a coordinate system for the graph, making sure to include the confidence limits around the fit (low and high) and leaving room for explanatory text to be placed on the plot [high + 0.05; xlim=c(0,30)]. The argument xaxt='n' suppresses the horizontal axis. This step and the remaining steps are shown (cumulatively) in the panels of Figure 7.11:

```
> plot(range(extraversion), range(c(low, high + 0.05)), type='n',
+       xlab='Introversion-Extraversion',
+       ylab='Probability of Volunteering',
+       xaxt='n', xlim=c(0,30))
>
```

   4. I use the axis function to add the horizontal axis to the plot, placing tick marks from 0 to 24 (and therefore allowing extra room to the right, since the horizontal axis runs to 30):

```
> axis(1, at=seq(0, 24, by=6))
>
```

   5. Looping through the five values of neuroticism, I draw a line on the graph for each value, and then place a label immediately to the right of the line, using the text function and setting adj=0[3]:

```
> for (neuro in 1:5){
+       lines(extraversion, prob[neuro,])
+       text(25, prob[neuro,25],
+               paste('N = ', neuroticism[neuro]),
+           adj=0)
+       }
>
```

   6. Next, I use the arrows function in R to place error bars around some of the fitted values; the variables extra and neuro hold the indices at which error bars are placed. The argument code=3 to arrows produces double-headed "arrows," angle=90 specifies arrow "heads" at

---

3. Loops and other programming constructs are described in the next chapter.

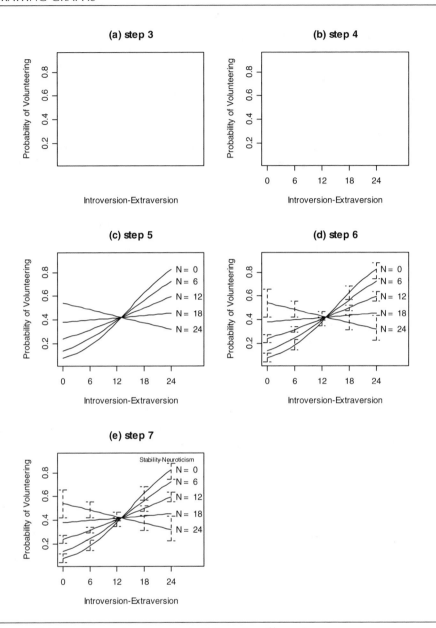

Figure 7.11   Successive steps in building the effect plot.

right angles to the shafts, and length=0.05 controls the length of the arrow heads:

```
> extra <- seq(1, 25, by=6)
> for (neuro in c(1, 3, 5)){
+        arrows(extraversion[extra], low[neuro, extra],
+            extraversion[extra], high[neuro, extra],
+            angle=90, code=3, lty=2, length=0.05)
+            }
>
```

Plotting Error Bars in S-PLUS

Recall that the `arrows` function in S-PLUS is not as capable as in R. In S-PLUS, we can plot error bars as vertical lines with `segments` or write our own simple function to add fancier error bars to plots.

---

7. The final step is to place the label 'Stability-Neuroticism' at the upper right of the graph. I use the mouse (via the `locator` function) to set the label on the plot; adj=1 right-justifies the text, making it easier to position the label, and cex=0.75 prints the label smaller than the rest of the text:

```
> text(locator(1), 'Stability-Neuroticism', adj=1, cex=0.75)
>
```

GRAPHICS DEVICES   7.3

Graphics devices in S send graphs to graphics windows, to files, or to "hard-copy" devices such as printers and plotters. It almost always makes sense to create graphs in windows, saving them to files, sending them to hard-copy devices, or copying and pasting them into other programs as desired. A new graphics window may be created directly in the Windows version of R with the `windows` function, and in S-PLUS with the `graphsheet` function.[4]

It is sometimes useful to have multiple graphics windows so that graphs can be juxtaposed on the screen. An alternative is to create several graphs on the same device [e.g., using par(mfrow=c(*rows, columns*))], to use graphsheets with multiple pages in S-PLUS, or to activate the graphics history in R. All these mechanisms are explained in the R and S-PLUS documentation.

If multiple devices are defined, only one is current at any given time. High-level graphics functions, such as `plot`, automatically open a graphics window if there is no current graphics device or clear the current device. The function `dev.list` returns a list of all open devices, `dev.cur` returns the number of the current device, and `dev.set` sets the current device. A newly created graphics device becomes the current device.

An R graphics window or S-PLUS graphsheet "page" may be copied to the clipboard when its window has the focus and then pasted into

---

4. There are other functions that create graphics devices, including `trellis.device`, which should be used with trellis graphics (created by functions in the `trellis` library in S-PLUS and `lattice` library in R).

another application, such as a graphics editor or word-processing program. Almost all of the graphs in this book were created in this manner. A graph also may be saved to a file in a variety of graphics formats or printed via the **File** menu (or, in R, by right-clicking in the graphics window).

CHAPTER 8

Writing Programs

This book is principally about using S to fit linear and generalized linear models, tasks that can be accomplished routinely by using the built-in capabilities of S and readily available libraries. Moreover, existing statistical procedures programmed in S extend far beyond the realm of linear and generalized linear models. Nevertheless, the main advantage of working in a statistical programming environment—rather than with a statistical package—is programmability.

S is a full-fledged programming language, with a variety of data and control structures. My object, however, is not to provide the background required to become an accomplished S programmer, but rather to convey the basic programming concepts and procedures that will enable you to use S more effectively in routine (and not-so-routine) data analysis. I have in mind primarily the "quick-and-dirty" programs that can facilitate your work in S rather than polished programs written for general use.

Further information may be found in several places, not least the documentation for R and S-PLUS. In addition, Venables and Ripley (2000) is an excellent advanced source on programming in S.

■ The first section of the chapter reviews function definition in S.

■ Matrix algebra is the common language of much of applied statistics. The second section shows how to perform a variety of matrix operations in S.

■ The S programming language provides a range of control structures. The third section takes up conditionals, loops, and recursion. This section also includes an extended illustration employing the programming techniques described in the chapter.

- The fourth section introduces the `apply` function and its relatives, which can be useful for avoiding loops in S programs, producing cleaner, and sometimes more efficient, programs.

- The fifth section describes class-based, object-oriented programming in S.

- The concluding section of the chapter provides some general advice about writing S programs.

The material in this chapter could have been placed earlier in the book, and from one point of view it would have been more logical to do so: After all, in the course of the preceding chapters, I occasionally introduced examples that made use of the programming concepts and structures described here. I feel, however, that this earlier material motivates the discussion in this chapter.

The data structures that we will require in this chapter—vectors, matrices, data frames, and lists—are already familiar (and were described in Chapter 2).

8.1   DEFINING FUNCTIONS

S is a functional programming language, and writing programs in S entails defining functions. Let us begin with a simple but useful example: Take a look again at Figure 6.5 on regression diagnostics. This is a scatterplot of hat values versus studentized residuals from a linear model; the points are plotted as circles with areas proportional to Cook's distances. Imagine that you want to draw this graph routinely for linear and generalized linear models, so that it makes sense to encapsulate the construction of the graph in a function. The following function does the trick, with a few bells and whistles:

```
> influence.plot <- function(model, scale=10, col=c(1,2),
+       labels=names(rstud), ...){
+       hatval <- hatvalues(model)
+       rstud <- rstudent(model)
+       cook <- sqrt(as.vector(cookd(model)))
+             # as.vector is needed for S3
+       scale <- scale/max(cook)
+       p <- length(coef(model))
+       n <- length(rstud)
+       cutoff <- sqrt(4/(n - p))  # for sqrt of Cook's D
+       plot(hatval, rstud, xlab='Hat-Values',
+           ylab='Studentized Residuals', type='n', ...)
+       abline(v=c(2, 3)*p/n, lty=2)  # reference lines
+       abline(h=c(-2, 0, 2), lty=2)  # reference lines
```

```
+       for (i in 1:n)    # loop over observations
+           points(hatval[i], rstud[i], cex=scale*cook[i],
+               col=if (cook[i] > cutoff) col[2] else col[1])
+       if (labels[1] != FALSE) identify(hatval, rstud, labels)
+       }
>
```

In practice, I would not enter a function definition directly at the command prompt, but rather would use an editor to compose the function, as explained in Chapter 1.

All the techniques employed in the `influence.plot` function, including control structures such as loops (`for`) and conditionals (`if`), are discussed later in the current chapter. Let us concentrate, for the present, on the general structure of this example.

Functions are defined using the `function` special form. The arguments to `function` specify the *formal* (or *dummy*) *arguments* of `influence.plot`, which include `model`, `scale`, `col`, `labels`, and `...`; these dummy arguments are matched to *real arguments* when the function is called, for example, in the following command:

```
> influence.plot(lm(prestige ~ income + education, data=Duncan))
```

The equals sign (=) is used to assign the *default value* of an argument in the function definition (e.g., `10` for `scale`), just as it is used to specify a value for the argument when the function is called. Here the result returned by the `lm` function matches the argument `model`; `scale`, `col`, and `labels` are unspecified and hence receive their default values; and `...` is simply missing from the function call.

The formal argument `...` is special, in that it may be matched by any number of real arguments when the function is called; within the function, `...` may be referenced as a local variable. In `influence.plot`, `...` serves to "soak up" extra arguments to be passed to the `plot` function; failing to specify `...` when `influence.plot` is called simply means that no additional arguments are passed to `plot`. Variables defined within the body of the function are also local to the function.

When a function is called, its arguments may be specified by position (i.e., in the order given in the function definition), by name, or by both. The usual convention is to specify the first one or two arguments by position and any remaining arguments by name; if arguments are skipped (either because they are not needed or because default values are to be used), then the remaining arguments must be specified by name, as must arguments that are supplied out of order. Named arguments may be abbreviated as long as the abbreviation is unique. For example, because no other argument to `influence.plot` begins with the letter *s*, the argument `scale` may be abbreviated to `scal`, `sca`, `sc`, or `s`.

Although formal arguments are associated with real arguments when the function is called, an argument is not *evaluated* until its first use. At that point, the argument is evaluated in the environment from which the function was called. In contrast, default values for arguments, if they exist, are evaluated in the environment of the function itself. This process of "lazy evaluation" frequently proves efficient and convenient—for example, the default value of one argument can depend on another argument or even on a value computed in the body of the function (e.g., the default value of `labels` in `influence.plot` references the local variable `rstud`)—but it can occasionally trip up the unwary programmer.

The remainder of the function definition is an S expression defining the *body* of the function. This is usually a compound expression, enclosed in braces, { }. The *value* returned by the function may be given in an explicit call to the `return` function or—more typically—is the value of the last expression executed in the function body.

The details of `influence.plot` should be largely self-explanatory, but note the following:

- The call to `plot` sets up the coordinate space for the graph.

- The function `abline` is used to place vertical and horizontal reference lines on the plot—the former at twice and three times the average hat value, and the latter at studentized residuals of −2, 0, and 2.

- So that the function will work both in R and in S-PLUS, the circles are plotted by calls to `points` in a `for` loop over the observation indices 1 to *n* (rather than in a vectorized call to `points`, as would be appropriate only in R).

- The relative diameters of the circles are controlled by the `cex` (character expansion) argument, set to be proportional to the square root of Cook's distance; the `scale` factor establishes the general size of the circles. (S3 requires that observation names be stripped by `as.vector` from the Cook's distances, before these quantities are passed to `cex`.)

- The circles are plotted in different colors, depending on whether Cook's D exceeds the cutoff $4/(n-p)$; the colors to be used are given by the `col` argument to the function.

- Finally, unless the `labels` argument is set to FALSE, the `identify` function is called to label points interactively; by default, the point labels are taken from the observation names associated with the studentized residuals. Because `identify` returns the indices of the identified points, and because this result becomes the value returned by the `if` statement that terminates the function, `influence.plot` returns these indices as well. Remember that points are identified by clicking the left mouse button; to exit from `influence.plot`, click the right button.

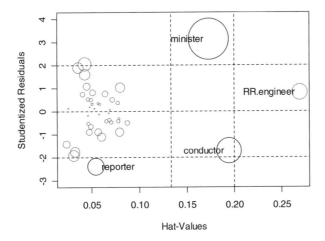

Figure 8.1   Graph produced by the influence.plot function. Several points were identified interactively with the mouse.

Let us try out influence.plot on Duncan's occupational-prestige regression:

```
> library(car)
> data(Duncan)
> influence.plot(lm(prestige ~ income + education, data=Duncan),
+     ylim=c(-3, 4), col=gray(c(0.5, 0)))
[1]   6   9  16  27
```

The resulting graph appears in Figure 8.1. I set col = gray(c(.75, 0) (i.e., medium gray and black) because the default colors in R (black and red) would not reproduce properly in the book; specifying ylim = c(-3, 4) expands the range of the vertical axis and is present to illustrate the use of an argument passed down to plot, via . . . .

WORKING WITH MATRICES*   8.2

S incorporates extensive facilities for matrix and linear algebra. This section concentrates on basic matrix operations.

Let us begin by defining some matrices via the matrix function; recall that matrix fills matrices by columns, unless the argument byrow is set to TRUE:

```
> A <- matrix(c(1, 2, -4, 3, 5, 0), 2, 3)
> B <- matrix(1:6, 2, 3)
> C <- matrix(c(2, -2, 0, 1, -1, 1, 4 ,4, -4), 3, 3, byrow=T)
```

```
> A
     [,1] [,2] [,3]
[1,]    1   -4    5
[2,]    2    3    0

> B
     [,1] [,2] [,3]
[1,]    1    3    5
[2,]    2    4    6

> C
     [,1] [,2] [,3]
[1,]    2   -2    0
[2,]    1   -1    1
[3,]    4    4   -4
```

Matrix addition, subtraction, negation, and the product of a matrix and a scalar use the usual operators; addition and subtraction require matrices of the same order:

```
> A + B
     [,1] [,2] [,3]
[1,]    2   -1   10
[2,]    4    7    6

> A - B
     [,1] [,2] [,3]
[1,]    0   -7    0
[2,]    0   -1   -6

> A + C  # A and C not of same order
Error in A + C : non-conformable arrays

> 2*A
     [,1] [,2] [,3]
[1,]    2   -8   10
[2,]    4    6    0

> -A
     [,1] [,2] [,3]
[1,]   -1    4   -5
[2,]   -2   -3    0
```

Using * to multiply two matrices forms the element-wise product (for matrices of the same order). The standard matrix product is formed with the inner-product operator, %*%, which requires that the matrices be conformable for multiplication:

```
> A %*% C
     [,1] [,2] [,3]
[1,]   18   22  -24
[2,]    7   -7    3
```

In matrix products, vectors are treated as row or column vectors, as required:

```
> a <- rep(1, 3)
> b <- c(1, 5, 3)
> C %*% a
     [,1]
[1,]    0
[2,]    1
[3,]    4

> a %*% C
     [,1] [,2] [,3]
[1,]    7    1   -3

> a %*% b
     [,1]
[1,]    9
```

The last example illustrates that the inner product of two vectors of the same length, a %*% b, is a scalar (actually, a 1×1 matrix). The outer product may be obtained via the outer function:

```
> outer(a, b)
     [,1] [,2] [,3]
[1,]    1    5    3
[2,]    1    5    3
[3,]    1    5    3
```

The outer function may be used with operations other than multiplication; an optional third argument, which defaults to '*', specifies the function to be applied to pairs of elements from the first two arguments.

The function t returns the transpose of a matrix:

```
> t(B)
     [,1] [,2]
[1,]    1    2
[2,]    3    4
[3,]    5    6
```

The solve function provides the inverse of a square, nonsingular matrix:

```
> solve(C)
            [,1] [,2]        [,3]
[1,] -2.4227e-16  0.5 1.2500e-01
[2,] -5.0000e-01  0.5 1.2500e-01
[3,] -5.0000e-01  1.0 6.2063e-17
```

As is typically the case in computer calculations with real numbers, there are small rounding errors, since the first and third diagonal entries should be 0; rounding the result makes it easier to read:

```
> round(solve(C), 3)
     [,1] [,2]  [,3]
[1,]  0.0  0.5 0.125
[2,] -0.5  0.5 0.125
[3,] -0.5  1.0 0.000
```

The `fractions` function in the `MASS` library is also helpful here:

```
> library(MASS)
> fractions(solve(C))
     [,1] [,2] [,3]
[1,]    0  1/2  1/8
[2,] -1/2  1/2  1/8
[3,] -1/2    1    0
```

The `solve` function may be used more generally to solve systems of linear simultaneous equations; for example, to solve $\mathbf{Cx} = \mathbf{b}$ for $\mathbf{x}$:

```
> solve(C, b)
[1] 2.875 2.375 4.500
```

In this example, the answer is simply $\mathbf{x} = \mathbf{C}^{-1}\mathbf{b}$, as we may easily verify:

```
> solve(C) %*% b
      [,1]
[1,] 2.875
[2,] 2.375
[3,] 4.500
```

If the system of equations is overdetermined, `solve` provides the least squares fit; for example, in

```
> D <- matrix(c(1, 2, 3, 5, 7, 8), 3, 2, byrow=T)
> D
     [,1] [,2]
[1,]    1    2
[2,]    3    5
[3,]    7    8

> solve(D, b)  # 3 inconsistent eqns., 2 unknowns
[1] -1.7848 1.9494
```

we obtain $(\mathbf{D}'\mathbf{D})^{-1}\mathbf{D}'\mathbf{b}$.

Underdetermined systems produce an error:

```
> solve(A, c(1,2))  # 2 eqns., 3 unknowns
Error in solve.default(A, c(1, 2)) : singular matrix 'a' in solve
```

Consider, now, finding the least squares coefficients for a linear model with model matrix $\mathbf{X}$ and response vector $\mathbf{y}$, using the Canadian occupational-prestige data as an example:

```
> data(Prestige)
> attach(Prestige)
> X <- cbind(1, as.matrix(Prestige[,1:3]))  # attach the constant
> y <- Prestige[,4]

> X[1:5,]  # first 5 rows
                       education income women
GOV.ADMINISTRATORS   1     13.11 12351 11.16
GENERAL.MANAGERS     1     12.26 25879  4.02
ACCOUNTANTS          1     12.77  9271 15.70
PURCHASING.OFFICERS  1     11.42  8865  9.11
CHEMISTS             1     14.62  8403 11.68

> y  # prestige
 [1] 68.8 69.1 63.4 56.8 73.5 77.6 72.6 78.1 73.1 68.8 62.0 60.0
[13] 53.8 62.2 74.9 55.1 82.3 58.1 58.3 72.8 84.6 59.6 66.1 87.2
 . . .
[97] 48.9 35.9 25.1 26.1 42.2 35.2
```

Notice that selecting a single column from the data frame (here, column 4, which is prestige) produces a vector rather than a one-column matrix: In indexing, S automatically drops dimensions with extent 1. We can circumvent this behavior by specifying drop=F (see Section 2.3.4 on indexing):

```
> Prestige[,4, drop=F]
                     prestige
GOV.ADMINISTRATORS     68.8
GENERAL.MANAGERS       69.1
ACCOUNTANTS            63.4
 . . .
TYPESETTERS            42.2
BOOKBINDERS            35.2
```

In this case, however, either a vector or a one-column matrix will do. The usual formula for the least squares coefficients is $\mathbf{b} = (\mathbf{X}'\mathbf{X})^{-1}\mathbf{X}'\mathbf{y}$. It is simple to write this formula directly as an S expression[1]:

```
> solve(t(X) %*% X) %*% t(X) %*% y

            [,1]
[1,] -6.7943342
[2,]  4.1866373
[3,]  0.0013136
[4,] -0.0089052
```

---

1. As mentioned above, solve(X, y) also produces the least squares fit, but my purpose here is to illustrate translating a familiar matrix formula into an S expression—and what is more familiar than the formula for the least squares coefficients?

This approach—forming and inverting $\mathbf{X}'\mathbf{X}$—will break down in certain instances, and there are numerically superior methods for solving least squares problems.[2] Unless the data are ill conditioned or the data set very large, however, the computation will go through just fine, as we may verify via the lm function for the current illustration:

```
> lm(prestige ~ education + income + women)
. . .

(Intercept)    education       income        women
   -6.79433      4.18664      0.00131     -0.00891
```

Among their other virtues (and despite their deficiencies), quick and dirty computations are often useful in learning how statistical methods work.

The eigen function calculates eigenvalues and eigenvectors of square matrices (including asymmetric matrices, which may have complex eigenvalues and eigenvectors). For example, an eigenanalysis of the correlation matrix for the predictors in the Canadian occupational-prestige regression is provided by the following commands:

```
> R <- cor(cbind(education, income, women))
> R  # correlation matrix
          education    income      women
education  1.000000   0.57758   0.061853
income     0.577580   1.00000  -0.441059
women      0.061853  -0.44106   1.000000

> eigen(R)
$values
[1] 1.69770 1.05964 0.24266


$vectors
             women     income  education
education  0.56106  -0.605273    0.56467
income     0.72125   0.022711   -0.69230
women     -0.40621  -0.795694   -0.44930
```

The eigenvectors—the columns of the list component $vectors—are each normalized to length 1, and therefore give the "loadings" for a principal-components analysis based on the correlations, while the eigenvalues give the collective variation accounted for by each component. Principal-components analysis can also be performed by the princomp and prcomp functions (in the mva library in R). Other matrix factorizations available in S include the singular-value, QR, and Cholesky decompositions: See the on-line help for svd, qr, and chol.

---

2. We may do a bit better in large data sets by forming squares and cross-products as crossprod(X) and crossprod(X, y), but computations via the QR decomposition of the model matrix X, for example, will be more numerically stable in ill-conditioned problems, for example, when the columns of X are nearly collinear (see Chambers, 1992). This is the default approach taken by the lm function.

The determinant of a square matrix may be computed in R or S4 by the function det; for example:

```
> det(R)
[1] 0.43653
```

Calculating Determinants in S3

The determinant function det does not exist in S3. A simple approach, which may break down in certain ill-conditioned problems, is to compute the determinant as the product of the eigenvalues:

```
> det <- function(X) prod(eigen(X, only.values=T)$values)
```

Depending on its argument, the function diag may be used to extract or to set the main diagonal of a matrix, to create a diagonal matrix from a vector, or to create an identity matrix of specified order:

```
> diag(R)  # extract diagonal
education    income     women
        1         1         1

> diag(R) <- NA  # set diagonal
> R
          education    income      women
education        NA   0.57758   0.061853
income     0.577580        NA  -0.441059
women      0.061853  -0.44106         NA

> diag(1:3)  # make diagonal matrix
     [,1] [,2] [,3]
[1,]    1    0    0
[2,]    0    2    0
[3,]    0    0    3

> diag(3)  # order-3 identity matrix
     [,1] [,2] [,3]
[1,]    1    0    0
[2,]    0    1    0
[3,]    0    0    1
```

The MASS library includes a function, ginv, for computing generalized inverses of square and rectangular matrices. Further facilities for matrix computation are provided by the Matrix library. At the time of writing, the Matrix library is available for R and for S3, but not for S4.

8.3   PROGRAM CONTROL: CONDITIONALS, LOOPS, AND RECURSION

8.3.1   Conditionals

The basic construct for conditional evaluation in S is the *if* statement, which takes one of the following two general forms:

1. if (*logical.condition*) *command*

2. if (*logical.condition*) *command* else *alternative.command*

   - In these constructions, if the first element of *logical.condition* evaluates to TRUE or to a nonzero number, then *command* is evaluated and its value is returned.

   - If *logical.condition* evaluates to FALSE or 0 in the first form, then NULL is returned.

   - If *logical.condition* evaluates to FALSE or 0 in the second form, then *alternative.command* is evaluated and its value returned.

   - In either case, *command* (or *alternative.command*) may be a compound S command, with the elementary commands that compose it enclosed in braces and separated by semicolons or new lines; when a compound command is evaluated, the value returned is the value of its last elementary command. (Some examples of compound commands appear below in the context of loops.)

The *if* statement is usually used in writing functions. Here, for example, is a simple function that returns the absolute value of a number:

```
> abs.1 <- function(x) if (x < 0) -x else x
> abs.1(-5)
[1] 5

> abs.1(5)
[1] 5
```

Of course, in a real application we would use the abs function in S for this purpose.

When abs.1 is applied to a vector, it does not produce the result that we (probably) intended, because only the first element in the condition x < 0 (which in the following illustration is TRUE) controls the action taken:

```
> abs.1(-3:3) # the first element, -3, controls the result
[1]  3  2  1  0 -1 -2 -3
```

The `ifelse` function in S provides a vectorized conditional, as required here:

```
> abs.2 <- function(x) ifelse(x < 0, -x, x)
> abs.2(-3:3)
[1] 3 2 1 0 1 2 3
```

The general format of `ifelse` is

`ifelse(`*vector.condition, true.vector, false.vector*`)`

The three arguments of `ifelse` are all vectors of the same length; wherever an element of *vector.condition* is TRUE, the corresponding element of *true.vector* is selected; where *vector.condition* is FALSE, the corresponding element of *false.vector* is returned.

More complex conditionals can be handled by cascading if/else statements. For example, the following function returns -1, 0, or 1 according to the sign of a number—negative, zero, or positive, consecutively.

```
> sign.1 <- function(x) {
+     if (x < 0) -1
+         else if (x > 0) 1
+             else 0
+     }

> sign.1(-5)
[1] -1
```

Once again, this is an artificial example, because this functionality is provided by the `sign` function in S.

The same technique may be applied to the `ifelse` function, for example, to provide a vector of signs:

```
> sign.2 <- function(x) {
+     ifelse (x < 0, -1,
+         ifelse(x > 0, 1, 0))
+     }

> sign.2(c(-5, 0, 10))
[1] -1  0  1
```

Alternatively, complex conditionals can be handled by the `switch` function (see the R or S-PLUS documentation for examples).

Loops (Iteration)   8.3.2

The `for`, `while`, and `repeat` statements in S are used to implement loops. Consider, for example, the task of computing the factorial of a nonnegative integer:

$$n! = n(n-1)\cdots(2)(1),$$

$$0! = 1.$$

```
> fact.1 <- function (x){
+    if (x <= 1) return(1)
+    f <- 1  # initialize
+    for (i in 1:x) f <- f * i  # accumulate product
+    f  # return result
+    }

> fact.1(5)
[1] 120
```

This, too, is an artificial problem: We can calculate the factorial of *n* very easily in S, either as gamma (n+1) or, for *n* > 0, as prod(1:n). Note how, in this example, I initialize the local variable f to 1, accumulate the factorial product in the loop, and implicitly return the product as the result of the function. It is also possible to return a result explicitly—for example, return(f).

Integer Arithmetic in S4

A subtle problem arises in S4 when the fact.1 function computes a large result: In S4, when all numbers in a calculation are integers, "integer arithmetic" (rather than "real arithmetic") is performed. This can cause an integer "overflow" if the result is a very large number. Try computing fact.1(15), for example. To circumvent this problem, we can initialize the computation at f <- 1.0 (rather than at f <- 1), which is represented internally by S4 as a real number, causing the computation to be done in real arithmetic.

The general format of the for statement is

```
for (loop.variable in values) command
```

In executing the loop, *loop.variable* successively takes on the values in the vector or list *values*; *command* is usually (but not in the preceding example) a compound command enclosed in braces, { }, and is evaluated each time through the loop using the current value of *loop.variable*.

In contrast, while loops iterate (repeat) as long as the specified condition holds true; for example:

```
> fact.2 <- function (x){
+    i <- f <- 1  # initialize
+    while (i <= x) {
+        f <- f * i  # accumulate product
+        i <- i + 1  # increment counter
+        }
```

```
+       f  # return result
+       }

> fact.2(5)
[1] 120
```

The general format of a `while` loop is

```
while (logical.condition) command
```

where *command*, which is typically a compound command, is executed as long as *logical.condition* holds.

Finally, `repeat` loops iterate until a `break` is executed:

```
> fact.3 <- function(x){
+       if ((!is.numeric(x)) || (x != floor(x))
+           || (x < 0) || (length(x) > 1))
+           stop('argument must be a non-negative integer')
+       i <- f <- 1  # initialize
+       repeat {
+           f <- f * i  # accumulate product
+           i <- i + 1  # increment counter
+           if (i > x) break  # termination test
+           }
+       f  # return result
+       }

> fact.3(5)
[1] 120

> fact.3(1.5)
Error in fact.3(1.5) : argument must be a non-negative integer
```

Note the use of the || (double-*or*) operator here: || differs from | in two respects:

1. | applies element-wise to vectors, while || takes single-element logical arguments.

2. || evaluates its right argument only if its left argument is FALSE. This second characteristic can be exploited to prevent the evaluation of an expression that would otherwise cause an error—in the illustration, `x != floor(x)` is not evaluated if x is not numeric, for example.

Similar comments apply to the && (double-*and*) operator: The right argument of && is evaluated only if its left argument is TRUE.

This example also illustrates how the `stop` function may be used to interrupt the execution of a function, signaling an error—in this case when the input to `fact.3` is inappropriate. As a general matter, checking input to a function is good programming practice.

The general format of repeat loops is simply

```
repeat command
```

If the loop is not to repeat endlessly, there must be a termination test in *command*, which is almost always a compound command.

8.3.3   Recursion

Recursion is at times an elegant alternative to looping; recursive functions are functions that call themselves:

```
> fact.4 <- function(x){
+      if (x <= 1) 1  # termination condition
+      else x * fact.4(x - 1)  # recursive call
+      }

> fact.4(5)
[1] 120
```

This recursive implementation of the factorial relies on the properties $n! = n \times (n - 1)!$ and $0! = 1! = 1$. A potential pitfall of the procedure, however, is that the name of the function can change by assignment (here to `factorial`):

```
> factorial <- fact.4
> remove(fact.4)
> factorial(5)  # tries to call the removed fact.4
Error in factorial(5) : couldn't find function "fact.4"
```

Consequently, a safer approach is to use the special `Recall` function (in place of the function's name) to implement the recursive call:

```
> fact.5 <- function(x){
+      if (x <= 1) 1
+      else x * Recall(x - 1)  # recursive call
+      }

> fact.5(5)
[1] 120

> factorial <- fact.5
> remove(fact.5)
> factorial(5)  # still works with fact.5 removed
[1] 120
```

An Extended Illustration: Binary 8.3.4
Logistic Regression*

With the exception of the introductory `influence.plot` function in Section 8.1, all of the preceding programming examples have been trivial; their purpose was transparency. The purpose of the current section is to illustrate how the programming techniques described in this chapter can be applied to a more complex problem. To this end, I develop two programs for fitting binary logistic-regression models. Although they are more realistic, these examples are in another sense artificial, because logistic regression is handled perfectly well by the `glm` function (as described in Chapter 5); indeed, checking results against `glm` will tell us whether my programs work properly.

Estimation by the Newton-Raphson Method

The *Newton-Raphson method* is a common iterative approach to estimating a logistic-regression model. The method may be succinctly described as follows:

1. Choose initial estimates of the regression coefficients, such as $\mathbf{b}_0 = 0$ (where the subscript 0 indicates that these are initial values).

2. At each iteration t, update the regression coefficients by the formula

$$\mathbf{b}_t = \mathbf{b}_{t-1} + (\mathbf{X}'\mathbf{V}_{t-1}\mathbf{X})^{-1}\mathbf{X}'(\mathbf{y} - \mathbf{p}_{t-1}),$$

where $\mathbf{X}$ is the model matrix, with $\mathbf{x}'_i$ as its ith row; $\mathbf{y}$ is the response vector (containing 0s and 1s); $\mathbf{p}_{t-1}$ is the vector of fitted response probabilities from the previous iteration, the ith entry of which is

$$p_{i,t-1} = \frac{1}{1 + \exp(-\mathbf{x}'_i\mathbf{b}_{t-1})};$$

and $\mathbf{V}_{t-1}$ is a diagonal matrix, with diagonal entries $p_{i,t-1}(1 - p_{i,t-1})$.

3. Step 2 is repeated until $\mathbf{b}_t$ is close enough to $\mathbf{b}_{t-1}$. At convergence, the estimated asymptotic covariance matrix of the coefficients is given by $(\mathbf{X}'\mathbf{V}\mathbf{X})^{-1}$, which is, conveniently, a by-product of the procedure.

Programming the Newton-Raphson method in S is straightforward:

```
> lreg <- function(X, y, max.iter=10, tol=1E-6){
+     # X is the model matrix
+     # y is the response vector of 0s and 1s
```

```
+        # max.iter is the maximum number of iterations
+        # tol is a convergence criterion
+        X <- cbind(1, X)  # add constant
+        b <- b.last <- rep(0, ncol(X))  # initialize coefficients
+        it <- 1  # initialize iteration counter
+        while (it <= max.iter){
+            p <- as.vector(1/(1 + exp(-X %*% b)))
+            V <- diag(p * (1 - p))
+            var.b <- solve(t(X) %*% V %*% X)
+            b <- b + var.b %*% t(X) %*% (y - p)  # update coef.
+            if (max(abs(b - b.last)/(abs(b.last) + 0.01*tol)) < tol)
+                break
+            b.last <- b  # update previous coef.
+            it <- it + 1  # increment counter
+            }
+        if (it > max.iter) warning('maximum iterations exceeded')
+        list(coefficients=as.vector(b), var=var.b, iterations=it)
+        }
>
```

The only slightly tricky point here is the test for convergence, which checks that the maximum absolute proportional change in the coefficients is less than some small tolerance, by default 10^{-6}: In calculating relative changes, I protect against dividing by numbers very close to 0 by adding a fraction of the tolerance to the denominator.[3] To protect against a runaway calculation, the argument max.iter specifies the maximum number of iterations (implemented in a while loop), which defaults to 10. The function begins by appending a column of 1s to the model matrix for the regression intercept. The function returns a list consisting of the regression coefficients, their estimated covariance matrix, and the number of iterations performed.

To illustrate the application of this function, I return to Mroz's labor-force participation data, employed as an example of logistic regression in Section 5.2.

```
> data(Mroz)
> attach(Mroz)
> Mroz[1:5,]  # first 5 obs.
  lfp k5 k618 age wc hc      lwg   inc
1 yes  1    0  32 no no 1.210165 10.91
2 yes  0    2  30 no no 0.328504 19.50
3 yes  1    3  35 no no 1.514128 12.04
4 yes  0    3  34 no no 0.092115  6.80
5 yes  1    2  31 yes no 1.524280 20.10
```

---

3. The convergence test could be incorporated into the termination condition for the while loop, but I wanted to illustrate breaking out of a loop. I invite the reader to reprogram lreg in this manner. Be careful, however, that the loop does not terminate the first time through, since b and b.last both start at 0.

The response variable, `lfp`, and two of the predictors, `wc` and `hc`, are factors. Because (unlike `glm`) the `lreg` function will not handle factors properly, these variables must be converted to numeric data.[4] This is easily done with the `recode` function in `car`:

```
> lfp <- recode(lfp, " 'yes'=1; 'no'=0 ", as.factor=F)
> wc <- recode(wc, " 'yes'=1; 'no'=0 ", as.factor=F)
> hc <- recode(hc, " 'yes'=1; 'no'=0 ", as.factor=F)
> mod.mroz <- lreg(cbind(k5, k618, age, wc, hc, lwg, inc), lfp)
>
```

Finally, I extract the coefficients from `mod.mroz` and compute their standard errors:

```
> mod.mroz$coefficients
[1]    3.182140 -1.462913 -0.064571 -0.062871   0.807274   0.111734
[7]    0.604693 -0.034446

> sqrt(diag(mod.mroz$var))
[1] 0.6443751 0.1970006 0.0680008 0.0127831 0.2299799 0.2060397
[7] 0.1508176 0.0082084
```

I invite the reader to compare these values with those computed by `glm` (as reported in Section 5.2).

Estimation by General Optimization

Another approach to fitting the logistic-regression model is to let a general-purpose optimizer do the work of maximizing the log-likelihood,

$$\log_e L = \sum y_i \log_e p_i + (1 - y_i) \log_e (1 - p_i),$$

where, as before, $p_i = 1/[1 + \exp(-\mathbf{x}_i'\mathbf{b})]$ is the fitted probability of response for observation i.

Optimizers work by evaluating the *gradient* (vector of partial derivatives) of the "objective function" (here the log-likelihood) at the current estimates of the parameters, iteratively improving the parameter estimates using the information in the gradient; iteration ceases when the gradient is sufficiently close to 0. Information on the matrix of second derivatives (the *Hessian*) may be used as well. Depending on the optimizer, expressions for the gradient and Hessian may be supplied by the user, or these quantities may be approximated numerically by taking differences; if expressions for the derivatives are available, then it is usually advantageous to use them.

---

4. If we were seriously programming a logistic-regression function, it would be desirable for the function to handle a model formula—a topic beyond the scope of this chapter.

In the current context, the gradient and Hessian are very simple:

$$\frac{\partial \log_e L}{\partial \mathbf{b}} = \sum (y_i - p_i)\mathbf{x}_i,$$

$$\frac{\partial \log_e L}{\partial \mathbf{b}\partial \mathbf{b}'} = \mathbf{X}'\mathbf{V}\mathbf{X},$$

where $\mathbf{X}$ is the model matrix, $\mathbf{x}_i$ is the ith row of $\mathbf{X}$ written as a column, and $\mathbf{V} = \text{diag}\{p_i(1 - p_i)\}$.

Several general optimizers are available in S, including the optim and nlm functions in R, and nlminb, nlmin, and ms in S-PLUS. I will illustrate how to proceed using optim; because, by default, optim *minimizes* the criterion function, I work with the *negative* of the log-likelihood (i.e., half the deviance) and the negative gradient:

```
> lreg.2 <- function(X, y, method='BFGS'){
+     X <- cbind(1, X)
+     negLogL <- function(b, X, y) {
+         p <- as.vector(1/(1 + exp(-X %*% b)))
+         - sum(y*log(p) + (1 - y)*log(1 - p))
+         }
+     grad <- function(b, X, y){
+         p <- as.vector(1/(1 + exp(-X %*% b)))
+         - apply(((y - p)*X), 2, sum)
+             }
+     result <- optim(rep(0, ncol(X)), negLogL, gr=grad,
+         hessian=T, method=method, X=X, y=y)
+     list(coefficients=result$par, var=solve(result$hessian),
+         deviance=2*result$value,
+         converged=result$convergence == 0)
+     }
>
```

In the lreg.2 function:

1. The negative log-likelihood and the negative gradient are defined as *local functions*, negLogL and grad, respectively. Like local variables, local functions exist only within the function in which they are defined.

2. Even though X and y are local variables in lreg.2, they are passed as arguments to negLogL and grad, along with the parameter vector b. In R, this is not strictly necessary, but it is in S-PLUS, and doing so allows me to show you how to pass additional arguments through the optimizer.[5]

---

5. A consideration of "scoping" rules for R and S-PLUS is above the level of this book; see, for example, Venables and Ripley (2000, Chapter 3) and a brief treatment in the Web appendix to the text.

3. The `optim` function in R provides several general optimizers. I have had good luck with the `BFGS` method for this kind of problem, so I have made this the default, but by providing an explicit `method` argument to `lreg.2`, and passing this argument down to `optim`, I also have made it easy to substitute another method. See `help(optim)` for details.

   ■ The first argument to `optim` gives start values for the parameters—in this case, a vector of 0s.

   ■ The second argument gives the objective function to be minimized (here, the local function `negLogL`), and the third argument gives the gradient (`gr=grad`). The first argument of the objective function and gradient must be the parameter vector (in this example, `b`).

   ■ Specifying `hessian=T` asks `optim` to return the Hessian, the inverse of which provides the estimated covariance matrix of the coefficients. The Hessian is computed numerically: `optim` does not allow us to supply an expression for the Hessian.

   ■ As explained, the `method` argument specifies the optimization method to be employed.

   ■ The two remaining arguments, `X` and `y` (the model matrix and the response vector), are passed by `optim` to `negLogL` and `grad`.

4. If the gradient is not given as an argument, `optim` will compute it numerically. As I mentioned, it is generally a good idea to supply an expression for the gradient, if one is available.

5. `optim` returns a list with several components. I pick out the parameters, the Hessian, the value of the objective function at the minimum, and a code indicating whether convergence has been achieved.

Trying out `lreg.2` on Mroz's data produces the following results:

```
> mod.mroz.2 <- lreg.2(cbind(k5, k618, age, wc, hc, lwg, inc), lfp)
> mod.mroz.2$coefficients
[1]   3.182114 -1.462898 -0.064569 -0.062870  0.807268  0.111731
[7]   0.604687 -0.034447

> sqrt(diag(mod.mroz.2$var))
[1] 0.6444435 0.1970014 0.0680002 0.0127858 0.2299802 0.2060394
[7] 0.1508174 0.0082086

> mod.mroz.2$converged
[1] TRUE
```

Optimization in S-PLUS

Unlike `optim` in R, the generally similar `nlminb` function in S-PLUS permits the specification of an expression for the Hessian. Here is a version of `lreg.2` that uses `nlminb`:

```
> lreg.2 <- function(X, y){
+       X <- cbind(1, X)
+       k <- ncol(X)
+       tri <- outer(1:k, 1:k, "<=")  # triangle
+       negLogL <- function(b, X, y) {
+           p <- as.vector(1/(1 + exp(-X %*% b)))
+           - sum(y*log(p) + (1 - y)*log(1 - p))
+           }
+       grad <- function(b, X, y, tri){
+           p <- as.vector(1/(1 + exp(-X %*% b)))
+           grad <- - colSums((y - p)*X)
+           hess <- (t(X) %*% diag(p*(1 - p)) %*% X)[tri]
+           list(gradient=grad, hessian=hess)
+           }
+       result <- nlminb(rep(0, ncol(X)), negLogL, gradient=grad,
+           hessian=T, X=X, y=y, tri=tri)
+       list(coefficients=result$par, deviance=2*result$objective,
+           var=solve(result$hessian), gradient=result$grad.norm,
+           message=result$message)
+       }
>
```

Notice that `nlminb` expects `grad` to return both the gradient and a vector giving one triangle of the Hessian.

Estimation by Iterated Weighted Least Squares

A third approach to the problem, which I will leave as an exercise for the reader, is to use iterated weighted least squares (IWLS) to compute the logistic-regression coefficients (as `glm` does). The relevant formulas (for binomial logistic regression) are given in Section 5.5.

8.4   `apply` AND ITS RELATIVES

Avoiding loops and recursion can make S programs more compact, easier to read, and sometimes more efficient in execution. S provides several facilities that we have already encountered—for example, matrix functions and operators and vectorized functions—that encourage us to write loopless expressions for tasks that would require loops in lower-level programming languages, such as FORTRAN and C. The `apply` function, and its relatives `lapply`, `sapply`, and `tapply`, can also help us to avoid loops or recursion.

The `apply` function invokes ("applies") another function along specified coordinates of an array. Although this is a useful facility for manipulating higher-dimensional arrays (for example, in working with multi-way contingency tables), in most instances the array in question is a matrix or data frame (treated as a matrix).

By way of example, consider the data frame `DavisThin` in the `car` library: The data represent the responses of 191 subjects to a seven-item "drive for thinness" summated-rating scale and are part of a larger data set for a study of eating disorders; each item is scored from 0 to 3. The scale is to be formed by summing the items (DT1 through DT7) for each subject:

```
> detach(Mroz)
> data(DavisThin)
> DavisThin[1:10,]   # first 10 rows
   DT1 DT2 DT3 DT4 DT5 DT6 DT7
1    0   0   0   0   0   0   0
2    0   0   0   0   0   0   0
3    0   0   0   0   0   0   0
4    0   0   0   0   0   0   0
5    0   0   0   0   0   0   0
6    0   1   0   0   0   0   0
7    0   2   2   0   2   2   0
8    2   3   3   2   3   3   3
9    0   0   0   0   3   0   0
10   3   3   2   1   3   3   0

> dim(DavisThin)
[1] 191   7
```

We can calculate the scale score for each subject by applying the `sum` function along the rows (the first coordinate) of the data frame:

```
> DavisThin$thin.drive <- apply(DavisThin, 1, sum)
> DavisThin$thin.drive
  1   2   3   4   5   6   7   8   9  10  11  12  13  14  15  16
  0   0   0   0   0   1   8  19   3  15  14   4   7  12  15   0
. . .
177 178 179 180 181 182 183 184 185 186 187 188 189 190 191
  0   3   6  14   0   0   0   0   6   2   0   7   2   4   0
```

The numbers above the sums are the row names (subject numbers) from the `DavisThin` data frame. Notice that I have chosen to add a variable (`thin.drive`) to the data frame, rather than to define the scale in the working data.

Similarly, if we are interested in the column means of the data frame, they may be simply calculated as follows, by averaging along the second (column) coordinate:

```
> apply(DavisThin, 2, mean)
      DT1        DT2        DT3        DT4        DT5
  0.46597    1.02094    0.95812    0.34031    1.10995
      DT6        DT7 thin.drive
  0.93194    0.56545    5.39267
```

To extend the example, imagine that some items comprising the scale are missing for certain subjects; to simulate this situation, I will eliminate the scale from the data frame and arbitrarily replace some of the data with NAs:

```
> DavisThin$thin.drive <- NULL  # remove thin.drive
> DavisThin[1,2] <- DavisThin[2,4] <- DavisThin[10,3] <- NA
> DavisThin[1:10,]  # first 10 rows
   DT1 DT2 DT3 DT4 DT5 DT6 DT7
1    0  NA   0   0   0   0   0
2    0   0   0  NA   0   0   0
3    0   0   0   0   0   0   0
4    0   0   0   0   0   0   0
5    0   0   0   0   0   0   0
6    0   1   0   0   0   0   0
7    0   2   2   0   2   2   0
8    2   3   3   2   3   3   3
9    0   0   0   0   3   0   0
10   3   3  NA   1   3   3   0
```

If we simply apply sum over the rows of the data frame, then the result will be missing for observations with any missing items, as we may readily verify:

```
> apply(DavisThin, 1, sum)[1:10]  # first 10
 1  2  3  4  5  6  7  8  9 10
NA NA  0  0  0  1  8 19  3 NA
```

A simple alternative is to average over the items that are present, multiplying the resulting mean by 7 (to restore 0 to 21 as the range of the scale); this procedure is easily implemented by defining an anonymous function in the call to apply:

```
> apply(DavisThin, 1, function(x) 7*mean(x, na.rm=T))[1:10]
      1       2       3       4       5       6       7       8       9
  0.000   0.000   0.000   0.000   0.000   1.000   8.000  19.000   3.000
     10
 15.167
```

Last, suppose that we are willing to work with the average score if more than half of the seven items are valid, but want the scale to be NA if there are four or more missing items:

```
> DavisThin[1,2:5] <- NA  # create some more missing data
> DavisThin[1:10,]  # first 10 rows
```

```
    DT1 DT2 DT3 DT4 DT5 DT6 DT7
1     0  NA  NA  NA  NA   0   0
2     0   0   0  NA   0   0   0
3     0   0   0   0   0   0   0
4     0   0   0   0   0   0   0
5     0   0   0   0   0   0   0
6     0   1   0   0   0   0   0
7     0   2   2   0   2   2   0
8     2   3   3   2   3   3   3
9     0   0   0   0   3   0   0
10    3   3  NA   1   3   3   0

> make.scale <- function(items){
+     if(sum(is.na(items)) >= 4) NA
+     else 7*mean(items, na.rm=T)
+     }

> apply(DavisThin, 1, make.scale)[1:10]   # first 10
       1      2      3      4      5      6      7       8      9
      NA  0.000  0.000  0.000  0.000  1.000  8.000  19.000  3.000
      10
  15.167
```

The lapply and sapply functions are similar to apply, but reference the successive elements of a list. To illustrate, I convert the data frame DavisThin to a list:

```
> thin.list <- as.list(DavisThin)
> thin.list
$DT1
  [1] 0 0 0 0 0 0 2 0 3 1 0 0 1 0 0 0 0 3 0 2 0 0 3 0 0 3 0 0 0
. . .
[181] 0 0 0 0 2 1 0 2 0 0 0

$DT2
  [1] NA 0 0 0 0 1 2 3 0 3 0 1 3 3 3 0 2 0 3 0
. . .
[181] 0 0 0 0 1 1 0 0 0 0 0 0

. . .

$DT7
  [1] 0 0 0 0 0 0 0 3 0 0 3 0 0 0 2 0 0 3 0 0 2 0 0 0 0 0 3 0 0 0
. . .
[181] 0 0 0 0 0 0 0 1 0 0 0
```

The list elements are the variables from the data frame. To calculate the mean of each element (eliminating missing data):

```
> lapply(thin.list, mean, na.rm=T)
$DT1
[1] 0.46597
```

```
$DT2
[1] 1.0263

$DT3
[1] 0.95767

$DT4
[1] 0.34392

$DT5
[1] 1.1158

$DT6
[1] 0.93194

$DT7
[1] 0.56545
```

Notice that additional arguments to the function that is applied may be specified (here, the na.rm argument to mean); this is true for apply as well.

The lapply function returns a list as its result; sapply works similarly, but tries to simplify the result, in this case returning a vector with named elements:

```
> sapply(thin.list, mean, na.rm=T)
    DT1      DT2      DT3      DT4      DT5      DT6      DT7
0.46597  1.02632  0.95767  0.34392  1.11579  0.93194  0.56545
```

Finally, tapply ("table apply") applies a function to each cell of a "ragged array" containing data for a variable cross-classified by one or more factors. I recall an example from Section 4.3, employing Moore and Krupat's conformity data:

```
> data(Moore)
> attach(Moore)
> Moore
   partner.status conformity fcategory fscore
1            low          8       low     37
2            low          4      high     57
3            low          8      high     65
.  .  .
44          high         10      high     52
45          high         15    medium     44
```

The factor partner.status has levels low and high; the factor fcategory has levels low, medium, and high; and the response, conformity, is a numeric variable. We may, for example, use tapply

to calculate the mean `conformity` for each combination of levels of
`partner.status` and `fcategory`:

```
> tapply(conformity,
+    list(Status=partner.status,
+        Authoritarianism=fcategory), mean)

        Authoritarianism
Status    high  low medium
   high 11.857 17.4 14.273
   low  12.625  8.9  7.250

> detach(Moore)
>
```

Because I did not explicitly order the levels of the factors, the levels
appear in alphabetical order—not what we probably would want.

OBJECT-ORIENTED PROGRAMMING IN S*   8.5

Object-oriented programming in S is based on simple procedures of
"object dispatch," where functions can be written to adapt their behavior
automatically to the classes of their arguments, as explained below. The
general notion of object dispatch is implemented differently in S versions
3 and 4. R, up to version 1.3.1 (the current version at the time that I am
writing), implements the S3 object-oriented programming system; there
are plans to incorporate S4 classes into R version 1.4.[6]

S Version 3   8.5.1

In S3, the `class` attribute of an object determines the specific behavior
of a *generic function* by invoking a *method function* appropriate to the
object's class. Not all objects in S have a `class` attribute, however. In
its simplest form, the `class` attribute of an object consists of a character
vector with a single element, giving the class of the object. For example,
the `lm` function returns a linear-model object of class `'lm'`:

```
> mod.prestige <- lm(prestige ~ income + education + women,
+    data=Prestige)
```

---

6. Rather than replacing the S3-style object system in R, the S4 object system will be implemented
primarily as a methods library.

```
> attributes(mod.prestige)
$names
 [1] "coefficients"  "residuals"      "effects"
 [4] "rank"          "fitted.values"  "assign"
 [7] "qr"            "df.residual"    "xlevels"
[10] "call"          "terms"          "model"

$class
[1] "lm"
```

The function class may be used to extract or (on the left-hand side of an assignment) to set an object's class:

```
> class(mod.prestige)
[1] "lm"
```

Generic functions are written to invoke methods determined (in most instances) by the class of their first argument. For example, the generic print function has the following definition:

```
> print
function (x, ...)
UseMethod("print")
```

When print is called with an argument of class 'lm', for example, it looks for a function named print.lm; if such a function exists, it is called as print.lm(x, ...). Indeed, it is perfectly proper to call print.lm directly; thus, all of the following commands are equivalent:

```
> mod.prestige
Call:
lm(formula = prestige ~ income + education + women,
    data = Prestige)

Coefficients:
(Intercept)       income    education         women
   -6.79433      0.00131      4.18664      -0.00891

> print(mod.prestige)
Call:
lm(formula = prestige ~ income + education + women,
    data = Prestige)

Coefficients:
(Intercept)       income    education         women
   -6.79433      0.00131      4.18664      -0.00891

> print.lm(mod.prestige)
Call:
lm(formula = prestige ~ income + education + women,
    data = Prestige)
```

```
Coefficients:
(Intercept)        income    education            women
   -6.79433       0.00131      4.18664         -0.00891
```

Recall that the `print` function is called automatically by any S statement that is not an assignment—for example, when we simply type the name of an object.

Suppose that we invoke the (hypothetical) generic function `fun` with argument `arg`; if there is no method function for `arg`'s class, or if `arg` has no class, then S looks for a method named `fun.default`. For example, classless objects are printed by `print.default`. If, under these circumstances, there is no default function, S reports an error.

Method selection is slightly more complicated for objects whose class-attribute vector contains more than one element. Consider, for example, an object returned by the `glm` function:

```
> mod.mroz <- glm(lfp ~ ., family=binomial, data=Mroz)
> class(mod.mroz)
[1] "glm" "lm"
```

If we invoke a generic function with `mod.mroz` as its argument, say `fun(mod.mroz)`, then S will look first for a method named `fun.glm`; if a function by this name does not exist, then it will search next for `fun.lm`, and finally for `fun.default`. We say that the object `mod.mroz` is of (primary) class "glm" and *inherits* from class "lm". Inheritance permits economical programming through generalization, but it can also get you into trouble (if, for example, there is no function `fun.glm`, but `fun.lm` is inappropriate for `mod.mroz` [7]).

"Quick-and-dirty" programming, which is the focus of this chapter, generally does not require writing object-oriented functions, but understanding concretely how the object system in S works is often useful. To this end, consider the following object-oriented version of my first logistic-regression program (from Section 8.3.4), which employs the Newton-Raphson algorithm:

```
> lreg.3 <- function(X, y, predictors=colnames(X), max.iter=10,
+          tol=1E-6, constant=TRUE){
+      if (!is.numeric(X) || !is.matrix(X))
+          stop('X must be a numeric matrix')
+      if (!is.numeric(y) || !all(y == 0 | y == 1))
+          stop('y must contain only 0s and 1s')
+      if (nrow(X) != length(y))
+          stop('X and y contain different numbers of observations')
+      if (constant) {
+          X <- cbind(1, X)
+          colnames(X)[1] <- 'Constant'
+          }
```

---

7. In a case like this, the programmer of `fun.lm` should be careful to create a function `fun.glm`, which calls the default method or reports an error (as appropriate).

```
+       b <- b.last <- rep(0, ncol(X))
+       it <- 1
+       while (it <= max.iter){
+           p <- as.vector(1/(1 + exp(-X %*% b)))
+           V <- diag(p * (1 - p))
+           var.b <- solve(t(X) %*% V %*% X)
+           b <- b + var.b %*% t(X) %*% (y - p)
+           if (max(abs(b - b.last)/(abs(b.last) + 0.01*tol)) < tol)
+               break
+           b.last <- b
+           it <- it + 1
+           }
+       dev <- -2*sum(y*log(p) + (1 - y)*log(1 - p))
+       if (it > max.iter) warning('maximum iterations exceeded')
+       result <- list(coefficients=as.vector(b), var=var.b,
+           deviance=dev, converged= it <= max.iter,
+           predictors=predictors)
+       class(result) <- 'lreg'
+       result
+       }
>
```

- As in Section 8.3.4, the first two arguments of `lreg.3` are the model matrix X and the response vector y, which contains 0s and 1s.

- In rewriting the function, I provided for predictor names, which, by default, are the column names of the model matrix X, and allowed the regression constant to be suppressed.

- The function begins by performing some checks on the data.

- Before returning an object (called `result` in `lreg.3`) containing logistic-regression coefficients, their covariance matrix, and so on, the function assigns to the object the class `'lreg'`.

Applying `lreg.3` to Mroz's data:

```
> mod.mroz.3 <- lreg.3(cbind(k5, k618, age, wc, hc, lwg, inc), lfp)
> class(mod.mroz.3)
[1] "lreg"

> mod.mroz.3
$coefficients
[1]  3.182140 -1.462913 -0.064571 -0.062871  0.807274  0.111734
[7]  0.604693 -0.034446

$var
              [,1]        [,2]        [,3]        [,4]        [,5]
[1,]   0.41521927 -0.06305186 -2.3035e-02 -7.6663e-03  0.01281877
[2,]  -0.06305186  0.03880924  1.9573e-03  1.2216e-03 -0.00454977
. . .
[7,]   0.00014344  2.2746e-02 -1.0779e-04
[8,]  -0.00048973 -1.0779e-04  6.7377e-05
```

```
$deviance
[1] 905.27

$converged
[1] TRUE

$predictors
[1] "Constant" "k5"        "k618"      "age"      "wc"
[6] "hc"        "lwg"       "inc"

attr(,"class")
[1] "lreg"
>
```

We may now write 'lreg' methods for standard generic functions, such as print and summary:

```
> print.lreg <- function(x) {
+       coef <- x$coefficients
+       names(coef) <- x$predictors
+       print(coef)
+       if (!x$converged) cat('\n *** lreg did not converge ***\n')
+       invisible(x)
+       }

> summary.lreg <- function(object) {
+       b <- object$coefficients
+       se <- sqrt(diag(object$var))
+       z <- b/se
+       table <- cbind(b, se, z, 2*(1-pnorm(abs(z))))
+       colnames(table) <- c('Coefficient', 'Std.Error', 'z', 'p')
+       rownames(table) <- object$predictors
+       print(table)
+       cat('\nDeviance =', object$deviance,'\n')
+       if (!object$converged)
+           cat('\n Note: *** lreg did not converge ***\n')
+       }

> mod.mroz.3
  Constant         k5      k618        age        wc        hc
  3.182140 -1.462913 -0.064571 -0.062871  0.807274  0.111734
       lwg        inc
  0.604693 -0.034446

> summary(mod.mroz.3)
           Coefficient Std.Error        z         p
Constant      3.182140 0.6443751  4.93834 7.8792e-07
k5           -1.462913 0.1970006 -7.42593 1.1191e-13
k618         -0.064571 0.0680008 -0.94956 3.4234e-01
age          -0.062871 0.0127831 -4.91826 8.7317e-07
wc            0.807274 0.2299799  3.51019 4.4778e-04
hc            0.111734 0.2060397  0.54229 5.8762e-01
lwg           0.604693 0.1508176  4.00943 6.0864e-05
inc          -0.034446 0.0082084 -4.19650 2.7107e-05

Deviance = 905.27
```

The print.lreg method prints a brief report, while the output produced by summary.lreg is somewhat more extensive. Note the use within these methods of print and cat to produce output. We are already familiar with the generic function print; the cat function may also be used for printed output: Each "new-line" character ('\n') in the argument to cat causes output to resume at the start of the next line. It is conventional for the first argument of a method to be the same as the first argument of the corresponding generic function (here x for print and object for summary).

It is also conventional for print methods to pass through their principal argument as an invisible result and for summary methods to create and return objects. According to this scheme, summary.lreg would produce an object of class lreg.summary, to be printed by a corresponding print method (i.e., print.lreg.summary, which I would then have to write), but that seems an unnecessary complication here.

8.5.2   S Version 4

The object system in S4, while broadly similar to that in S3, is more formal, consistent, and pervasive. There is, however, backward compatibility to S3 classes, so that most software written in the older object-oriented style still works (including the example developed in the previous section).

In S4, every object belongs to one and only one class.[8] Classes are defined globally, via the setClass function. Adapting the earlier example, I define a class of 'lreg' objects to contain the results of a logistic regression:

```
> setClass('lreg',
+     representation(coefficients='numeric', var='matrix',
+         iterations='numeric', deviance='numeric',
+         predictors='character'))
>
```

---

8. That some objects in S3 do not have a class attribute can occasionally be a cause of inconvenience. Suppose, for example, that we want to define a method fun.matrix for the generic function fun to be applied to matrix objects. Matrices in S3, however, are unclassed objects. The data.class function can often be of help here: data.class returns the class of an object, if it has one; otherwise, it returns another identifier, such as 'matrix' for a matrix object or 'numeric' for a numeric vector. Thus, a generic function might be written in the following manner to accommodate objects with and without a class attribute:

```
> fun <- function(object, ...){
+ if (is.null(class(object))) class(object) <- data.class(object)
+ UseMethod('fun', object)
+ }
```

The first argument to setClass is the name of the class being defined, here 'lreg'. The second argument calls the representation function to define the *slots* that compose objects of class 'lreg'; each argument to representation is a slot name that identifies the kind of data (e.g., a numeric vector, a matrix, a character vector) that the slot is to contain.

My S4 object-oriented logistic-regression program uses the Newton-Raphson algorithm (as explained in Section 8.3.4):

```
> lreg.4 <- function(X, y, predictors=colnames(X),
+     constant=T, max.iter=10, tol=1E-6){
+     if (!is.numeric(X) || !is.matrix(X))
+         stop('X must be a numeric matrix')
+     if (!is.numeric(y) || !all(y == 0 | y == 1))
+         stop('y must contain only 0s and 1s')
+     if (nrow(X) != length(y))
+         stop('X and y contain different numbers of observations')
+     if (constant) {
+         X <- cbind(1, X)
+         colnames(X)[1] <- 'Constant'
+         }
+     b <- b.last <- rep(0, ncol(X))
+     it <- 1
+     while (it <= max.iter){
+         p <- as.vector(1/(1 + exp(-X %*% b)))
+         V <- diag(p * (1 - p))
+         var.b <- solve(t(X) %*% V %*% X)
+         b <- b + var.b %*% t(X) %*% (y - p)
+         if (max(abs(b - b.last)/(abs(b.last) + 0.01*tol)) < tol)
+             break
+         b.last <- b
+         it <- it + 1
+         }
+     if (i > max.iter) warning('maximum iterations exceeded')
+     result <- new('lreg',coefficients=b,var=var.b,iterations=it,
+         deviance=-2*sum(y*log(p) + (1 - y)*log(1 - p)),
+         predictors=predictors)
+     result
+     }
>
```

This function creates the class 'lreg' object result by calling the general object-constructor function new and supplying the contents of each slot; lreg.4 terminates by returning the object result.

Let us try out lreg.4 on Mroz's data:

```
> mod.mroz.4 <- lreg.4(cbind(k5, k618, age, wc, hc, lwg, inc), lfp)
> class(mod.mroz.4)
[1] "lreg"

> mod.mroz.4
An object of class "lreg"

Slot "coefficients":
[1]   3.182140 -1.462913 -0.064571 -0.062871  0.807274  0.111734
[7]   0.604693 -0.034446
```

```
Slot "var":
              Constant           k5          k618            age
Constant   0.41521927 -0.06305186 -0.023034861 -7.6663e-003
      k5  -0.06305186  0.03880924  0.001957324  1.2216e-003
    k618  -0.02303486  0.00195732  0.004624113  3.7474e-004
. . .

     lwg  -0.00673674  0.00014344  0.022745938 -1.0779e-004
     inc  -0.00025326 -0.00048973 -0.000107789  6.7377e-005

Slot "iterations":
[1] 5

Slot "deviance":
[1] 905.27

Slot "predictors":
[1] "Constant" "k5"       "k618"     "age"      "wc"
[6] "hc"       "lwg"      "inc"
```

In S3, typing the name of an object (or entering any statement that is not an assignment) causes the generic print function to be invoked; similarly, in S4, typing the name of an object invokes the show function. Because I have not yet defined a 'show' method for objects of class 'lreg', the default method—which in S4 is the function simply named show—is invoked; show has the following definition:

```
> show
## automatic display of the value of a task. This is a generic
## with default method a call to 'print()'
function(object)
{
    print(object)
    invisible(NULL)
}
```

I proceed to define a 'show' method for objects of class 'lreg' by calling the setMethod function:

```
> setMethod('show', signature(object='lreg'),
+     definition=function(object){
+         coef <- object@coefficients
+         names(coef) <- object@predictors
+         print(coef)
+         }
+     )
>
```

■ The first argument to setMethod gives the name of the method that we wish to create (here, 'show').

- The second argument indicates the *signature* of the method—that is, the kind of objects to which it applies. In S4, methods can have complex signatures that depend upon the classes of several arguments; in this instance, however, the show method has only one argument, object, and the method is meant to apply to objects of class 'lreg'.

- The final argument to setMethod defines the method function; this may be a preexisting function or, as here, a function defined "on the fly." Methods in S4 have to employ the same arguments as the generic function (e.g., the single argument object for a 'show' method). Notice that the operator @ (the at sign) is used to extract the contents of a slot (much as $ is used to extract a list element).

Let us verify that the new method works properly:

```
> mod.mroz.4
  Constant       k5      k618        age       wc       hc      lwg
    3.1821  -1.4629  -0.064571  -0.062871  0.80727  0.11173  0.60469


       inc
 -0.034446
```

The 'show' method for objects of class 'lreg' reports only the regression coefficients. I next define a 'summary' method that outputs more information about the logistic regression:

```
> setMethod('summary', signature(object='lreg'),
+     definition=function(object, ...){
+         b <- object@coefficients
+         se <- sqrt(diag(object@var))
+         z <- b/se
+         table <- cbind(b, se, z, 2*(1-pnorm(abs(z))))
+         colnames(table) <- c('Coefficient', 'Std.Error', 'z', 'p')
+         rownames(table) <- object@predictors
+         print(table)
+         cat('\nDeviance =', object@deviance,'\n')
+         }
+     )
>
```

Because the generic summary function has two arguments, object and ..., so must the method, even though ... is never used in the body of the method. (In a generic function, the argument ... can be used to "soak up" different arguments for different methods.) Applying summary to the model produces the desired result:

```
> summary(mod.mroz.4)
          Coefficient Std.Error        z          p
Constant     3.182140 0.6443751  4.93834  7.8792e-007
      k5    -1.462913 0.1970006 -7.42593  1.1191e-013
    k618    -0.064571 0.0680008 -0.94956  3.4234e-001
```

```
 age   -0.062871 0.0127831 -4.91826 8.7317e-007
  wc    0.807274 0.2299799  3.51019 4.4778e-004
  hc    0.111734 0.2060397  0.54229 5.8762e-001
 lwg    0.604693 0.1508176  4.00943 6.0864e-005
 inc   -0.034446 0.0082084 -4.19650 2.7107e-005
```

Deviance = 905.265914855628

Finally, a word about inheritance in S4: Recall that in S3 an object can have more than one class. The first class is the object's primary class, but if a method for a particular generic function does not exist for the primary class, methods for the second, third, and so on, classes are searched for successively. In S4, in contrast, each object belongs to one and *only one* class. Inheritance is (as it should be) a relationship between classes and not a property of objects. If one class *extends* another class, then the first class inherits the methods of the second. Inheritance is established by the `setIs` function: `setIs('classA', 'classB')` asserts that `classA` extends, and therefore can inherit methods from, `classB`; put another way, objects of class `'classA'` also belong to class `'classB'`.

The object-oriented programming system in S4 is more complex than that in S3—indeed, I have only scratched the surface here, showing how to do in S4 what we previously learned to do in S3. The S4 object system is quite new; whether its added complexity will prove productive for developing statistical software remains to be seen. At the moment, almost all object-oriented software in S uses the older approach.

8.6   WRITING S PROGRAMS

Programming is a craft. Like most crafts, it is a combination of art and science; and as is true of most crafts, facility in programming is partly the product of experience. The purpose of this section is to give general, miscellaneous, and mostly unoriginal, advice about the craft of programming in S, organized as brief points:

■ *Program experimentally.* One of the advantages of programming in an interpreted environment is the ability to type S statements and have them immediately evaluated. You can therefore try out key parts of your program, and correct them, before incorporating them into the program. Often, you can simply copy a debugged statement from the *R Console* (or S-PLUS *Commands* window) into your program editor.

■ *Work from the bottom up.* You will occasionally encounter a moderately large programming project. It is almost always helpful to break a large project into smaller parts, each of which can be programmed as an independent function. In a truly complex project, these functions may be organized hierarchically, with some calling others. If some of these small functions are of more general utility, then you can maintain them as independent programs and reuse them; if the small functions are unique to the current project, then they may eventually be incorporated as local functions. Traditionally, large projects were programmed "from the top down"—beginning with the highest level of generality—but a functional, interpreted programming language such as S makes it easier to "build the language up" to the program.[9]

■ *If possible and reasonable, avoid loops.* Programs that avoid loops are generally easier to read and often are more efficient, especially if a loop would be executed a very large number of times. Some processes, such as numerical optimization, are intrinsically iterative, but in many other cases loops can be avoided by making use of vectorized calculations, matrix operations, functions such as `apply`, or even recursion. Sometimes, however, a loop will be the most natural means of expressing a computation.

■ *Test your program.* Before worrying about speed, memory usage, elegance, and so on, make sure that your program provides the right answer. Program development is an iterative process of refinement, and getting a program to function correctly is the key first step. In checking out your program, try to anticipate all of the circumstances that the program will encounter and test each of them. Furthermore, in "quick-and-dirty" programming, the time that you spend writing and debugging your program will probably be vastly greater than the time the program spends executing. Remember the programmer's adage[10]: "Make it right before you make it faster." (And emphasize the "quick"—in the sense of quick program development—as opposed to the "dirty.")

■ *Learn to use debugging tools.* It is rare to write a program that works correctly the first time that it is tried, and debugging is therefore an important programming skill. Working in an interpreted environment simplifies debugging: As explained in Section 1.1.7, the `traceback` function can help you to locate the source of an error. Often, all that is required to pinpoint the error is to add statements to the program that call the `print` or `cat` functions to print out partial results. Similarly, inserting calls to the `browser` function in a program (see the on-line help) allows interactive inspection of local variables. Both R and S-PLUS also provide a variety of more sophisticated debugging tools: In

---

9. See Graham (1994, 1996) for an eloquent discussion of these points in relation to another functional programming language—Lisp.

10. This dictum, and a great deal of other good advice on programming, originates in Kernighan and Plauger (1974); see also Kernighan and Pike (1999).

particular, take a look at the documentation for the debug function in R and the inspect function in S-PLUS.

■ *Document the program.* Unless your program is to be used only once and then thrown away, its use should be documented in some manner. The best documentation is to write programs in a transparent and readable style—use descriptive variable names; avoid clever but opaque tricks; do not pack too many operations into one line of program code; indent program lines (for example, in loops) to reveal the structure of the program. You can also add a few comments to the beginning of a function to explain what the function does and what its arguments mean (look back at the lreg function in Section 8.3.4, for example). It is my assumption that you are programming for yourself, rather than for others, and this decreases the burden of preparing documentation, but you want to understand your own programs when you return to them a month or a year later.

References

Agresti, A. (1984). *Analysis of ordinal categorical data.* New York: Wiley.

Agresti, A. (1990). *Categorical data analysis.* New York: Wiley.

Atkinson, A. C. (1985). *Plots, transformations and regression: An introduction to graphical methods of diagnostic regression analysis.* Oxford, UK: Oxford University Press.

Becker, R. A., Chambers, J. M., & Wilks, A. R. (1988). *The new S language: A programming environment for data analysis and graphics.* Pacific Grove, CA: Wadsworth.

Berndt, E. R. (1991). *The practice of econometrics: Classic and contemporary.* Reading, MA: Addison-Wesley.

Bowman, A. W., & Azzalini, A. (1997). *Applied smoothing techniques for data analysis: The kernel approach with S-Plus illustrations.* Oxford, UK: Oxford University Press.

Box, G. E. P., & Cox, D. R. (1964). An analysis of transformations. *Journal of the Royal Statistical Society, Series B 26,* 211–252.

Box, G. E. P., & Tidwell, P. W. (1962). Transformation of the independent variables. *Technometrics 4,* 531–550.

Breusch, T. S., & Pagan, A. R. (1979). A simple test for heteroscedasticity and random coefficient variation. *Econometrica 47,* 1287–1294.

Campbell, A., Converse, P. E., Miller, W. E., & Stokes, D. E. (1960). *The American voter.* New York: Wiley.

Chambers, J. M. (1992). Linear models. In J. M. Chambers & T. J. Hastie (Eds.), *Statistical models in S* (pp. 95–144). Pacific Grove, CA: Wadsworth.

Chambers, J. M. (1998). *Programming with data: A guide to the S language.* New York: Springer.

Chambers, J. M., Cleveland, W. S., Kleiner, B., & Tukey, P. A. (1983). *Graphical methods for data analysis.* Belmont, CA: Wadsworth.

Chambers, J. M., & Hastie, T. J. (1992). Statistical models. In J. M. Chambers & T. J. Hastie (Eds.), *Statistical models in S* (pp. 13–44). Pacific Grove, CA: Wadsworth.

Chambers, J. M., & Hastie, T. J. (Eds.). (1992). *Statistical models in S.* Pacific Grove, CA: Wadsworth.

Cleveland, W. S. (1993). *Visualizing data.* Summit, NJ: Hobart Press.

Cleveland, W. S. (1994). *The elements of graphing data.* (rev. ed.). Summit, NJ: Hobart Press.

Clogg, C. C., & Shihadeh, E. S. (1994). *Statistical models for ordinal variables.* Thousand Oaks, CA: Sage.

Cook, R. D. (1993). Exploring partial residual plots. *Technometrics 35,* 351–362.

Cook, R. D. (1996). Added-variable plots and curvature in linear regression. *Technometrics 38*, 275–278.

Cook, R. D. (1998). *Regression graphics: Ideas for studying regressions through graphics.* New York: Wiley.

Cook, R. D., & Weisberg, S. (1983). Diagnostics for heteroscedasticity in regression. *Biometrika 70*, 1–10.

Cook, R. D., & Weisberg, S. (1999). *Applied regression including computing and graphics.* New York: Wiley.

Cowles, M., & Davis, C. (1987). The subject matter of psychology: Volunteers. *British Journal of Social Psychology 26*, 97–102.

Davis, C. (1990). Body image and weight preoccupation: A comparison between exercising and non-exercising women. *Appetite 15*, 13–21.

Davison, A. C., & Hinkley, D. V. (1997). *Bootstrap methods and their application.* Cambridge, UK: Cambridge University Press.

Duncan, O. D. (1961). A socioeconomic index for all occupations. In A. J. Reiss, Jr. (Ed.), *Occupations and social status* (pp. 109–138). New York: Free Press.

Efron, B., & Tibshirani, R. J. (1993). *An introduction to the bootstrap.* New York: Chapman & Hall.

Ericksen, E. P., Kadane, J. B., & Tukey, J. W. (1989). Adjusting the 1990 Census of Population and Housing. *Journal of the American Statistical Association 84*, 927–944.

Fienberg, S. E. (1980). *The analysis of cross-classified categorical data* (2nd ed.). Cambridge, MA: MIT Press.

Fox, J. (1987). Effect displays for generalized linear models. In C. C. Clogg (Ed.), *Sociological methodology 1987* (Vol. 17, pp. 347–361). Washington, DC: American Sociological Association.

Fox, J. (1997). *Applied regression analysis, linear models, and related methods.* Thousand Oaks, CA: Sage.

Fox, J., & Guyer, M. (1978). "Public" choice and cooperation in *n*-person prisoner's dilemma. *Journal of Conflict Resolution 22*, 469–481.

Fox, J., & Monette, G. (1992). Generalized collinearity diagnostics. *Journal of the American Statistical Association 87*, 178–183.

Freedman, D., & Diaconis, P. (1981). On the histogram as a density estimator. *Zeitschrift fur Wahrscheinlichkeitstheorie und verwandte Gebiete 57*, 453–476.

Freedman, J. L. (1975). *Crowding and behavior.* New York: Viking.

Graham, P. (1994). *On Lisp: Advanced Techniques for Common Lisp.* Englewood Cliffs, NJ: Prentice Hall.

Graham, P. (1996). *ANSI Common Lisp.* Englewood Cliffs, NJ: Prentice Hall.

Hastie, T. J., & Tibshirani, R. J. (1990). *Generalized additive models.* London: Chapman & Hall.

Kernighan, B. W., & Pike, R. (1999). *The practice of programming.* Reading MA: Addison-Wesley.

Kernighan, B. W., & Plauger, P. J. (1974). *The elements of programming style.* New York: McGraw-Hill.

Landwehr, J. M., Pregibon, D., & Shoemaker, A. C. (1980). Some graphical procedures for studying a logistic regression fit. *Proceedings of the Business and Economics Statistics Section, American Statistical Association, 15–20.*

Little, R. J. A., & Rubin, D. B. (1987). *Statistical analysis with missing data.* New York: Wiley.

Loader, C. (1999). *Local regression and likelihood.* New York: Springer.

Long, J. S. (1997). *Regression models for categorical and limited dependent variables.* Thousand Oaks, CA: Sage.

Long, J. S., & Ervin, L. H. (2000). Using heteroscedasity consistent standard errors in the linear regression model. *American Statistician 54,* 217–224.

Monette, G. (1990). Geometry of multiple regression and interactive 3-D graphics. In J. Fox and J. S. Long (Eds.), *Modern methods of data analysis* (pp. 209–256). Newbury Park, CA: Sage.

Moore, D. S., & McCabe, G. P. (1993). *Introduction to the practice of statistics* (2nd ed.). New York: Freeman.

Moore, J. C., Jr, & Krupat, E. (1971). Relationship between source status, authoritarianism, and conformity in a social setting. *Sociometry 34,* 122–134.

Mosteller, F. W., & Tukey, J. W. (1977). *Data analysis and regression: A second course in statistics.* Reading, MA: Addison-Wesley.

Mroz, T. A. (1987). The sensitivity of an empirical model of married women's hours of work to economic and statistical assumptions. *Econometrica 55,* 765–799.

Nelder, J. A., & Wedderburn, R. W. M. (1972). Generalised linear models. *Journal of the Royal Statistical Society, Series A 135,* 370–384.

Ornstein, M. D. (1976). The boards and executives of the largest Canadian corporations: Size, composition, and interlocks. *Canadian Journal of Sociology 1,* 411–437.

Pinheiro, J. C., & Bates, D. M. (2000). *Mixed-effects models in S and S-PLUS.* New York: Springer.

Powers, D. A., & Xie, Y. (2000). *Statistical methods for categorical data analysis.* San Diego: Academic Press.

Pregibon, D. (1981). Logistic regression diagnostics. *Annals of Statistics 9,* 705–724.

Sall, J. (1990). Leverage plots for general linear hypotheses. *American Statistician 44,* 308–315.

Schafer, J. L. (1997). *Analysis of incomplete multivariate data.* New York: Chapman & Hall.

Silverman, B. W. (1986). *Density estimation for statistics and data analysis.* London: Chapman & Hall.

Stine, R., & Fox, J. (Eds.). (1997). *Statistical computing environments for social research.* Thousand Oaks, CA: Sage.

Swayne, D. F., Cook, D., & Buja, A. (1998). XGobi: Interactive dynamic data visualization in the X Window system. *Journal of Computational and Graphical Statistics 7,* 1–20.

Therneau, T. M., & Grambsch, P. M. (2000). *Modeling survival data.* New York: Springer.

Tierney, L. (1990). *Lisp-Stat: An object-oriented environment for statistical computing and dynamic graphics.* New York: Wiley.

Tukey, J. W. (1977). *Exploratory data analysis*. Reading, MA: Addison-Wesley.

United Nations. (1998). *Social indicators*. Available on line at http://www.un.org/Depts/unsd/social/main.htm.

Venables, W. N., & Ripley, B. D. (1999). *Modern applied statistics with S-PLUS* (3rd ed.). New York: Springer.

Venables, W. N., & Ripley, B. D. (2000). *S programming*. New York: Springer.

Wang, P. C. (1985). Adding a variable in generalized linear models. *Technometrics 27*, 273–276.

Wang, P. C. (1987). Residual plots for detecting nonlinearity in generalized linear models. *Technometrics 29*, 435–438.

White, H. (1980). A heterskedastic consistent covariance matrix estimator and a direct test of heteroskedasticity. *Econometrica 48*, 817–838.

Williams, D. A. (1987). Generalized linear model diagnostics using the deviance and single case deletions. *Applied Statistics 36*, 181–191.

Index of Data Sets

The following data frames are all in the car library.

Index of Functions, Operators, Control Structures, and Other Symbols

Functions in the `car` library are marked [`car`].

Author Index

Subject Index

About the Author

JOHN FOX is Professor of Sociology at McMaster University in Hamilton, Ontario, Canada. He was previously Professor of Sociology and of Mathematics and Statistics at York University in Toronto, where he also directed the Statistical Consulting Service at the Institute for Social Research. Professor Fox earned a Ph.D. in sociology from the University of Michigan in 1972. He has delivered numerous lectures and workshops on statistical topics, at such places as the summer program of the Inter-University Consortium for Political and Social Research and the annual meetings of the American Sociological Association. His recent and current work includes research on statistical methods (for example, work on three-dimensional statistical graphs) and on Canadian society (for example, a study of political polls in the 1995 Quebec sovereignty referendum). He is author of many articles, in such journals as *Sociological Methodology, The Journal of Computational and Graphical Statistics, The Journal of the American Statistical Association, The Canadian Review of Sociology and Anthropology*, and *The Canadian Journal of Sociology*. He has written several other books, including *Applied Regression Analysis, Linear Models*, and *Related Methods* (Sage, 1997), *Nonparametric Simple Regression* (Sage, 2000), and *Multiple and Generalized Nonparametric Regression* (Sage, 2000).